DATE DUE

The
HANDPLANE
Book

The
HANDPLANE
Book

GARRETT HACK

Photographs by John S. Sheldon

The Taunton Press

for fellow enthusiasts

First printing: 1997
Printed in the United States of America

A FINE WOODWORKING Book

FINE WOODWORKING ® is a trademark of The Taunton Press, Inc.,
registered in the U.S. Patent and Trademark Office.

The Taunton Press, Inc., 63 South Main Street, PO Box 5506,
Newtown, CT 06470-5506
e-mail: tp@taunton.com

Library of Congress Cataloging-in-Publication Data

Hack, Garrett.
   The handplane book / Garrett Hack.
      p.   cm.
   "A Fine woodworking book" — T.p. verso.
   Includes bibliographical references and index.
   ISBN 1-56158-155-0
   1. Planes (Hand tools).   2. Woodwork.   I. Title.
 TT186.H33   1997
 684'.082 — dc21   97-7943
                                                          CIP

About Your Safety

Working wood is inherently dangerous. Using hand or power tools improperly or
ignoring standard safety practices can lead to permanent injury or even death.
Don't try to perform operations you learn about here (or elsewhere) unless you're
certain they are safe for you. If something about an operation doesn't feel right,
don't do it. Look for another way. We want you to enjoy the craft, so please keep
safety foremost in your mind whenever you're in the shop.

To Helen and Vinny who saw the possibilities,

Ned who encouraged me, and

Hope who has kept me tuned and planing true

ACKNOWLEDGMENTS

No one can hope to bring together a book like this without help. Very few of us will ever own all of the planes discussed within these pages; the range and numbers of different ones are simply too vast. Some are so scarce and expensive that they are beyond the means of most of us. Luckily, there's no shortage of people who love and collect planes willing to share them. I'm appreciative of all those who offered their tools, books, and insights into the different types of planes and how they're used. Equally important were the people who gave advice or encouragement along the way.

Helen Albert, for her insights and encouragement from the beginning

Jonathan Binzen

M. S. Carter, a special collector of miniature planes

Violinmaker Jonathan Cooper

Auctioneer Richard Crane, who's seen more tools than most of us ever will

Michael Dunbar, a chairmaker knowledgeable about all hand tools

Deborah Federhen, Curator of Collections, Bennington Museum, Bennington, Vermont

Jay Gaynor of the Colonial Williamsburg Foundation, Williamsburg, Virginia, who together with Joseph Hutchins made planes as art

Barbara Hamblett, Polly Mitchell, and the Shelburne Museum, Shelburne, Vermont

Gerry and Jane Haviland, eternal springs of encouragement

Bill Hildebrandt

Ted Ingraham, a plane maker and savant of 18th-century woodworking skills and tools

Tool historian and collector Paul Kebabian

Vincent Laurence, a wonderful friend and teacher

Leonard Lee

Tom Lie-Nielsen and the crew of Lie-Nielsen Toolworks, Warren, Maine, redefining how fine new planes can be

John Lively, who challenged and encouraged my ideas

Noel Perrin, for his insights about all things besides tools

Jack Playne

Violinmaker David Polstein

Cooper Ron Raiselis and the Strawbery Banke Museum, Portsmouth, New Hampshire

Mark and Jane Rees, writers and lovers of old woodworking tools

Gordon Riesdel

Plane maker Leon Robbins

Ken Roberts

Photographer John Sheldon, for his enthusiasm, spirit, and creativity

Richard Starr, inspiring kids to use hand tools

Charles Stirling, of Bristol Design, Bristol, England

Plane maker Jeff Warshafsky, ever curious about the fine points of planes and planing

Caroline and Bill Wilkins, astute collectors and gracious hosts

Windsor Precision Museum, Windsor, Vermont

Dean Zoerheide, for his workingman's appreciation of planes

And for my support at The Taunton Press:

Peter Chapman
Jim Chiavelli
Rick Peters
Joanne Renna
Carol Singer

CONTENTS

INTRODUCTION

A man who wants to work must attach value to the best tools.

–Goethe

Handplanes have become such an integral part of my furniture making that I cannot imagine working without them. This isn't to cling to some romantic image of the past—I'm still a practical Yankee with a shop full of machines. The simple truth is that a plane works better and more efficiently than a machine in many situations. What machine can fit a drawer as well as a plane, one thin and thoughtful shaving at a time?

Learning to use planes can improve your craftsmanship. No tool matches the clarity and polish of a surface cut with a plane. No machine leaves a better glue surface or cuts such a tight-fitting joint. There are so many varieties of planes— panel raisers, molding planes, and chamfer planes to name but a few—that using them can't help but encourage you to work in new ways or add interesting details. And if that isn't enough, planes are a lot more pleasurable to use than machines and will make your shop a quieter and cleaner place to work.

Learning to tune and use planes isn't difficult. Any woodworker has the skills but maybe not all of the necessary information. No planes I've ever bought came with an owner's manual, although it would be nice if they had. Maybe then my first attempts wouldn't have been so frustrating—the plane ending up so thoroughly clogged that it did more damage than good. Few books were helpful; they focused more on the history of planes than on offering practical information for the contemporary wood-worker. So I've set out to remedy that.

I like to think of this book as a plane owner's manual. It explains the basics of how a plane cuts and describes how to tune, sharpen, and adjust a plane to work better than you ever thought possible. Every type of plane you'll ever likely need is discussed, along with planing techniques for each, from holding the plane to clamping the work and troubleshooting problems. I've also included the especially useful information that ordinary manuals never seem to discuss, such as how to read the grain of a board and plane figured wood, how to decide which planes are essential for your shop, and how to know where to look and what to look for when buying them.

Specific planes and techniques are introduced as you might use them in building a piece of furniture. The planes are grouped according to the work they do: truing and preparing stock, cutting joinery, smoothing surfaces, and cutting moldings or other shaped decoration. The range runs from essential bench planes to such oddities as a spill plane, where producing a useful shaving—not an improved surface—is the intent.

The final chapters offer a different perspective on planes. Here are the plane-making techniques of a handful of contemporary craftsmen, advice from an auctioneer 30 years in the tool business, and the stories of a few incurable collectors.

Planes were once one of the most important tools in a carpenter's chest, making possible a whole range of techniques difficult or impossible with other tools. They are no less relevant today. Use this book as a guide and no matter what you know about planes, it will help you gain greater confidence and skill and experience greater pleasure working wood.

1

WHAT IS A PLANE?

Many woodworking operations which we take for granted would be impossibly laborious without Planes. A worker with the right Plane for a particular task has only to concentrate on holding it in the correct attitude in contact with the workpiece, and he can then push away freely until the task is completed.

—R. A. Salaman, *Dictionary of Woodworking Tools,* 1975

If you'd looked inside the tool chest of an 18th-century colonial joiner, you'd have found chisels, gouges, a bit stock and bits, handsaws, hammers, squares, gimlets, a hand adz, and an assortment of planes. Some of the tools were imported from England, while others were made locally. Planes for special tasks were bought from other joiners who produced them as a sideline to their furniture work, or from skilled commercial plane makers. A stout smoothing plane, a long jointer, and

many of the molding planes the joiner likely cut himself from yellow birch and beech and fitted with thick imported cast-steel irons. Essentially, these were wooden tools for working the resources of a land rich in timber, for creating the wooden essentials for the settler, villager, and town dweller alike—from buildings to bridges, wagons to hay forks, barrels to sap buckets, furniture to spoons.

Before the development of the planers and table saws common in most shops today, everything was made by hand.

When a colonial joiner built a case of drawers, for example, he first marked out all the different parts on the boards and sawed them apart with a handsaw. The real work began in earnest with planing the parts to size, leveling and smoothing each surface, and working each part down to uniform thickness. For this he would have pulled from his chest a heavy jack plane—a stock of beech a little over a foot long fitted with a double plane iron and an open, curved handle at the rear. It was a tool little changed from that familiar to a Roman joiner, nor much different from one likely made of cast iron instead of wood found in a wood-working shop today.

It is hard to imagine truing and dimensioning the case and drawer parts by hand without using planes. Leveling

The concept of a plane is a simple one—a chisel wedged into a solid body—but the tool takes many different forms. Shown here are a Norris panel plane with steel sides and sole and rosewood infill, used for truing edges and flattening surfaces, and rare Norris wooden molding planes with shaped soles and single irons.

5

An 18th-century joiner's tool chest would have held an assortment of planes, including many molding planes, a jack plane, and a coffin-shaped smoother, as well as chisels, bit brace and bits, and measuring tools.

and smoothing can be done with a hand adz and chisels, in much the same way that a large chisel or slick is used, but such work requires great skill controlling the cuts, and a lot of energy besides. Even in skilled hands it's easy to gouge the surface and leave the parts uneven enough to make joining or fitting them closely together difficult. Wedge the same chisel iron in a block of wood at a pitch of say 45°, and you've given the craftsman a plane—a tool that allows him great flexibility to control the cut while focusing his energy on driving the tool. The simplest of planes has a flat "sole" or base with the cutting iron projecting through it. By tapping on the plane body or iron its depth can be adjusted to take

an aggressive cut to level the surface quickly or to take a finer cut for final smoothing. The straight and flat sole guides and controls the cutting of the iron so that high spots are planed off progressively lower until the plane takes a continuous shaving from end to end and creates the plane the name of the tool suggests.

Classes of Planes

Planes can be broadly grouped according to the work they perform: truing and sizing stock, cutting and fitting joints, finishing or smoothing surfaces, and shaping. An 18th-century joiner had specific planes in his tool chest for each of these different planing tasks. Although

he did not have the variety of planes common a century later, each of his tools was general enough to do the work needed; if it was not, he cut a new plane or reshaped an old one.

The need for a greater variety of planes evolved with the gradual specialization and separation of the different woodworking professions. The joiner who completed the interior woodworking of a building needed more specialized planes than the carpenter who cut the frame—molding planes for shaping trim and crown moldings, sash and door planes for building windows and doors, and grooving and panel-raising planes for wainscoting. Within each trade, planes evolved to satisfy the particular demands of both the craft and the craftsman. Coopers took the jack plane and curved it into a more practical topping plane, so it could better follow the top of a barrel when leveling the ends of the staves. Similarly, stairbuilders shortened and altered molding planes to follow the tight curves of handrails. Up until nearly a century ago many hundred styles and types of planes were in daily use. Basic planes such as the jack were used throughout the woodworking trades. Others were so specific—coachmaking tools, for example—that the exact function of some of them has unfortunately been lost with the passing of the coachmaker's craft.

BENCH PLANES FOR TRUING AND SIZING

Of all the work that planes perform, the most basic of truing and sizing stock falls to a class of planes called bench planes. As their name suggests, these planes are used mainly at a bench for planing stock held with clamps, dogs, or within a vise. For an 18th-century woodworker, these were the most important planes he owned, used throughout the working day from leveling and thicknessing parts to jointing edges and initially smoothing surfaces. Bench planes are no less useful today, although with readily available dimensioned lumber and woodworking machinery common in nearly every shop, they are used less for the rough sizing of parts and more for final dimensioning, jointing, and fitting.

Early bench planes, made from well-seasoned stocks of quartersawn beech, yellow birch, or more rarely dense tropical hardwoods, vary in length from the 7-in.- to 9-in.-long smooth plane to the 26-in. to 30-in. jointer plane. Between them are at least two more sizes: a 14-in. to 16-in. jack plane and a trying or fore plane somewhat shorter

than the jointer. The sizes and styles vary widely due to regional differences and each plane maker's preferences. The longer the plane, the truer or straighter the surface the plane cuts; a jointer is a better choice for truing long board edges than the shorter jack. Bench planes have flat soles and an iron bedded at an angle of 45° to 50° to it, the steeper angle being preferred for harder woods. A handle or tote of many forms behind the iron allows a firm hold on the tool to deliver power to it through the cut. (For more on the anatomy of bench planes, see Chapter 3.)

Toward the end of the 19th century wooden bench planes began to give way to cast-iron planes patented by Leonard Bailey and others (see the top photo on p. 8). Making such cast-iron planes demanded a whole new method of manufacture and an understanding of casting technology that once developed

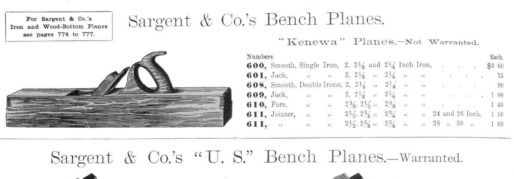

For Sargent & Co.'s Iron and Wood-Bottom Planes see pages 774 to 777.

Sargent & Co.'s Bench Planes.

"Kenewa" Planes.—Not Warranted.

Numbers.							Each.
600, Smooth, Single Iron,	2,	2⅛ and 2¼ Inch Iron,			. . .		$0 60
601, Jack,	"	"	2,	2⅛ " 2¼	"	"	. . . .	75
608, Smooth, Double Irons,	2,	2⅛ " 2¼	"	"	. . . .		90
609, Jack,	"	"	2,	2⅛ " 2¼	"	"	. . . .	1 00
610, Fore,	"	"	2⅜, 2½ " 2⅝	"	"	. . . .		1 40
611, Jointer,	"	"	2½, 2⅝ " 2¾	"	" 24 and 26 Inch,		1 50
611, "	"	"	2½, 2⅝ " 2¾	"	" 28 " 30 "		1 60

Sargent & Co.'s "U. S." Bench Planes.—Warranted.

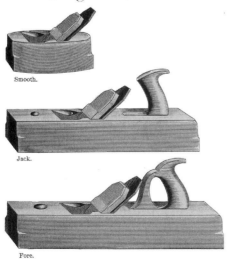

Smooth.

Jack.

Fore.

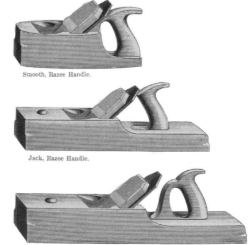

Smooth, Razee Handle.

Jack, Razee Handle.

Jointer, Razee Handle.

These wooden bench planes sold by Sargent & Co. of New Haven, Connecticut, are typical of the various sizes and styles available from commercial plane makers just over 100 years ago.

led to the production of vast numbers of inexpensive planes. These planes have popular features such as an easy mechanical adjuster for iron alignment and depth, and flat, long-wearing soles that are sometimes grooved or corrugated for reduced friction. Even though some woodworkers still prefer the feel of a wooden plane, cast-iron planes far outlast their wooden cousins whose soles need periodic reflattening due to hard use and changing seasons.

Bailey and others patented another style of bench plane, a combination wooden-soled and cast-iron plane meant to satisfy craftsmen who were not so willing to part with their all-wood planes. These so-called "transitional" planes (see the bottom photo at left) combine the feel of a traditional wood plane with the mechanical advantages of a cast-iron plane—easy adjustment of the cutting iron and a movable frog. It's natural to think that wood-bottomed planes were a stage in the evolution of the cast-iron plane and were transitional in this way, but they were made right along with all-cast-iron planes for almost 75 years. Their appeal was their availability in a wide selection of sizes for about half the cost of an all-cast-iron plane and their ability to hold up to rough use. Since the plane's sole is still wood, it is worn down by use and needs regular reflattening. Nevertheless, transitional planes have appealed to many generations of craftsmen who appreciate the subtle feel of a wood plane for varied bench-planing work.

Transitional planes have mostly wooden bodies (usually beech) and cast-iron parts, combining the smooth planing of a wooden sole and the adjustability of a cast-iron plane.

Among the many designs of planes for cutting and fitting joints are a Stanley #90A bullnose rabbet plane (at rear), one of the rarest of planes, and a Sargent #1508½ "Lady bug" bullnose fillister rabbet plane with fence and depth gauge.

Combination planes evolved from plow planes to perform a variety of tasks, including cutting dadoes, rabbets, grooves, and tongues. These two early designs are a Stanley #46 with skewed cutters (at rear) and a Siegley combination plane.

PLANES FOR CUTTING AND FITTING JOINERY

Once the stock is prepared, a second group of planes is brought to the work to cut and adjust the joinery that fits the parts together. Except for the long bench planes, which could be included in this group for shooting straight edges for edge joining, joinery planes tend to be smaller and specialized. These planes include rabbet, dado, and fillister planes for cutting rabbets and wide grooves or dadoes (see the photo above); plow and grooving planes for cutting grooves in the edges of boards; dovetail planes for cutting sliding-dovetail joints; shoulder and bullnose planes for finely adjusting joints; and low-angle planes for trimming miters and end grain. Combination planes often combine the joint-cutting functions of a number of these planes.

For work across the grain, the iron is bedded at 20° or less, with the bevel upwards; other joinery planes have irons bedded at 45° (with the bevel down), similar to bench planes, or steeper still. Some of these planes are designed to cut cross-grain with the help of sharpened spurs or nickers ahead of the iron to slice the fibers cleanly.

An 18th-century craftsman had to make do with only a few of these specialized joinery planes; he would likely have had a few sizes of dado planes, a fillister or large rabbet plane, and a plow plane. With the development of more complex planes and their expanded industrial production by such makers as Stanley, a craftsman could afford to buy any number of specialized cast-iron planes for cutting and fitting joints. It wasn't that the new planes could cut more complex joints, but they were

easier to use and worked more accurately than their wooden counterparts.

As with bench planes, shapers, routers, and similar woodworking machines have largely replaced many of these tools in the woodworking trades. Sadly, too, strong traditional joints have given way to the more quickly machine-cut biscuit or dowel joint. Still, some of these joinery planes are just as useful today to fine-tune joints cut by hand or with a machine.

PLANES FOR SMOOTHING

Among the most useful tools in any contemporary shop are the third class of planes: those used for the final leveling and smoothing of surfaces. Because they are no different in design and are used in a similar way at the bench, smoothing

English smoothing planes are among the most beautiful planes ever made, and they work as well as they look. Shown here are an A6 Norris (at rear) from the famous company of T. Norris of London and a smoothing plane by Spiers of Ayr, Scotland, the first commercial maker of such planes.

Scrapers are versatile tools that can smooth surfaces that are difficult to plane. The simplest scraper is a piece of sawblade, but easier to use are handled scrapers such as the ram's head scraper at rear, a spokeshave-type scraper in the foreground, and a small, specially made tool for scraping a convex profile.

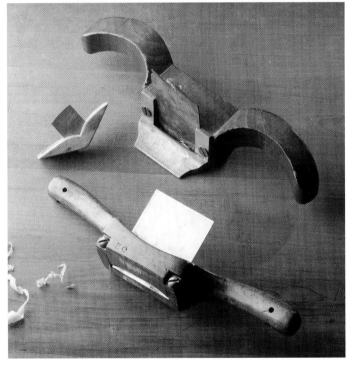

for the final leveling of a surface already worked on by other planes, their small size is an advantage for easy maneuvering as their weight helps them hug the surface. A light cut, a heavy iron, and the overall massiveness of the plane result in chatter-free smoothing cuts and a polished surface.

Scrapers and scraper planes, versatile smoothing tools that complement smoothing planes, are included in this third class. Although they look and work slightly differently from planes with a chisel-like iron, they are essentially plane tools. With a thin steel iron held at a high angle to the surface, scrapers can cut or scrape fine shavings from wildly figured or difficult wood—often better than any other tool. Shape the iron, and scrapers can "scratch" shallow profiles similar to a molding plane along straight or curved edges. Substitute a toothed iron, and this tool is useful for roughing veneers for a good glue bond or for aggressive leveling of very difficult woods. Because they are so useful, scrapers are found in many forms throughout the woodworking trades.

PLANES FOR SHAPING

A final group of planes shape surfaces or edges. These tools are as varied as molding planes that cut the wood with shaped irons and corresponding shaped soles (see the top photo on the facing page), panel-raising and chamfering planes with straight irons held at an angle to the work with the aid of a shaped sole, and compass planes with curved soles and straight or curved irons. Shaping planes could be further divided into those that shape decoration (molding planes) and those that work curved surfaces (compass planes). Categorizing some of these planes is hard because nearly all of them do more than just cut shapes. For example, a compass plane shapes the surface and

planes are sometimes included with the bench planes. How they do differ is in the way they are tuned and in the degree to which smoothing planes have evolved on their own to suit their specific purpose—to such beautiful tools as

dovetailed steel, brass, and rosewood Norris planes capable of smoothing the most difficult woods (see the photo at top). Whether of wood, metal, or some combination, smoothing planes tend to be small and heavy, with a tight mouth and a finely set iron. Since they are used

can also leave it as smooth as if finished with a smoothing plane. This points out the basic difficulty of trying to put planes neatly into groups; many will do varied work depending upon how they are tuned and in whose hands they are used. Some just don't fit neatly into any group. Where would Stanley's Universal Plane #55 fit in these categories, "a planing mill within itself" capable of cutting joints, moldings, truing and shaping edges, plowing grooves, and more besides? Or how about an ice plane (see the bottom photo at right)?

Of the many types of planes in production and in use up until the middle of this century, very few are still being made today. Even the best woodworking catalogs list at most a couple of dozen planes, compared to the many hundreds in all sizes and types that Stanley Tools and others once offered. With few new, quality planes available, one might well believe that planes are steadily and slowly passing from the woodworking trades. To an extent this is true. With the simultaneous development and marketing of routers, shapers, jointers, and every imaginable woodworking machine, planes are used less often for the tedious and strenuous tasks many were designed for.

Yes, gone are the days when each craftsman made many of his own wooden planes and a fancy inlaid tool chest to store them in as a rite of passage and learning the joinery trade. As artifacts of our culture, some of these handmade tools—beautifully made boxwood and brass plows, fillisters, and complex molding planes—are better left to be admired and studied by collectors and historians. That still leaves a wealth of usable planes of every description. To find out the real story about the vitality of these tools today, go to any tool auction and you'll be amazed at how

One might have found a stack of molding planes with matched pairs of hollows and rounds like this for sale at a tool dealer a century or more ago. The soles on the outside were visible, and as long as the stack was even, chances were good that each tier was a matched pair.

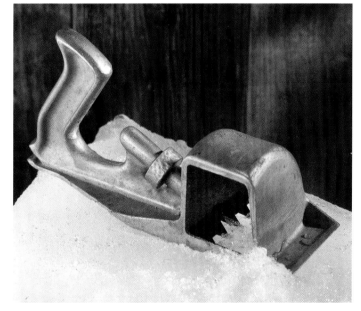

This odd tool looks and works like a plane, except that it shaves ice rather than wood (maybe for the first slush drinks?). The iron is sharply toothed like a saw, and the body is made of aluminum to prevent rusting.

eagerly sought out are planes once common 50 or more years ago. Planes that once sold for a few dollars can now bring a hundred times as much. Or use one of Lie-Nielsen's new planes, recast and better engineered versions of earlier

Stanley planes, and try to resist its beauty and smooth cutting. Better yet, talk with any good craftsman and chances are he has a toolbox full of favorite planes that he can't imagine working without.

2
HISTORY OF PLANES

The invention of the Plane was the most important advance in the history of woodworking tools in the last two thousand years.

—R. A. Salaman, *Dictionary of Woodworking Tools*, 1975

Early in my adventure with planes it was easy to appreciate the wide range of work that planes could do, but they were still just some of the many tools I used during the course of a day. It wasn't until I started using a noble old Scottish smoothing plane, a heavy and beautiful Spiers of steel, rosewood, and bronze, that I became really curious about the history of these tools and planes in general. Here was a plane so different from my Bailey smoothing planes that clearly embodied the exceptional skill of

its maker of over a century ago. Into the worn and polished wood was stamped the maker's name along with the name of the craftsman who had owned and used this plane. Why did this tool work so well, and where did the design come from? What was the inspiration of the plane maker that combined his skills, knowledge, and artistry in this plane? Who were the craftsmen who used such tools when other furniture makers chose cast-iron "Bailey-pattern" planes?

Understanding how planes have evolved will deepen your appreciation of these tools and offer much insight into the creativity of the toolmakers who made them, the craftsmen who used them, and the society that shaped them both.

Early Toolmaking

Man the toolmaker has always been trying to improve his tools. Ever since prehistoric man chipped a crude cutting edge from a hunk of flint, he had a tool to scrape wood or work other materials. The next logical step was to shape a handle and lash it to the sharpened flint with strips of animal hide and he had an ax. Every advance created better tools that extended the natural motion of his arms, hands, or body. However

This early-15th-century illumination from the *Bedford Book of Hours*, entitled "Building the Ark," shows medieval tools, including planes, at work. (Photo used by permission of The British Library, London.)

sophisticated the hand tools of later ages, they don't deviate from this very simple purpose.

The further development of tools was limited only by the materials they were made of—how difficult the material was to work and how durable the finished tool. A handled stone hammer was a big improvement over a stone held in the hand, but it wasn't until man learned how to smelt copper, and later bronze from copper and tin ore, that toolmaking could make the next leap forward. Copper was easily freed from the ore and could be worked into useful cutting tools, but bronze was more useful still. Bronze is a hard metal that melts easily, can be cast in many forms, and can be sharpened to hold a better edge than any copper tool. It was during the Bronze Age that some of the basic carpenter's tools evolved: the ax, chisel, adz, and saw.

Most of the tools familiar to us today did not develop until the discovery of ways to smelt iron from hematite ore ushered in the Iron Age some 3,000 years ago. Here was a material far more available than bronze, a material that could be hammered and shaped, that held a good edge, and that could be easily resharpened. But iron is a complex metal that doesn't yield its secrets easily. Smelting the ore results in a weak iron full of impurities. Only by repeatedly heating and hammering the metal can these impurities be worked out and "wrought" (meaning worked) iron be made. Each time wrought iron is heated in a charcoal fire and hammered, it absorbs some carbon and gradually becomes steel, which is much better for toolmaking. Steel in this form is tough but unfortunately too brittle. It wasn't until sometime during the Roman era that two processes were discovered that allowed the forging of truly useful tool steel: quenching and tempering.

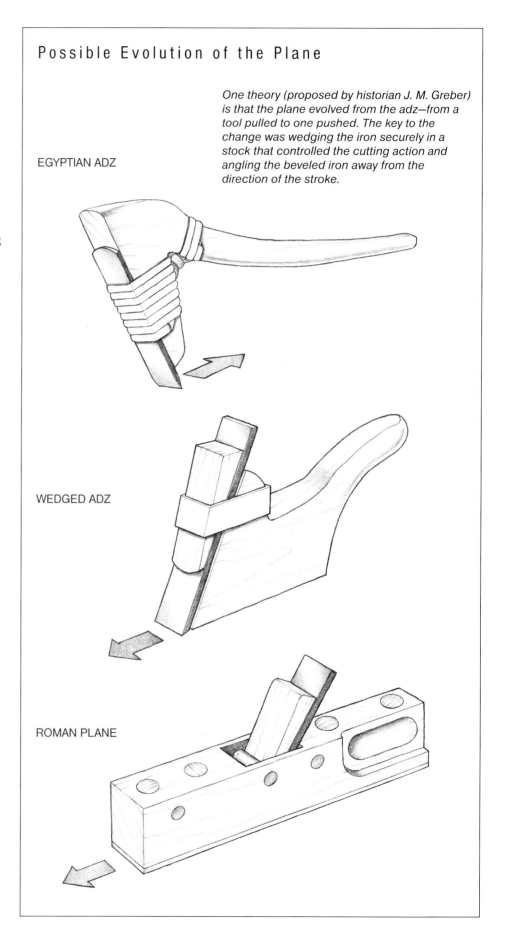

Possible Evolution of the Plane

One theory (proposed by historian J. M. Greber) is that the plane evolved from the adz—from a tool pulled to one pushed. The key to the change was wedging the iron securely in a stock that controlled the cutting action and angling the beveled iron away from the direction of the stroke.

EGYPTIAN ADZ

WEDGED ADZ

ROMAN PLANE

Quenching, rapidly cooling the red hot metal in water or oil, hardens the steel. Tempering, reheating the steel to a low temperature, softens this hardness enough to create tough cutting edges that are not too brittle and likely to crack or chip in use.

The known origins of the plane follow this understanding of turning iron into tool steel. The earliest discovered planes are Roman, but it is possible that the plane was a tool known to earlier cultures (see the drawing on the facing page). What is strange is how fully formed the plane is when it appears, without any clear antecedent. Yet well over 1,000 years before, Egyptians were building furniture as sophisticated as that of any age since, with dovetails, mortise-and-tenon joints, inlays of ivory and gold, veneers, frames and inset panels, and decorative moldings. Was all of this fitting and smoothing done entirely with saws, chisels, adzes, rasps, and sanding stones? We know that the Egyptians had bronze chisels with hammer-hardened cutting edges, which

could have been held in some sort of wood body and used like a plane, but to date no such tools or pictures of them have been found to establish that Egyptians might have invented the plane.

The First Planes

The earliest known planes, dating from A.D. 79, were found preserved in the ash at Pompeii. Enough similar Roman planes and plane irons have been unearthed elsewhere to give us a good idea of how these tools looked and worked. The simplest of these tools are made entirely of wood with an iron cutter wedged against a cross-bar—very much like any basic wooden plane made even today. Some surviving Roman planes have bodies made of wood partially covered over with iron and riveted together, forming the sole and the sides of the body (see the photo above). A simple handhold is cut into the wood at the rear. The Roman plane maker was probably well aware of the long-wearing sole and overall durability of an iron-clad plane that more than

justified the added trouble to make it. Another form of Roman plane is all wood except for iron plates reinforcing the sides of the plane at the throat.

It's amazing how little these early planes have changed from the tools used by a carpenter today. A modern plane is more likely to be made of cast iron, the steel in the iron is tougher and holds an edge better, and the iron can be adjusted more easily than in the earlier tools, but the basic concept has not changed. The concept is a simple one—a tool with a cutting iron wedged in a plane body that allows good control of the cutting action.

Little is known about how planes were used or what they looked like from Roman times through the Middle Ages and into the early Renaissance. Since hardly any planes have survived, what we do know comes from secondary sources such as carvings, stained-glass windows, and illuminated manuscripts. In one such illumination, *Building the Ark* (see the photo on p. 12), we see that planes are in common use and little changed from Roman prototypes. From other

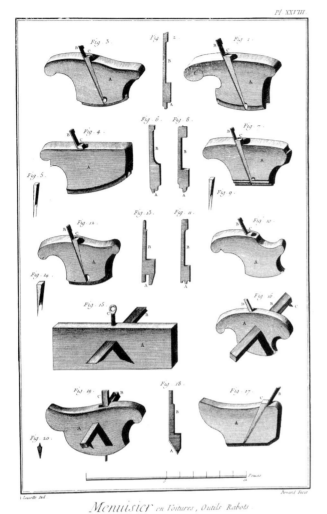

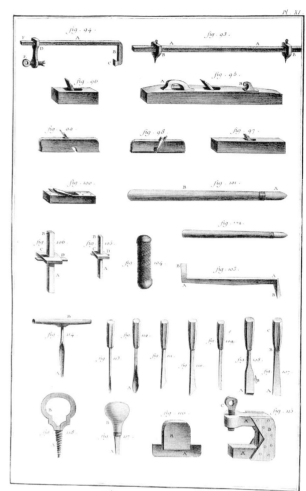

Engravings from works such as Denis Diderot's *Encyclopédie* give an idea of the types of planes in use in the 18th century.

sources we know that planes had evolved in a range of sizes, and specialty planes such as molding and rabbet planes had begun to appear. Wood was used to build nearly everything from ships to military machinery, and planes must have been important tools throughout this period.

One of the greatest impediments to change in tool design and methods of working was the power of the guilds, which began to form among artisans and merchants during the Middle Ages. Guilds grew out of the gradual division and specialization within the woodworking trades, into such groups as carpenters, furniture makers, shipwrights, and wagonmakers. Guilds regulated every aspect of each craft, from the training of apprentices to establishing wages and prices for finished goods, and they guarded trade secrets and working methods as well. Apprentices copied masters in what became an inflexible system, discouraging innovation and stifling the evolution of new tools and ideas. It's no wonder, then, that the basic tools and ways of working wood remained essentially unchanged until the strength of the guilds waned in the early 18th century.

We do have a glimpse into guilds, the woodworking trades, and the range of planes in use at the time through Joseph Moxon's *Mechanick Exercises, or The Doctrine of Handy-Works,* published in London in 1678. It is the original "how-to" book, but written more for the curious gentleman than for the workman trying to learn the trade of house carpenter, joiner, or turner. Nevertheless, it is one of the first books to illustrate the tools in use for these trades and to explain how to set up and use bench, rabbet, plow, and molding planes. We can learn even more from two books published about a century later: Denis Diderot's *Encyclopédie* and André-Jacob Roubo's *L'Art du Menuisier* (The Skill of the Cabinetmaker). Diderot describes nearly every trade, and includes extensive engravings of their shops, tools, and methods. All three books give clear insight into woodworking tools and methods before great changes took place in the 19th century.

Through these books and other sources, we know of at least two subtle changes in plane design that had occurred: The iron was wedged into place in tapered grooves (or abutments) cut into the sides of the body rather than against a cross-bar, and handles were evolving to designs common today. Wedging the iron in tapered grooves with a more thinly shaped wedge—a method still used for most wooden planes—reduced the plane's tendency to clog. Subtle changes in the throat shape helped the plane work better, too.

Whereas Roman planes had a handle formed in the plane body and later ones had a simple rear handle, handles were gradually evolving to the more upright open or closed tote we know today. For a more positive and comfortable grip, Continental craftsmen added an upright handle in the shape of a horn to the toe of the plane. Over time this became the sculpted, rounded cow's horn still common on German and Austrian planes (see the photo below). Continental craftsman were also apt to decorate their tools with personal touches—carved or stamped initials and dates, punched or chip-carved designs, and gracefully carved throats. Meanwhile English planes, which would later influence American tools, maintained simple, restrained lines.

These two horn planes show the upright handle and decorative detailing characteristic of European planes.

The Development of Modern Planes

Many changes occurred within the woodworking trades and society in both England and America during the last half of the 17th century into the 18th century, and with these changes began the evolution of modern woodworking tools.

One of the most far-reaching changes was the gradual specialization and sophistication of the woodworking trades. This happened first in England and later in the Colonies due to a growing population, changing tastes, increased wealth, and demand for all types of goods. The changes in building tastes illustrate this quite clearly. As houses in America followed the sophisticated English Georgian style, the hewn house frame was covered with paneling and trim. No longer were just the skills of a carpenter required, whose work was now confined to erecting the frame and the sheathing, but also the talents of a joiner completing the interior. Besides the basic tools of the carpenter, the interior finish required planes to cut fielded panels, to plow grooves for these panels, to cut crown and other moldings of all sizes, and to build window sash and doors. The cabinetmaker who built the furnishings needed special planes, too, as tastes changed from heavy, simple solid-wood furniture to sophisticated inlaid and veneered furniture of exotic or wildly figured woods.

It is possible that one early specialization within the woodworking trades was plane making, although there is no evidence of this until about 1700. Thomas Granford of London was the first plane maker known to "sign" his work. This was a profound change that has had an effect right up until the

Stamping plane irons with the maker's mark was an early form of advertising. "Warranted Cast Steel," stamped on these two irons, was known for its superior quality and its ability to hold a keen edge.

present, that of separation between the plane maker and the plane user. Before this time, individual craftsmen made their own planes as the need arose, with the irons coming from a local blacksmith or from small specialized manufacturers. It was fairly simple work for a craftsman to fashion a new bench plane as the work demanded. As it was, wooden planes needed to be regularly replaced, because they lasted only so long under hard use. Whether due to normal wear or regular reflattening of the sole, the mouth of the plane eventually grew too wide and the plane worked poorly.

Another change hastened the shift from each craftsman making his own planes to specialized makers: the need for more complex tools and more tools in general. As the work of a joiner demanded planes to cut moldings, raise panels, and the like, he increasingly turned to individual plane makers with the tools and ability to make them. Whereas a jack plane was easily made, complex molding planes and plow planes took skills and tools not easily acquired. As the population grew and with it the demand for more goods of greater variety, more craftsmen were needed for the work. Since this was well before industrialization, this meant a growing

The introduction of the double iron, as on this unusual molding plane for heavy work, was a major development in the history of plane design.

need for planes and woodworking tools. Specialized plane makers moved to fill this market, eventually leading to the gradual conformity of sizes and shapes of planes.

Paralleling the trade of specialized plane maker was the ironworker who made plane irons, files, and other edge tools. Since the late Middle Ages, Sheffield, England, had become an important center in the steel-making trade, due in large part to its experienced smiths and plentiful river power to turn water wheels and grindstones. Importing Swedish iron because of its purity, small manufacturers forged an array of superior-quality plane irons and

edge tools in many shapes and sizes. Benjamin Huntsman's process of making crucible cast steel further improved the quality of edge tools from 1742 onward, to the end that Sheffield irons were regularly exported throughout the world (see the sidebar on p. 45). Throughout the 19th century many types of Sheffield-made plane irons and steel plane parts made to the highest standards were offered for sale through the catalogs of American plane makers. Even as late as 1939, Stanley proudly states in its catalog of that year that its irons are stamped from the "best English steel."

Blacksmithing skills and an understanding of iron arrived in the Colonies with English immigrants, but it was a long time before domestically forged irons could equal those of Sheffield. Wrought iron was made from naturally occurring bog iron as early as 1719, but it was unsuitable for cutting edges. To make a good plane iron, a steel edge, most likely imported from Sheffield, was forge-welded to the wrought-iron blank. Early plane irons show this distinct weld line between the different materials. When the cutting edge was worn down by use and sharpening, a blacksmith would "steal" it, or weld on a new one.

Through all of this time, each trade used a greater variety of planes, but the basic physics of the tools was essentially unchanged from centuries earlier. Sometime late in the 18th century came a major improvement that did change plane design—the introduction of the double iron (see the photo on p. 19). A slightly curved cap iron screwed to the cutting iron greatly improves the plane's ability to cut difficult wood. Not only is the double iron heavier, more rigid, and more stable, but the cap iron also supports the cutting edge and helps curl the shavings and breaks them as they are planed. This simple mechanical advantage reduces tearout and leaves a smoother surfaces. Many specialized planes had a single iron, but most of the hardest working bench planes were fitted with double irons, costing roughly twice that of a single iron.

EARLY PLANE MAKING IN AMERICA

Before plane making became a specialized trade in America early in the 18th century, most tools were imported from England or arrived with immigrants. What tools the colonial craftsman didn't buy from England he made himself and most likely fitted with imported irons. England offered a greater variety of tools, and as some craftsmen felt, superior quality, too. Planes of all sizes and shapes were imported, along with plane irons and plane parts: fillister and plow plane depth stops, iron soles for smoothing planes, and plow skates. With close trading ties and a shared history, English tools set the pattern for and influenced American tools well into the 19th century. It wasn't until the Civil War that this changed significantly, although even today English tools still have a special appeal.

The earliest plane makers in America worked either in or close to coastal towns important as trading or population centers. The Colonies lagged behind England in the specialization of the plane maker for a number of reasons. There was less demand for the tools from a smaller population, good tools could be easily imported, and craftsmen were initially concerned more with creating the necessities of life rather than decorative furniture or fancy buildings, which required specialized tools. Deacon Francis Nicholson, working in Wrentham, Massachusetts, from about 1728 to 1753, is the first documented colonial plane maker. Many Nicholson planes, along with those of his son John, his black slave Cesar Chelor, and a handful of others, have survived. Except for slight differences in length and wedge finials, and the use of yellow birch instead of the more usual beech, they could easily be confused with contemporary English planes.

One of the few ways we can follow the development of the plane-making trade in America is through the name that each maker stamped into the toe of his planes (see the photo at left). Some makers included their town in a form of early advertising. By studying census

Early wooden-plane makers boldly stamped their names and towns into the toe of their planes. Shown here (from left) are a Nicholson plow plane with a fence riveted to the arms, a Chelor panel raiser, a Nicholson crown molder, and (in the foreground) a simple round.

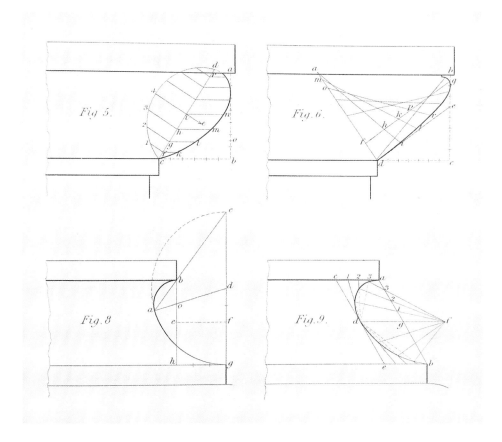

work on architecture, his *American Builder's Companion.* The changes in molding styles he proposed were as different as the new Federal style.

Typical molding profiles before then were based on Roman prototypes and arcs of circles. Benjamin's moldings were based on quite different Grecian models—the soft and subtle curves of parabolas, ellipses, and hyperbolas (see the illustration at left). His book explains simple mechanical methods for laying out the new ovolos, astragals, and ogees that were to become the basic molding forms right into the 20th century. Now carpenters and furniture makers needed a whole new set of molding planes in the latest style, which a growing number of plane makers readily supplied. While these were sweeping changes, it was nothing like what would occur with industrialization and the development of the cast-iron plane later in the century.

The Golden Age of Planes

By the end of the 18th century the Industrial Revolution was well under way in England. Even so, with a surplus of labor and lingering effects of the strong guilds, hand methods of work persisted. English sawyers effectively resisted powered sawmills long after they were a common sight in America, turning out millions of board feet of lumber, shingles, and clapboards from its vast forests. Industrialization was quickly

records, probates, indenture agreements, and the like, we can date individual makers. Some makers immigrated from Europe and continued working, giving us insight into differences between the plane-making trade here and in England. The irony of studying any planes is that the ones that have survived are the ones that were less used for some reason; planes well used wore out and usually did not survive.

As the population grew and colonial society matured, changing tastes once again give us insight into the demand for specific planes and their gradual evolution. One way that changing tastes were popularized was through architecture books, both those for the craftsman and those for wealthy gentlemen builders. Two of the most important were Batty Langley's *The City and Country Builder's and Workman's Treasury of Designs,* initially published in

1740, and Thomas Chippendale's *The Gentleman and Cabinet-Maker's Director* of 1754. With such books, carpenters and joiners could learn rules for proportion and common classical moldings. As references, they guided the craftsman in selecting or making appropriate molding planes in accord with prevailing international tastes. Such books also served the needs of molding-plane makers, allowing them to keep abreast of changing architectural styles and produce planes that cut moldings in the latest fashion.

The Federal style was the first wholly American style. With advances in movable-type printing presses and the plummeting price for paper, information about the new style was easily dispersed through design books and penny magazines. In 1806, Asher Benjamin published the first original American

The Woods planing machine (c. 1830) was one of the earliest water-powered machines used to plane stock flat. The heavy wood frame supports a circular cutterhead with two gouge-like steel cutters set into the outer rim. (The machine shown here is housed in the Windsor Precision Museum, Windsor, Vermont.)

embraced here by a society independent of guilds, with a strong entrepreneurial spirit and a shortage of labor. Imaginations were captured by the possibilities of machines. It was just a matter of time before turbines (and sound hydraulic principles) would be applied to textile manufacturing and eventually to woodworking machines of all types.

The development of machines brought far-reaching changes to the woodworking trades in village and city alike. With a growing population and demand for all types of wooden goods came the incentive to develop machines to speed production and take over some of the laborious tasks. Work once done entirely by hand was now done by machine. It wasn't long before whole shops were mechanized, planing wood, cutting moldings, or building sashes, doors, and blinds. Along with industrialization came a better transportation network and the end of the largely self-sufficient community.

Rather than heralding the end of hand tools, initially mechanization only increased the demand. Hand tools were needed to build machines made largely of wood, and they still had a flexibility that machines lacked. Ironically, plane makers were among the first to see the possibilities of the machine, as a way to increase their production and create new and varied tools. Planers sped up the milling of wooden plane stocks that could then be further worked upon with circular saws and mortisers. Once industrialization was under way, fascination with the machine and machine processes drove tool design forward. As the century progressed, toolmakers turned their attention to new materials and to creating the new tools needed by craftsmen relying on machines.

CAST-IRON PLANES

Cast iron was one of the new materials toolmakers turned their attention to. While not exactly new—the Greeks and people of India had used cast iron—it wasn't until the mid-19th century that it was used for planes and other tools. Cast iron is simply molten iron with some impurities and a carbon content between 2% and 5% that is poured into a mold to cool. Its advantages for making planes are obvious: The plane body is stable, the sole is long-wearing, the throat stays consistent, and each plane is identical and inexpensive.

Hazard Knowles was the first to try casting planes. Interestingly, his 1827 patent was the first significant plane patent in America, and it was for a cast-iron plane that wouldn't be popularly accepted for another 50 years. Many other makers experimented with casting planes, either as complete planes or in combination with wood as in later transitional types; initially, none could make planes in sufficient quantities or economically enough to compete with wooden planes. It wasn't until past mid-century that the man we associate most with cast-iron planes, Leonard Bailey, got started. It took the huge advances in production technology spurred by the Civil War to finally establish cast-iron planes as a superior alternative to wood.

The necessity of making armaments during the Civil War accelerated the development of machines, machine processes, and the technology associated with interchangeable parts. These developments required factories. Making cast-iron planes required the same organized production system to turn out large numbers of identical parts. Leonard Bailey started making cast-iron planes with Stanley in 1869. In the 1870 catalog Stanley offered an impressive line of 28 different sizes and types, both cast iron and wood-bottomed. Even though

Pocket catalogs were one of Stanley's many ways of advertising its tools. Made for carpenters and woodworkers to carry in their toolboxes, catalogs were for handy reference or to thumb through during breaks when dreaming about future purchases.

such planes were unknown to most craftsmen and the wooden-plane business was firmly established, by the end of the century Stanley was selling millions.

Leonard Bailey was one of the brilliant inventive minds behind the success of cast-iron planes. It was from firsthand experience as a cabinetmaker that he was interested in improving his tools. From his first patent in 1855 to 1869 when Bailey, Chaney and Company was bought by Stanley Rule and Level, Bailey experimented with and improved many designs for bench planes and scrapers. He invented such things as the depth adjuster and the lever cap still common on planes today. In fact, the

design of the "Bailey-pattern" bench plane has remained essentially unchanged for well over a century.

The agreement between Stanley and Bailey didn't last. In 1875 Bailey broke away and started making a line of planes under the trade name "Victor." What followed was years of disagreement between them, as Stanley continued to get larger (typically by buying up competitors such as Victor) and Bailey finally gave up making planes.

What did last was Bailey's contribution to cast-iron planes and Stanley's incredible success with them. Success was not immediate though. For one thing, the planes were expensive compared with wooden ones. In 1870, the first year they were offered, #5 bench planes sold for $7.50 each; a premium wooden jack was closer to $1.50. As production increased, the next year the price dropped to $6.00, and by 1892 the same plane was $3.75. Stanley aggressively marketed its planes through pocket catalogs, trade magazines, store displays, and exhibitions. The advantages of the planes were so compelling that sales gradually rose. In the words of a contemporary catalog, "Increased sales meant increased production, increased production meant better facilities, better facilities meant better goods and lower prices..." and the promise of factory production of cast-iron planes was fulfilled. The demise of the wooden plane was just a matter of time.

THE DEMISE OF WOODEN PLANES

Wooden planes were in peak production when Stanley first started producing cast-iron planes. But during the last quarter of the 19th century three influences drastically cut the demand for wooden planes: the success of cast-iron planes, a gradual decrease in the need for handwork with the increasing availability and variety of woodworking machines, and the consolidation of the wooden-plane industry into a few large makers.

Once they became readily available and inexpensive enough to compete with wooden planes, cast-iron planes soon won out. They were simply easier to use and adjust; they stayed true and needed little sole maintenance. Wooden planes couldn't compete with the incredible variety of cast-iron planes that Stanley and others introduced year after year. Why carry a toolbox full of wooden molding planes when a Stanley #55 combination plane could do it all and

then some? Meanwhile, molding and milling machines reduced the demand for the work wooden planes usually did. The final blow to wooden planes was the demise of the small maker who could no longer compete against a few large manufacturers. Only major toolmakers such as Ohio Tool, Auburn Tool, and Chapin-Stevens could afford the factories and large-scale production necessary to make wooden planes economically. Auburn even competed by using prison labor! By World War I there were few buyers left for wooden planes.

The bright side is that wooden planes never disappeared entirely. They persisted longer in England, again because of the conservatism of the trades and a surplus of labor. That is why English molding planes can be found that cut Victorian moldings, whereas in this country such moldings were typically machine made. European makers such as Primus and E.C.E. never stopped making wooden planes either, although there seem to be fewer and fewer available in woodworking catalogs these days. Old wooden planes can still be found at any flea market or auction or from tool dealers. So many were made that there is likely to be a good supply for a long time to come.

Whereas few wooden planes are still made in America, Continental European plane makers continue to produce them, such as this Primus plane made of pear with a lignum-vitae sole and unique adjusters.

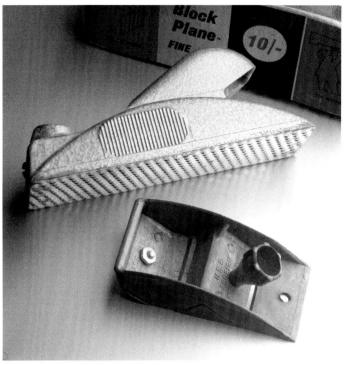

In the immediate post–World War II period, economics drove the market to low-cost and low-quality tools. Shown here (from rear) are a cast-aluminum Sargent #600 with "4-Edge Blade"; a Stanley "Handyman" in the famous two-tone colors, also with a replaceable "Ready-Edge Blade"; and a Millers Falls #8900 of traditional design with dark painted knobs and tote to resemble the rosewood once common.

Two unique 20th-century planes are a Surform (c. 1956), thought by some to be the only modern advance in plane technology, and, in the foreground, a razor plane that uses a disposable razor blade as a cutter, eliminating the need for sharpening.

From the Golden Age of Planes to the Present

Stanley dominated the market in the Golden Age of planes, from 1870 up to World War II. It's hard to convey the incredible range of planes Stanley made, literally hundreds, and many that no one else did, such as curved rabbet planes, dovetail planes, and beltmaker's planes. Stanley's Bed Rock line of bench planes was the best on the market. Other manufacturers such as Sargent, Union Tool, and Millers Falls competed with their own lines of cast-iron planes, either of their own innovation or patterned after expired Stanley patents. Only Sargent came close to Stanley in the variety of planes it offered, and they were every bit as well made, too. But it was inevitable that the demand for planes would diminish. Other than in a few specialized trades, a craftsman using hand tools just couldn't compete economically with machine-produced products.

Stanley continued to offer many of its planes right up until World War II, even though by then the market was much smaller. It hung on because it still aggressively marketed its tools, not only in America but now throughout the world. In England, Stanley competed with Edward Preston, a maker of fine-quality cast-iron tools, and later Record. In the United States, demand had persisted beyond the turn of the century because the population was still growing and moving westward. Carpenters building the housing still needed a few basic planes. Only a few specialized trades—furniture makers, stairbuilders, and others—used any more than these. Building had become a process of assembling component parts—dimensioned lumber of all sorts and sizes, machine-made moldings, doors, and windows. Stationary powered shop tools were readily available, and by World War II, portable electric wood-working machines, too. By mid-century only a few of the basic bench planes were in demand and thus economically viable to keep producing. Our long history of working with hand tools, while not entirely over, was vastly different from even a few generations before.

Millers Falls smoothing planes include (at rear) a deluxe #209 of c. 1940 vintage and a "Buck Rodgers" #709 with 1950s' streamlined styling, polished chromed parts, Tenite plastic handles, and solid plane physics.

Even if the demand for planes was diminishing, Stanley, Sargent, and others kept on making them. The planes were mostly the standard bench-plane sizes, block planes, and a few specialty planes such as rabbet planes. Generally the quality was poor. To keep costs down, castings were rough, the parts were poorly finished, and the handles were plastic or stained wood. These weren't tools for craftsmen, but for the newly expanding "do-it-yourself" market. Stanley even called one of its line of planes "Handyman" (see the photo at left on p. 25). To make some of these

planes even easier to use, Stanley revived the old idea of a disposable blade. No sharpening was necessary—you just had to put in another "Ready-Edge Blade." How frustrating it must have been to do good work with some of these tools.

In amongst these postwar planes there actually were some good ideas. The most novel is the "Surform," which is part rasp and part plane (see the photo at right on p. 25). Hundreds of hardened teeth "plane" the surface in any direction, without clogging. Then there are the "Buck Rodgers" smoothing planes made by Millers Falls, so thoroughly imbued with 1950s' style: red Tenite handles,

chrome-nickel finish, streamlined shaping, and oversized adjuster wheel (see the photo above). Clearly they were styled by a talented industrial designer, but they look as though they work wonderfully, too.

Although these postwar planes might look similar to those of the past, they are as different as the societies that created them. Hand tools are cultural artifacts that broadly reflect society overall. Planes of over a century ago, especially wooden ones, tell us much about the inventiveness, skills, and artistic sense of their makers. The craftsmen who used the tools valued these skills and the plane maker's artistry; perhaps this is what I love about my old Spiers smoothing plane. Most new planes no longer show the special care and talent of an individual maker, expressing instead our emphasis on production, uniformity, and affordability.

If not long ago beautiful planes of all descriptions could be bought by every type of craftsman for any imaginable need, it was because demand created a supply of good tools. After the turn of the century demand gradually lessened, until by World War II portable wood-working tools dominated the market for new tools. If many of the planes made since have plastic handles, are poorly machined and poorly finished, it's only because until recently this is what the market was willing to pay for. Those craftsmen who wanted good tools sought out the best old tools. They often still do.

While today the demand for planes is not staggering, it is by no means insignificant. Every craftsman needs at least a few planes, and not everyone has the skills or desire to restore old ones. Only a handful of makers are still making a line of common bench planes, nearly all of which resemble Leonard Bailey's planes of the 1870s. While there is also some demand for more specialized planes, modern manufacturing methods often require higher production runs, exceeding the limited demand. Fortunately, a number of Renaissance plane makers have tooled up. For example, Tom Lie-Nielsen of Warren, Maine, makes high-quality cast-iron and manganese-bronze planes based on Stanley patterns (see Chapter 12). But he doesn't just make copies; he has re-engineered and improved upon the originals. In fact, isn't this what plane makers since the Romans have been doing all along?

Modern Stanley planes include (from rear) an RB10 rabbet plane similar to the original #10 with a replaceable edge iron; a #9½A block plane; and a very new RB5 chisel and block plane, also with a replaceable edge iron. Wood is no longer used on any of these planes.

Lie-Nielsen's bronze #1 bench plane (in the foreground) is one of the best-quality planes made today. The plane at rear is a basic contemporary Russian plane of the same size with a single iron, more like an early cast-iron plane of more than a century ago.

3

PLANE MECHANICS

The amount of force required to work each plane is dependent on the angle

and relation of the edge, on the hardness of the material, and the

magnitude of the shaving; but the required force is in addition greatly

influenced by the degree in which the shaving is bent for its removal in the

most perfect manner.

— Charles Holtzapffel, *Turning and Mechanical Manipulation,* 1875

I t sounds like a child's joke: What has a toe, a heel, and a sole, two cheeks, a mouth, and a frog in its throat? And it's sliding across the bench toward you! All trades have specific names for things, and, in thinking about the parts of a plane, I wonder why many of these names correspond to parts of our bodies. Is there any connection between these anatomical names and the beautiful heads carved in the throats of early European planes? I believe we relate names to parts of our bodies because we can readily understand them. If I told

you a plane had a toe, a heel, and a sole and you had never seen one before, most likely you could imagine a tool shaped like your foot and right away know which end was the toe and which the heel. Even if you already know where the heel of a plane is, take a minute or two to familiarize yourself with the parts of a plane (shown in the drawings on pp. 30-31). Speaking the same language will help to avoid misunderstandings in this chapter, which explains how the different parts relate to the functioning

of a plane, and in later chapters on tuning and using planes.

Although they have similar parts, planes come in lots of shapes, styles, and sizes, are made of different materials, and have an iron held in various configurations. Yet one thing planes all share is the same basic cutting dynamics. If a plane is essentially an iron secured in a plane body, then its performance is a function of certain physical characteristics: the mass of the plane, how the iron is secured, how sharp it is, its pitch or angle to the sole and bevel angle, the width of the throat opening, the depth of the cut, and how the plane is oriented to the cut. Naturally these factors are all interrelated. For example, you will see later how skewing the plane has the same effect as lowering the pitch of the iron, giving a better cut. This

Shavings are as different as the tools that produce them. Shown here are translucent, gossamer-thin smoothing-plane shavings and coarse scrub-plane shavings, barely curled and looking almost as if they were gouged from the surface.

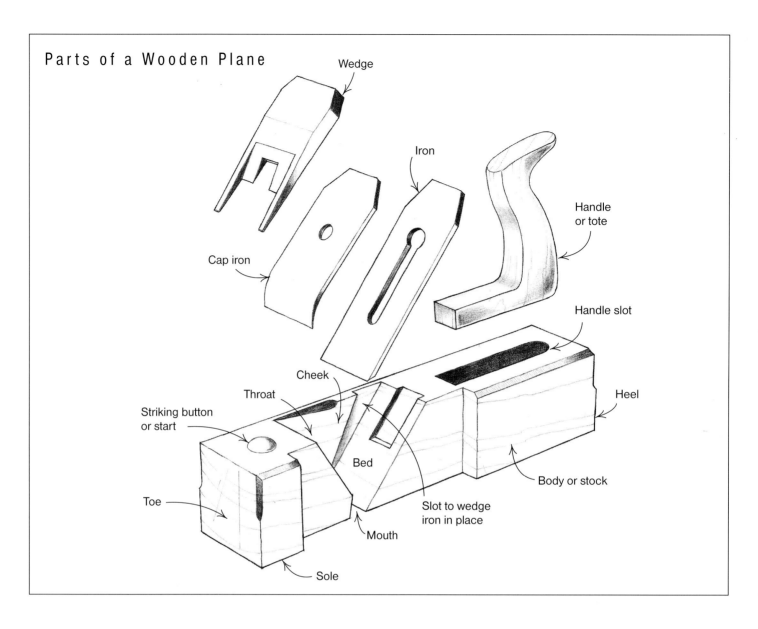

Parts of a Wooden Plane

Wedge

Iron

Handle or tote

Cap iron

Handle slot

Cheek

Throat

Heel

Striking button or start

Bed

Body or stock

Toe

Slot to wedge iron in place

Mouth

Sole

chapter explains how each of these characteristics affects a plane's performance, which will not only help you understand better how a plane cuts, but also help you choose the right plane for the job and tune it to do the best work possible.

Plane Anatomy

There are three general classes of planes, each with a somewhat different anatomy. What distinguishes them are the materials their plane bodies are made from: wood, metal (often cast iron), or some combination of the two, as in

transitional planes. The drawings above and on the facing page show the parts of a simple bench plane in both wood and cast iron.

WOODEN PLANES

The wood-bodied plane has a one-piece body or stock, which is cut into to create a throat, a mouth, a bed for the iron, and slots in the cheeks to wedge the iron in place. On such a plane there is usually a single handle or tote (to the English, a "toat") securely mortised or fastened in the rear of the body. This is usually the only handle on wooden bench planes, although earlier planes had a "grip" just

back from the toe. On better-quality traditional wooden bench planes there is a small button let into the top of the body at the toe, called a striking button or start, which is hit to free the iron and wedge, or to adjust the cutting depth rather than hitting and marring the plane stock. Starts can be boxwood, ebony, or steel—tough materials that can take the pounding. Some newer wooden planes have a start set into the end grain at the heel. Altogether, the wooden bench plane is a simple design that has changed little over the past two millennia.

The iron on the bench plane shown in the drawing is a double iron made up of

Parts of a Cast-Iron Plane

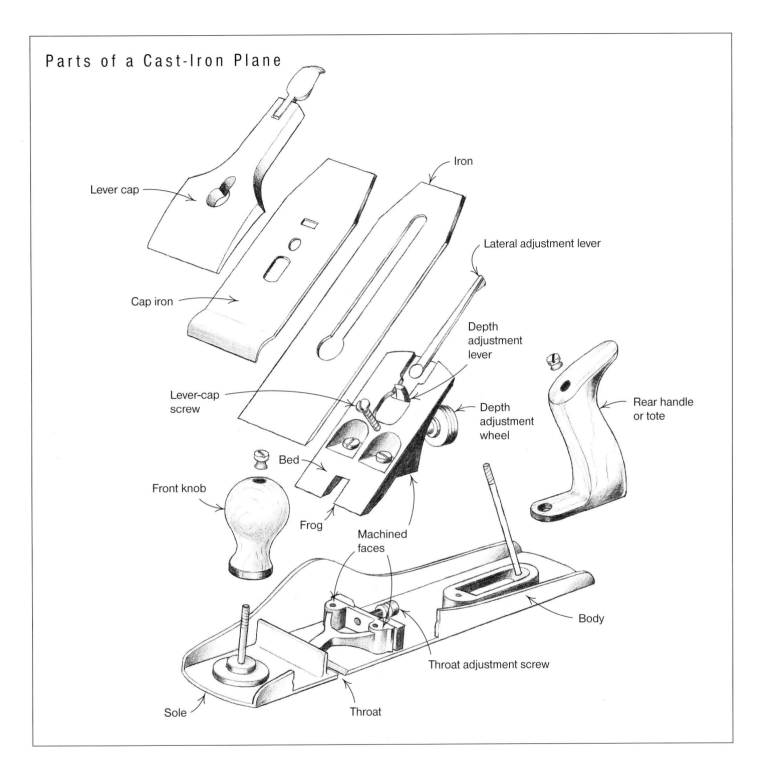

Lever cap

Iron

Cap iron

Lateral adjustment lever

Lever-cap screw

Depth adjustment lever

Depth adjustment wheel

Rear handle or tote

Front knob

Bed

Frog

Machined faces

Body

Throat adjustment screw

Sole

Throat

a cap iron bolted to the cutting iron; the two irons are held in place with a wooden wedge let into tapered slots cut into the throat cheeks. Over the years many wedge designs have been tried to hold the iron securely in place and allow the smooth escape of the shavings. Before about 1760 wooden bench planes would have had a single thick iron, as some still do, wedged in a similar way as the double iron. Eastern planes use a variation of this wedging system; they have very thick and short single irons wedged into place against a cross-bar, sometimes with either a wooden or steel wedge that does some of the same work as a cap iron.

CAST-IRON PLANES

Cast-iron bench planes might look different from their wooden counterparts, but the parts are basically the same. The one-piece cast-iron body has sides machined square with the sole, a mouth and a throat that the shavings pass through, a rear handle and a front knob bolted on, and machined faces where the frog attaches. The frog, a separate casting machined to mate with the plane body and screwed to it, forms the bed for the cutting iron. Except for the very earliest bench-plane designs, most frogs have some sort of adjustment screw to shift the frog's position. Besides the cost savings to cast and machine the plane body and frog separately, an adjustable frog allows the throat opening to be fine-tuned by moving the frog forward or backward.

Often the difference in performance between one cast-iron plane and another is directly related to how positively the frog mates with the plane body to support and stabilize the iron (see the sidebar on p. 47). The iron in the cast-iron bench plane shown in the drawing on p. 31 is also a double iron, but it's much thinner than those common in wooden planes. Whereas double irons perform better in hard-working bench planes, single irons are usual in other metal planes such as block and shoulder planes making light, accurate cuts. Whether the iron is single or double, a lever cap locks the iron down against the frog through a screw that allows for variable tension.

There is one small but very important difference between a cast-iron bench plane and a wooden bench plane: Most cast-iron bench planes have an adjuster that regulates the depth of the cut and the alignment of the iron, whereas few wooden planes do. We have a stroke of genius by Leonard Bailey to thank for this detail (see the sidebar at right). On the back of the frog are two adjusters. One is a steel lever with its lower end engaged in a slot in the iron that pivots side to side and brings the iron into alignment with the sole. This is the so-called lateral adjustment. Cutting depth is adjusted through two parts: an adjuster

PLANE-IRON ADJUSTERS

In the middle of the 19th century, with a growing interest in machines, invention, and cast-iron planes, there was a parallel interest in ways to adjust the iron more easily. The earliest adjuster designs were developed on wooden planes, most naturally because these were the planes in daily use. Lateral adjustment wasn't difficult—the iron could be tapped to either side to align it—but depth adjustment was trickier and took more care and a light touch.

Part of the challenge with wooden planes was coming up with a design that could move the iron while it was wedged in place. Some ideas worked by first unwedging the iron; more successful designs devised new ways to hold the iron that still allowed it to slide up and down. Many designs used some sort of threaded adjuster attached to both the plane body and the iron. While many of these early adjusters worked, they seem awkward compared with the ease of modern adjusters.

With the birth of cast-iron planes came inventive ideas for adjusting their irons. One

of the earliest, a Leonard Bailey design, used a lever behind the iron with a small nib that engaged with a plate riveted to the iron; rocking the lever raised and lowered the iron. From here it wasn't a big leap to an adjuster similar to ones still commonly used on block planes, with a wheel mounted on a vertical post that raised and lowered a lever or pin engaged with the iron.

Stanley competitors Union Tool, Chaplin, Sargent, and others came up with their own versions with large gears, levers that swing laterally under the iron, or a means to move the iron assembly on a carriage via a threaded rod. By the end of the century most cast-iron bench planes were using a version of the simple and successful Bailey adjuster that we know today.

Adjuster invention still goes on today. Primus wooden planes (see the photo on p. 24) use an adjuster that looks simple enough and works well, but it's almost too complicated to describe. More interesting is that they feel their planes need an adjuster to compete in the marketplace today.

Early adjusters for wooden planes look awkward to modern eyes. Shown here are Gladwin's 1858 patent smoothing plane (at rear), which has a brass lever cam that locks and unlocks the double iron, and Worrall's patent block plane, which adjusts with a screw at the heel of the plane.

Many innovative approaches were tried for adjusting the irons of cast-iron planes. On Chaplin's improved patent bench planes a large nickel-plated lever moves the "saddle" that holds the iron in or out.

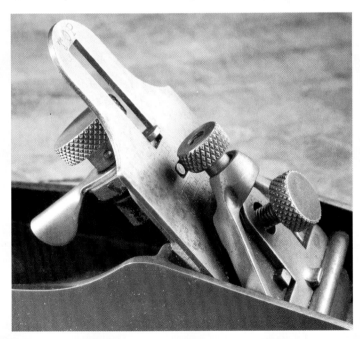

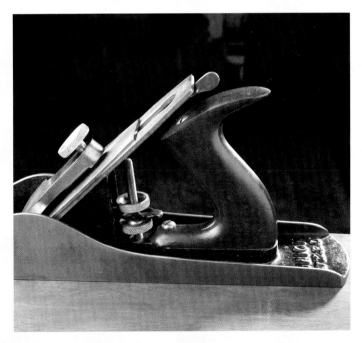

Sargent's VBM (Very Best Made) "auto-set" adjuster has a knurled nut that adjusts the depth of the cut and a large lever for lateral alignment.

Union Tool's vertical post adjuster is somewhat slower to adjust than a Bailey plane adjuster, but it is extremely positive.

A steel toe plate fitted to the toe of a shopmade wooden smoothing plane makes the throat adjustable for the finest work and keeps the sole from wearing.

Transitional planes are part wooden plane and part cast iron. This exploded view shows the number of parts that make up one plane, each identical and interchangeable with parts on similar planes.

wheel mounted on a horizontal post on the back of the frog and a Y-shaped fork captured by the adjuster wheel. The adjuster fork passes through the frog and engages with the cap iron; as the adjuster pivots, it moves the iron in or out. Some block planes have a modification of this same system, with the adjuster wheel mounted on a vertical threaded post set into the plane's sole.

Some wooden and cast-iron planes, a low-angle block plane being one, have another adjustable feature that's very useful for refining the cut of the plane: an adjustable throat regulated by a movable part of the sole ahead of the iron (see the top photo at left). It's handy to be able to adjust the throat for different planing jobs—a wide opening for coarse work and planing thick shavings and a tightly set opening for fine work and thin shavings. The advantage of the movable sole is the ease with which adjustments can be made; by backing off a nut or screw on the top of the plane you can loosen the sole piece and slide it forward or backward. For cast-iron planes without an adjustable throat, the alternative is to loosen and move the frog, which often entails removing the iron first. At one time cast-iron toe plates, for an adjustable throat, or complete iron soles could be bought separately and fitted to a shopmade wooden smoothing plane.

TRANSITIONAL PLANES

Although not all that different from wooden or metal bench planes, transitional planes have a unique anatomy. They combine the beech plane body of a wooden plane with the upper half of a cast-iron plane. Often they are mistakenly thought to be transitional in the sense that they mark a step in the evolution from older wood-bodied planes to newer cast-iron planes. In fact, metal and wood have been combined in planes since the time of the Romans (see the photo on p. 15). Stanley offered transitional planes the same year it started selling Bailey cast-iron bench planes, recognizing that some craftsmen preferred the lower cost and sweet action of a wood sole, along with the convenience of a metal plane's depth and lateral adjustment.

The wood body of a transitional plane is thinner than that of an all-wood bench plane, but with the same throat and rear handle. The iron casting that forms the upper half of the plane contains the same working parts as a metal bench plane: a similar frog, mechanisms for lateral and depth adjustment of the iron, a lever cap, a double iron, and a front knob. These planes are preferred by some for their lightness and easy planing, but they share the same limitations as all-wood planes. The sole naturally wears over time and can warp out of true with seasonal humidity changes. Early versions had another problem: The frog screwed right into the wooden body and would work loose over time and no longer support the iron rigidly. A later improvement screwed the frog into threaded bushings set into the plane body.

MATERIALS

Wood has always been an important material used in plane making, whether the plane is all wood, primarily cast iron, or somewhere between the two as in transitional planes. Beech is the most common wood, used in all types of wooden bench and molding planes because of its stability, toughness, and density. Some early American plane makers made planes of yellow birch, a wood similar to beech, for probably no other reason than to be different and distinguish their planes from English prototypes. More rare are beautiful planes of apple, boxwood, or bird's-eye maple.

These transitional planes were made by the Gage Tool Company, of Vineland, New Jersey, which was eventually bought by Stanley. Beech was the standard wood (background), but for a small premium, apple was substituted for a longer-wearing, more beautiful plane (foreground). The knob and handle are rosewood.

Dense tropical woods make stunning and long-wearing planes. Ebony planes, such as this low-angle English miter plane, are relatively uncommon.

Schoolboy planes were made to be nearly indestructible, either with thick castings or made from pressed steel or malleable cast iron.

sides of expensive British and American wood-and-metal planes (see the photo on p. 42).

Boxwood is a hard, long-wearing wood that has been used in many ways in plane making. Imported from Turkey or cut from hedges, boxwood works fairly easily and is so fine grained that it almost appears to have none. Small and expensive specialty planes are sometimes made entirely of boxwood, although its chief use has been for the parts of molding planes or plow-plane fences subject to hard wear. What has become known as "boxing" is inlaying boxwood (or lignum vitae or other hard tropical wood) where maximum wear occurs down the length of the sole of molding planes or where the profile is particularly fine and fragile. Boxing styles are as variable as the personalities of the makers, yet all are replaceable or repairable when needed. (Boxing is explained further in Chapter 10.)

Nearly any dense hardwood will make a good plane body, but for dimensional stability it is important that it be straight grained and quartersawn. Look at any wooden plane and you'll usually find the growth rings parallel with the sole and the sides showing quartersawn figure. Usually the plane blank is oriented so that the grain gently rises from the heel to the toe, so that in use the fibers are smoothed down rather than worked against (see the drawing on p. 30). Since many plane makers believed that the hardest part of the tree is closest to the bark, this side of the body became the sole. Sometimes the green plane blanks were boiled for a day or longer to speed the seasoning process and bring out the rich color of the wood. At the very least the blanks were seasoned for many years (sometimes as long as eight years). Seasoning the stock, choosing the right blank for a particular plane, and

In coastal towns and colonial shipbuilding centers, lignum vitae was the preferred wood for bench planes, most likely because tropical woods were regularly shipped to the Colonies through trade with Central and South America and the West Indies. Such a hard and dense wood (the only one that doesn't float) makes good tools that stand up to heavy use and wear. Other exotic tropical woods are also found in planes: Rosewood, cocobolo, and ebony have been used for knobs, handles, fences, and entire planes, such as the high-end plow planes. These tools are often further decorated with ivory, brass, or even silver details. Rosewood, ebony, and beech have been commonly used to "infill" or stuff within the metal sole and

orienting it properly have all been important parts of the wooden-plane maker's craft.

Whereas wooden-plane makers had a variety of woods to choose from, metal-plane makers have historically used only a few materials. Once the technology of cast iron had been sufficiently mastered, it became (and still is) the most common material for metal planes. The chief virtues of cast iron are its workability, its adaptability to many applications, and its low cost. It has another nice quality—cast iron is porous enough to absorb wax into the sole for considerably easier planing. If you've ever dropped a cast-iron plane you know very well its main limitation—its brittleness. Drop-forged and pressed-steel plane bodies are more durable alternatives to cast iron and good choices for schoolboy planes and carpenter's block planes subjected to rough use (see the photo on the facing page). Another limitation of cast iron is that it rusts. To overcome this, Stanley produced a few lightweight aluminum planes for a short time between the wars, but they never became popular.

The sole and sides of early British smoothing, miter, and panel planes (mid-length bench planes) are made from steel or gunmetal plates ingeniously and nearly invisibly dovetailed together. Rosewood, ebony, or beech fills the interior space and forms the throat, bed, front knob, and handle, with a gunmetal lever cap and tightening screw. Gunmetal is a common name for any brasslike alloy, be it brass, bronze, or true gunmetal, so named for its original use for casting cannons. Gunmetal is a beautiful bronze alloy of copper and tin in the ratio of 8:1 that's harder than iron and is easily cast and worked. Unfortunately, brass soles can leave smudges on the planed surface, so for this reason and added wear resistance a thin steel sole is often soldered on. Manganese bronze, an alloy containing almost no tin but a high proportion of zinc, has become the material of choice for many contemporary specialty plane makers. It has the same beauty and easy workability as gunmetal, as well as the nice advantage of weighing slightly more than cast iron. Since bronze is not a porous metal, bronze soles need frequent waxing for smooth, easy planing.

HANDLE STYLES

Not only does the plane maker have a wide range of materials to choose from, but he also has the freedom to shape the parts to suit his comfort or aesthetic. As a way to grasp the plane, to direct force to it, and to steer it, handles are one such element that takes many forms. They're as individual as each craftsman or plane maker, ranging from the functional to the beautifully sculptural.

The simplest "handle" is nothing more than a comfortably shaped plane body that affords a grasp. Wooden smoothing and block planes are held this way, as are metal block planes with the Stanley "Hand-y" feature—oval recesses milled in the plane's sides for a finger hold (as shown in the photo of the block plane at left). Small one-handed planes

Stanley experimented with aluminum for only a few years, making planes of this material quite unusual and uncommon. Shown here are a Stanley #45, #78, and block plane.

The simplest "handle" is a comfortably shaped plane body. The Little Victor (foreground) and the Stanley #101½ (center) are held by two or three fingers alone. The owner-made handle added to the Stanley #101 bullnose plane (rear) provides a place to rest the palm for added control.

Hammacher Schlemmer violinmaker's planes, shown here in a fitted case, have detachable tail handles that screw into the frog. The tool in the background is a peg shaper, which works like a tapered pencil sharpener or spoke pointer.

have rounded knobs, "squirrel tail" handles, or pistol grips. My favorite block plane, a Stanley #9¾, has a rosewood ball-tail handle, just comfortable enough to grasp and to use the plane one-handed, or to help balance the other hand on the front knob. To hold the smallest block planes, a squirrel-tail handle is the best, which as a Stanley catalog notes, "just fits nicely into the palm of the hand." Pistol-grip handles allow a lot of control steering the cut, either with one or two hands, as is common with coachmaker's planes (see the top photo on p. 217). Some violinmaker's planes have one further handle variation—a rounded palm grip on a rod that extends well behind the heel of the plane (see the photo at right above).

Of all planes, bench planes are the hardest working and most in need of a stout handle or a means of getting a firm grip. An early handle on wooden planes, if you can even call it that, was no more than a rounded support behind the blade that one's hand would stop behind to push the plane. The other hand would just grab the front stock of the plane. On later cast-iron planes a low or high knob was bolted on near the toe for a more comfortable and surer grip. Gradually the rear handle became longer and higher, eventually evolving to the shapely and comfortable open tote we know today. For greater strength, the same style tote is "closed" in what is also known as a "D" handle.

Cast-iron handles, formed as part of the plane body as in cast-iron plow planes and the Stanley #45 and #55, are almost always closed. This gives the tool good balance, an important attribute of any handle, and greater strength to survive hard use. Besides strength considerations, whether a plane has an open or closed handle is a matter of personal choice, assuming there is adequate room behind the iron for either style. I don't know if 19th-century craftsmen had small hands or if I have large hands, but I never seem to be able to fit more than three or four fingers comfortably around either style of handle. This might be an actual advantage; the odd finger comes in handy for adjusting the iron's depth on the fly, and laid along the side of the plane it gives an added bit of control.

If you look closely at an old cast-iron bench plane tote, you can't help but be struck by its beautiful, sculptural shape. You might also notice that the tote cants forward toward the throat of the plane. This subtlety gives an added measure of control by not only directing the plane forward but also pressing it downward into the cut.

Where once these totes and knobs were commonly rosewood, walnut, or cocobolo (or aluminum or hard rubber for replacing broken handles in school shops), today you'll find beech, stained maple, or plastic. None of the latter materials have quite the same feel or beauty as richly grained rosewood polished smooth over time, certainly not plastic, as durable as it is. Furthermore, plastic handles come one size fits all and they aren't so easily shaped to fit one's hand. Whatever your plane handles are

made of, don't be afraid to shape them for a better fit or to smooth the edges for comfort. More will be said about tuning handles in Chapter 4.

The Physics of Planing

Planes are more than just a collection of parts fitted together. Clearly some planes work a whole lot better than others. Why is this? Why can one plane curl up shaving after shaving from obstinate curly maple and leave a surface with an almost polished smoothness, where another plane chatters and clogs after a few uneven planing strokes? Certainly it's a matter of tuning and a certain harmony among the parts, a sharp iron, choosing the right plane for the work, and knowing how to use it. But it's more than this. Some planes just have physics in their favor.

The dynamics of the cut is fairly basic physics. The plane's cutting iron contacts the wood, driving a shaving into the throat that curls and breaks against the cutting edge of the iron (and against the cap iron, too, if the plane has one). Every part of the plane in contact with the shaving affects the physics: the sharpness of the iron, the size and smoothness of the throat opening, the pitch of the iron, and its bevel angle. Understanding some of the subtle aspects of this physics will really help in fine-tuning your planes, or it might inspire you to build a "better" plane.

A plane iron is really no different from a chisel; the plane body supports the iron in a way that allows good control of the cutting action. Imagine driving a chisel into a block of wood along the grain: Not only will the fibers be cut, but some splitting will occur as well. Areas where the grain splits out (otherwise

The closed "D" handle of this rare Miller's Improved Joiner's plow plane, in gunmetal with beautiful floral decoration, is formed as part of the casting.

Cutting Dynamics

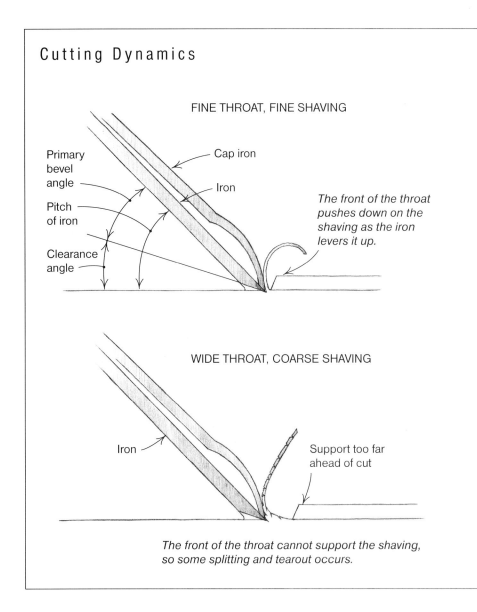

FINE THROAT, FINE SHAVING

Primary bevel angle

Pitch of iron

Clearance angle

Cap iron

Iron

The front of the throat pushes down on the shaving as the iron levers it up.

WIDE THROAT, COARSE SHAVING

Iron

Support too far ahead of cut

The front of the throat cannot support the shaving, so some splitting and tearout occurs.

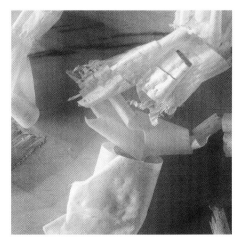

Fine shaving

Coarse shaving

known as tearout) are rough; cut areas are considerably smoother. The physics of a plane is simply an attempt to control the splitting in favor of cutting for a smooth final surface.

The quality of the cut is affected by the hardness of the material or its resistance to being cut, the cutting angle or pitch that the cutting edge makes with the surface, the direction of the wood grain, and the thickness of the shaving. If this same chisel had an acute edge similar to a knife, the wood was straight grained and easily worked, and a fine rather than a coarse shaving was cut,

then very little splitting would occur and the resulting surface would be quite smooth. Working with the grain, any splitting ahead of the cut would be above the final cut surface and be of minor significance. Also, less force is needed to cut with an iron with a thin edge profile. In theory, this is how a low-angle plane or spokeshave works.

The problem comes in cutting anything other than well-behaved woods with the grain, which is where a plane has distinct advantages over a chisel. Forcing the shaving into the throat of the plane causes it to be curled and repeatedly broken in a levering action

that limits potential tearout. The drawing above shows the cutting edge lifting a chip, forcing it upwards, and breaking it against the forward part of the throat as this part of the sole exerts downward pressure. Some splitting is bound to happen when planing against the grain; the best you can do is keep the tearout as fine as possible. A sharp iron, cutting a thin shaving, and a tight throat will all help. This makes it easier to understand why a wide throat (caused by wear or inattention) often does not give good performance—the chip is supported too far ahead of the cut and too much splitting goes on. Of course,

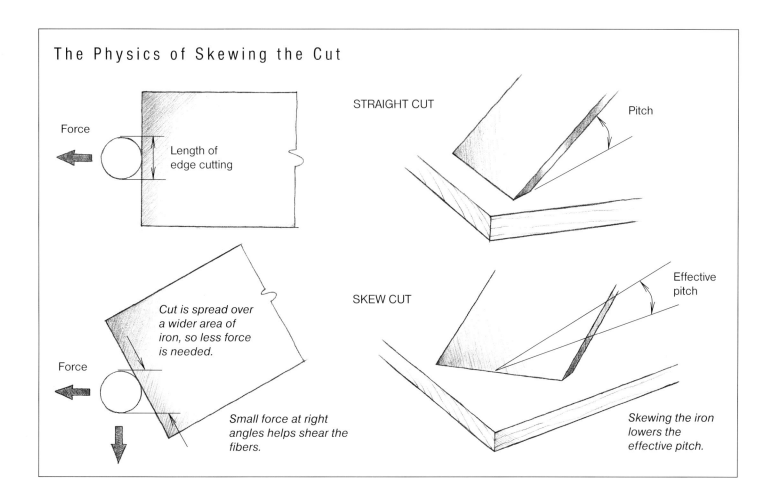

The Physics of Skewing the Cut

Force

Length of edge cutting

STRAIGHT CUT

Pitch

Cut is spread over a wider area of iron, so less force is needed.

Force

SKEW CUT

Effective pitch

Small force at right angles helps shear the fibers.

Skewing the iron lowers the effective pitch.

for rough work and planing thick shavings, a wider throat is necessary.

Effectively curling and breaking the shaving depends on more than just the width of the throat, but also on the inclination of the iron to the sole, or pitch, and the presence or absence of a cap iron. For hard or figured woods a steeper pitch is necessary for good results. The steeper the pitch, the more abruptly the shaving is curled and, assuming the fibers are pressed downward by the front of the throat, splitting out ahead of the cut is less likely. But the pitch of the iron has a dramatic effect on the force required to drive the plane; the steeper the pitch, the more force needed. This can be more easily understood by comparing the force needed to cut a shaving with a knife edge at a low angle to the surface (a thin wedge at 25° pitch) to the force needed

to cut with a chisel held at a high angle to the surface (a thick wedge at 45° or higher pitch).

A cap iron (also known as a chip breaker) presents a steeper angle than the pitch of the cutting iron and helps curl and break the shaving, but at the cost of slightly greater resistance. The closer the cap iron is set to the cutting edge, the more effective the cap iron. Most important is that the leading edge of the cap iron lie completely flat against the cutting iron to help stabilize it and not allow any shavings to lodge between the two and clog the smooth escape of new shavings.

SKEWING THE IRON

Skewing the cut is one way to have your cake and eat it too, so to speak—good performance and reduced cutting force. Rotating or skewing the plane at either a

slight or great angle noticeably improves the cutting dynamics. Three things happen: The effective cutting angle is lowered, the iron presents a smaller profile to the cut so there is less resistance, and a slicing force is added to the cut (see the drawing above).

Skewing is an incredibly effective strategy, especially for beginning a stroke smoothly. Skewing in one direction will often make a very noticeable difference over cutting the opposite way, especially in areas of swirled figure or knots. Increasing the skew of the plane can sometimes help, too, although with too much skew the plane is making only a narrow cut. At this angle the dynamics can also be so different that with some woods you start to get some tearout. The key is to experiment.

Characteristics that Affect Plane Performance

Once you've grasped the basic physics, you can better understand the characteristics of each plane that affect the way it cuts. Moreover, these characteristics are all interrelated: It doesn't matter what the pitch of the iron is if the iron can't hold a good edge, or how good the edge is if the iron vibrates and chatters under cutting pressure. Subtle changes in the plane's physical characteristics—using a heavier iron, a different bevel angle, or adding a microbevel—will often make a noticeable difference in performance. Being aware of the contribution of each of these factors will make it easier to understand how to tune planes, give you greater insight into ways to alter any plane, and help you decide which plane to buy for a specific need. One of the easiest factors to understand is how the mass of the plane affects the way it cuts.

MASS

When it comes to the plane's mass, all things being equal, a heavier plane is more stable, better able to support the iron and dampen cutting vibration, and able to cut a lot more smoothly. Taken to the extreme, we would all want planes about as heavy as we could comfortably lift, cast from pure kryptonite or some other incredibly dense space-age material. Such planes might work amazingly well, but we'd get pretty tired after a few minutes. What's important is to balance adequate mass for good functioning with how the plane feels during extended use.

Where the mass is balanced within the plane is every bit as important as how heavy it is. I am really conscious of a

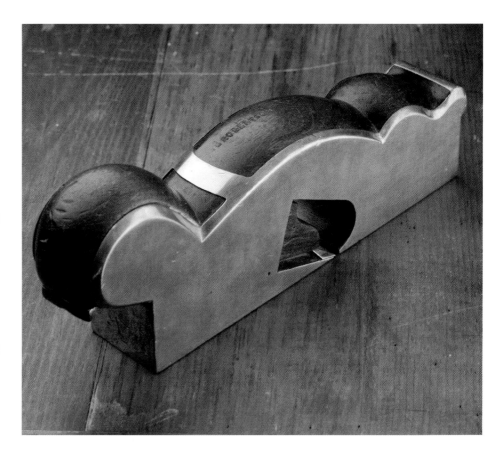

This beautiful English shoulder plane has a gunmetal body infilled with mahogany, which adds mass to the plane for superior performance.

plane's balance when raising it with one hand at the end of the stroke (as the other hand clears the throat of shavings). A casting heavier toward the toe, or a tote further to the heel, and the balance doesn't feel right. After a century of refinement, Bailey-pattern cast-iron bench planes strike the right balance between weight, where the weight is distributed, and the placement of the tote and knob. Although much lighter overall, most wood-bodied planes have the same fine balance gained by generations of refinement.

The mass of the plane relates directly to its inertial stability—its ability to maintain momentum as grain changes resist the cut. A plane cuts more smoothly with continuous and consistent speed, which explains why the longer bench planes perform well,

often just because they are heavier. A low center of gravity is another nice virtue, to help the plane hug the surface.

Mass has historically been added to planes in many ways. One way is to cut the plane body from naturally heavy materials, such as dense tropical hardwoods (see the bottom photo on p. 35). Using cast iron, steel, or manganese bronze can make a plane heavier still. Thicker castings can add even more mass and still keep the center of gravity low. But the best way to add mass is the oldest and the most time-consuming construction method that yields planes beautiful to look at and use: infilling a cast-iron, steel, or gunmetal body with rosewood or some other heavy and dense wood (see the photo above). Some of the earliest Roman planes were made in this way, as are traditional British miter, shoulder, smoothing, and panel planes. Overall they're about double the weight of similar wood-bodied planes and, other things being equal, perform twice as well, too.

A heavy cap iron and lever cap add little to the overall weight of a plane, but because they are right at the heart of the cutting action, their contribution can be important. A beefier cap iron is more likely to be rigid and better able to support the iron, especially the thin irons common on most bench planes. Similarly, a heavy lever cap or wedge is better able to help resist the same stresses as it locks down the iron.

SMOOTH AND CORRUGATED SOLES

Although less massive than cast-iron planes, wood-bodied planes have always had a natural advantage with their sweet action of wood upon wood. With a bit of wax on their soles, they work with an ease that is quite wonderful—I'm sure it's a factor in their enduring appeal. Waxing the sole of cast-iron planes (except for jointers or planes cutting surfaces to be glued) gives nearly the same satisfying feel. Many early cast-iron plane makers, being the tinkerers they were, felt they had to try ways to reduce the friction on the sole even more to make the work less tiring and their planes more competitive with wooden planes.

One of the earliest ideas was to inlay dovetailed strips of rosewood down the length of the sole (as shown in the top photo at right). One innovative maker milled zigzags down the sole's length, another cast large holes in the sole, and still another cast his name in a pattern of raised letters (see the bottom photo at right). Stanley tried corrugations, long grooves milled down the sole that started and stopped just shy of the heel, throat,

Each of these three early patented cast-iron planes has a different sole design to reduce friction: from the back, Steer's rosewood strips dovetailed into the sole; Rodier's wavy corrugations; and Birdsill's smooth plane with drilled holes.

Corrugated soles could serve as advertising, too, as on this mid-1870s plane by the Bailey Tool Company of Woonsocket, Rhode Island. This company was started by Selden Bailey, not the better-known Leonard Bailey.

A Japanese laminated iron and cap iron (bottom) is considerably more massive than the standard Stanley thin iron (center) and the thicker iron typical of old wooden bench planes (top).

and toe. Such planes were sold with the idea that they might work better in pitchy woods and the corrugated sole would eliminate any "suction" increasing friction. Another amusing explanation was that the corrugations were meant to hold wax and thus would constantly rewax the sole under use.

I've never had much use for corrugated soles and find them no different in use than a smooth sole. Moreover, small surfaces being planed can sometimes fall into the corrugations. Others must have agreed with me; corrugated planes are far less common, even though new they cost no more than smooth soles. Because of their rarity, corrugated planes

sell for a premium today. Perhaps their only advantage is the ease with which the sole can be lapped flat.

PLANE IRONS

A more massive plane iron has the same positive effect on performance as greater overall mass of the plane body. In most bench planes, it's easy to substitute a heavier iron for a difference that will amaze you. Eastern planes take this concept to the extreme; the wooden plane body is relatively light with a short massive iron—quite the opposite of traditional Western bench planes.

Since the iron is taking the full force of the cut, its ability to remain stable has a direct effect on the way the plane feels while cutting and on the quality of the

cut surface. Driving the iron into the cut changes the pressure on the cutting edge, which can cause it to distort and vibrate. Changes in the grain direction in figured woods, the naturally variable grain in any board, the size of the shaving, or working the plane at a skew all affect the pressure upon the iron. Of course, a dull iron increases the pressure, too. The thicker the iron, the stiffer it is and the better able it is to resist flexing and vibrating.

The invention of the double iron was a major advance in the evolution of the plane. The curved end of the cap iron not only helps curl the shaving better than a single iron alone, but the cap iron also supports the cutting edge. In the days when plane irons were commonly thick and heavy, a cap iron was less important because the iron was rigid enough on its own. But when Bailey and Stanley introduced a very thin iron (presumably because it was easier to grind and hone), a well-fitting cap iron became very important for best results.

Before thin irons became standard issue, two versions of a thick iron were common: parallel or gauged irons and tapered irons. As the name implies, a parallel iron is of equal thickness from end to end. Today's thin irons are parallel, too, but only about one-third the thickness of the older irons. Tapered irons have a distinct taper from a thick cutting edge to a thinner top end. Functionally, there is no difference between parallel irons and tapered irons. There is one subtle difference, however; over the decades of grinding and honing the tapered iron gets shorter and the cutting edge advances into a thinner section of the iron. This has the same effect as gradually widening the throat.

Japanese irons are typically tapered and, as with older Western irons, are made by forge-welding a steel cutting edge to a wrought-iron or mild-steel blank. Both materials are heated red hot and hammered together at the anvil. Originally this method in the West was born out of economy, because quality edge steel was usually imported and thus more expensive and less available than native wrought iron. But there is an added advantage to laminated blades. The wrought iron has a natural ability to dampen cutting vibration and makes for a stronger iron by supporting the harder and more brittle cutting edge. Because of the support the mild steel gives, laminated irons can be harder (Rc62 on the Rockwell hardness scale) than irons of high-carbon cast steel (Rc58-60) or a modern alloy, and hold a better edge as a result.

The hardness of the cutting edge has a major effect on its durability, how easily it can be sharpened, and its optimum bevel profile—certainly very important characteristics. Hardness is always a balance between a hard, long-lasting edge that is also brittle and likely to chip when forced into a knot or particularly unyielding grain, and a softer edge that has the necessary strength but doesn't sharpen quite as keenly and dulls more quickly with use. The harder the steel, the larger the bevel angle necessary to support the cutting edge. Honing a steeper microbevel or honing a back bevel are two ways to create a more durable edge and improve performance (see Chapter 4).

How do you go about choosing a good plane iron if you need one? Fortunately, few of us will wear out an iron in our working lifetime; if we do, it will probably be a common size for a bench plane. Certainly there are irons available in many modern steel alloys, each with slightly different working characteristics. With modern steelmaking processes and sophisticated means of hardening and tempering, plane irons have probably

THE QUALITY OF AN IRON

The search for the ideal steel for plane irons has been a difficult one. Iron is a very complex material. Even though smelting iron and forging it into tools has been known for 3,000 years, it wasn't until the 18th century that steelmaking was mastered. Only a little over a century ago with the invention of the Bessemer process was steel finally available in both large quantities and consistent quality.

Two problems plagued early attempts at smelting iron and refining it into steel: getting rid of the natural impurities in the iron and achieving the high heat necessary for making steel. Also necessary is a carbon content between 0.5% and 1.5%, which gives the steel the magical ability to be hardened and tempered. But as the carbon content drops, higher and higher temperatures are needed, requiring sophisticated furnaces and vessels to contain the molten iron.

Cast steel, a superior tool steel, was first made in 1742 by Benjamin Huntsman, a clockmaker searching for a method of making steel for springs of absolute regularity. He took pieces of blister steel (Swedish iron low in impurities heated in charcoal to absorb some carbon), melted them in a clay crucible, and cast the steel into bars.

This steel had a more consistent structure, perfect for forging into edge tools. Initially only small amounts could be made at a time, so it was expensive. Because of this, many early plane irons and edge tools have a noticeable weld line where an edge of cast steel was forged to a wrought-iron blank. As the cast-steel-making process improved, costs came down. Later irons were entirely cast steel and were so stamped to mark them as of high quality.

There is no equal to cast steel for its ability to take and hold a keen edge. A modern plane iron is almost certainly a steel alloy—some combination of carbon steel and a small percentage of tungsten, vanadium, chromium, or any of a half-dozen other elements. Alloying elements are added for many reasons: to increase the steel's hardness and hardening ability, wear and shock resistance, tensile strength, or resistance to corrosion. It is an incredibly complex and subtle process, where slight changes in composition affect the quality of the finished steel. Add to this the uncertainty of the hardening, quenching, and tempering of the iron and you can easily see why the quality of an iron is often a matter of luck.

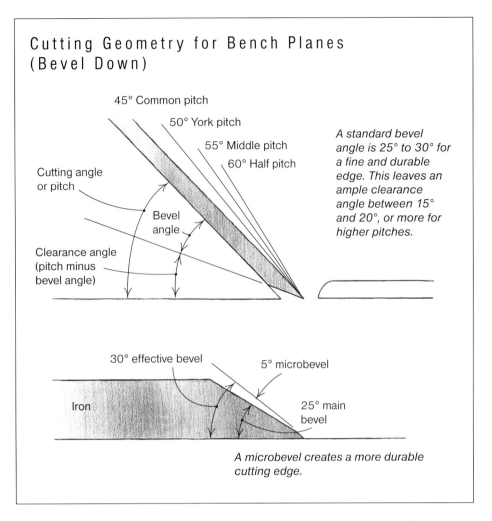

Cutting Geometry for Bench Planes (Bevel Down)

45° Common pitch

50° York pitch

55° Middle pitch

60° Half pitch

Cutting angle or pitch

Bevel angle

Clearance angle (pitch minus bevel angle)

A standard bevel angle is 25° to 30° for a fine and durable edge. This leaves an ample clearance angle between 15° and 20°, or more for higher pitches.

30° effective bevel

5° microbevel

Iron

25° main bevel

A microbevel creates a more durable cutting edge.

become more consistent, but no better than a good cast-steel iron of one hundred or more years ago.

Plane-iron metallurgy must involve an element of magic. Some irons are just excellent—they sharpen easily and hold a keen edge. Other irons range from adequate to useless. Two irons that look identical might sharpen and hold an edge quite differently. This is due in part to the differences in the way an iron is made today—whether it is stamped out of a sheet of steel or carefully hammered and forged by craftsmen who worked a lifetime to learn this subtle art. I always look for older cast-steel irons (usually stamped "warranted cast steel"), and the thicker the better (see the photo on p. 18). Two of my favorite irons were bought new on a whim at a hardware store in Singapore for less than $3! There is no easy answer as to where to find a great iron, but you'll certainly know it when you do.

Bedding the iron

Whether thick or thin, double or single, all irons need to have stable support from the plane body to cut well. Supporting the iron is the function of the bed or frog. On most planes the bed is cut forward of center so that there's more of the body mass behind and supporting the iron. On wooden and transitional planes the bed is cut right into the wood body; cast-iron planes have a separate frog cast and machined and then screwed to the sole of the body casting. The bed of wood-bodied and transitional planes is cut at a consistent angle right to the bottom of the sole, which gives the iron support over its whole length and helps dampen vibration. Any problems occur when the bed is not true or is warped in such a way that the iron doesn't sit flat and get full support.

Two-piece frogs have their own advantages and disadvantages. If the casting and finishing are done well, the bed is a true surface and will probably stay flat. Before it is screwed firmly to the sole, the frog can be slid forward or backward to fine-tune the throat opening. Better planes allow for adjustment of the frog without removing the iron, which is a definite advantage. Any weakness in the system comes from the rigidity of the connection of the frog to the sole. The larger the surface area between the two parts, the more stable the connection. This is clearly seen in the difference between Stanley's Bailey line of bench planes and the top-of-the-line Bed Rocks (see the sidebar on the facing page). Metal frogs have one further drawback; the bed is not a consistent angle right to the sole unless the frog is set in one exact position, which works counter to moving it to adjust the throat. This problem is discussed further in Chapter 4 (see pp. 57-61).

Pitch and bevel angle of the iron

The pitch of the iron is the angle it makes with the sole; the bevel angle is the angle ground and honed into the cutting edge of the iron (see the drawing above). The two characteristics are separate but related. The pitch is often a given—some planes are high angle, some are low angle, and most fall between the two. The bevel angle is variable within

When Stanley designed a new line of premium bench planes, they introduced them with typical bravado, declaring the Bed Rock "the best plane ever made." And they were right; Bed Rocks were the best bench planes Stanley or any of its competitors ever made. Although out of production by World War II, today they are eagerly sought after by collectors and users alike.

Bed Rocks might have been in production as early as 1895, but they first show up as a new product in catalog #28 (1902). Initially there was little difference between the Bed Rock and Bailey line of bench planes—they even looked the same—except for one important improvement: The frog of the Bed Rock was greatly refined. Not only did the new frog mate with the sole over a wider area milled to close tolerances, but it also fitted into a groove machined to receive it. This eliminated distortion or potential misalignment between the parts and resulted in a frog that was securely bedded to provide rigid support to the iron. The plane worked a lot better because of it.

Bed Rocks soon had another improvement. Initially the frog was secured to the plane with bolts, just as it still is in the Bailey line. With the bolts loosened, a fine-threaded captured nut behind the frog adjusts the frog forward or backward. After 1911 Bed Rocks used a more secure clamping system with two pins through the frog into the sole. Each pin has a cone-shaped dimple in its side. As the two screws with tapered ends behind the frog engage with the dimples, the pins are drawn tightly down. By just backing out the screws, the frog could be moved without first removing the iron as it would need to be in a Bailey plane.

Many of Stanley's patents in the early 20th century involved improvements to bench planes that first appeared in Bed Rocks. Still, Bed Rocks were very similar to Bailey planes; they shared some of the same parts and were about as heavy. To further distinguish their Bed Rock line, after 1914 Stanley squared off the tops of the sides and used a higher front knob. Numbered #602 through #608 (a #1 size was never made), Bed Rocks could be bought with flat or corrugated soles. The rarest of all is the #602C (corrugated), but the other sizes can be found and are well worth the search.

Bed Rock planes were made in a range of sizes from #602 to #608, with flat or corrugated soles.

The Bed Rock frog (left) was an improvement on the Bailey pattern frog (right). It has a large, accurately milled bearing surface, a groove to locate the frog, and two large pins to secure it.

Because trademarks are apt to change over time, they are useful for both tool collectors and historians as a means of dating manufacturing or ownership changes. One such trademark stamped on some of my plane irons had always piqued my curiosity: an "S.W." surrounded by a round heart. Just above the heart is the word "Stanley" outlined by a rectangular box.

This is the so-called "Sweetheart" trademark first used in 1920 to commemorate the merger of the Stanley Rule and Level Company into Stanley Works. Stanley Works was a huge manufacturing company, producing a line of goods from hardware to bulk steel. Stanley Rule and Level was manufacturing its well-known line of carpenter's and mechanic's tools, rules, and levels. Stanley Works started using the heart on its hardware line in 1915 to honor William Hart, president of the company from 1884 to 1915. It wasn't until after the merger of the two companies that the combined trademark was stamped on plane irons, and it continued to be used until 1934. Today some collectors buy only tools made during this brief period, creating demand at the yearly sale of at least one dealer where everything is Sweetheart vintage.

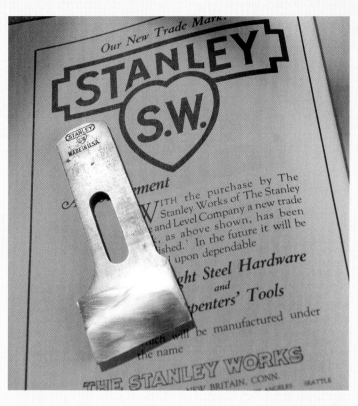

The Sweetheart trademark, shown with the catalog announcing the acquisition of Stanley Rule and Level by the larger Stanley Works.

limits, depending upon the hardness and other characteristics of the iron, and how the iron will be used. Generally the more acute the bevel angle, the more easily the iron will penetrate and cut, but at the risk of a more fragile cutting edge that can chip. The more blunt the bevel, the stronger and more durable the edge, but also the more resistance to the cut. Depending on the bevel angle and the pitch, some planes will cut hardwood with excellent results, whereas others will work softwoods more easily. Small differences in either can be quite noticeable.

Most bench planes have a 45° pitch (known as common pitch), which is a compromise between good all-around performance and relatively low cutting resistance. The drawing on p. 46 shows typical cutting angles at this pitch with the bevel down and the iron sharpened at 25° with a 5° microbevel. Lowering the pitch has the advantage of easier cutting (a finer edge "wedge"), but unless the throat is very tight or the wood easily cut, some splitting rather than all cutting of the fibers is going to happen. For highly figured or hard woods where tearout is a concern, a higher pitch of 50° (York pitch), 55° (Middle pitch), or 60° (Half pitch) works noticeably better. The higher pitch curls and breaks the fibers more abruptly before they split. For common-pitched bench planes, the effective pitch or cutting angle can be raised by honing a back bevel onto the iron (see the top drawing on the facing page). Unfortunately, a disadvantage of a higher pitch is that the cutting edge will also drag more and cut with a scraping action that can heat and dull the iron more quickly.

So far in this discussion we have been looking at pitch and bevel angles for cutting along the grain of the board. The mechanics for cutting end grain are quite different (see the bottom drawing on the facing page). When cutting the ends of the wood fibers, a low angle theoretically works the best. Tearout is much less of a problem, as is concern about curling the shavings, because end-grain shavings are naturally weak and break apart themselves. The lower the cutting angle and the lighter the cut, the more easily the end-grain fibers will cut, rather than deform and break. This is the physics of low-angle planes. Commonly without a cap iron and with the iron bevel up, low-angle planes work well for more than just end grain, especially if they have an adjustable throat.

The limiting factor with low-angle planes is the bevel angle of the iron. Again it comes down to edge durability versus the easier cutting of a fine bevel. Good irons can be beveled at 20° and possibly even a few degrees less without risk of chipping the edge. Assuming the pitch of the body is a given, the only other way to improve performance further is to back-bevel the iron 5° or so. This reduces the clearance angle and further reduces the cutting angle, while still keeping the overall bevel angle at 20°.

While back bevels are quite useful, I find that I rarely hone my irons with them. By the time I learned and understood the technique, I had already collected and tuned an assortment of high-angle planes that worked extremely well. I use scrapers often, too. With no new bench planes available with a pitch above 47½°, back bevels might make the difference in some woods between a smooth or torn-out surface. If I had a limited number of planes to work with, I would certainly back-bevel the iron on a heavy smoothing plane and keep it handy for when nothing else seemed to work.

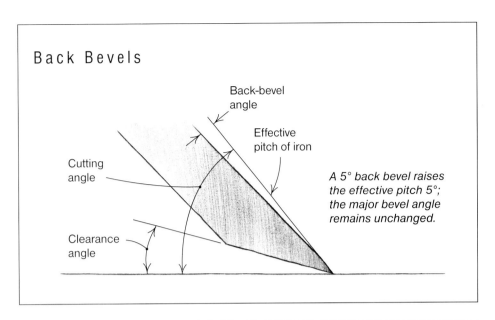

Back Bevels

Back-bevel angle

Effective pitch of iron

Cutting angle

Clearance angle

A 5° back bevel raises the effective pitch 5°; the major bevel angle remains unchanged.

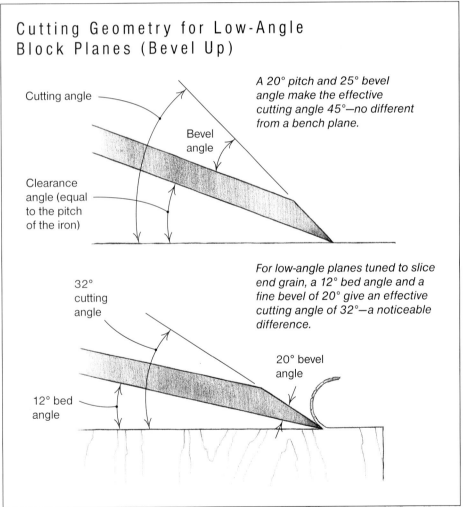

Cutting Geometry for Low-Angle Block Planes (Bevel Up)

Cutting angle

Bevel angle

Clearance angle (equal to the pitch of the iron)

A 20° pitch and 25° bevel angle make the effective cutting angle 45°—no different from a bench plane.

32° cutting angle

12° bed angle

20° bevel angle

For low-angle planes tuned to slice end grain, a 12° bed angle and a fine bevel of 20° give an effective cutting angle of 32°—a noticeable difference.

4
TUNING A PLANE

But before you come to use your planes, you must know how to grind, and whet them, for they are not fitted when they are bought, but every Workman accomodates [sic] them to this purpose, as if it be an hard wood he is to work on, he grinds his basil to a more obtuse angle, than he would do for soft wood.

— Joseph Moxon, *Mechanick Exercises* (3rd. ed.), 1703

Planing with a well-tuned plane can be one of the most sublime pleasures of working wood. And tuning a plane isn't all that difficult. Anyone who works with wood has the practical skills necessary; what is often missing is the information about what to do and how to do it.

Every plane needs tuning sometime. Just because a plane is new doesn't mean that the sole is flat or that the parts were properly adjusted into harmony at the factory. You expect that the iron needs sharpening, but when you start checking, chances are you'll find other parts that need tuning to achieve that smooth performance you're striving for. Just because a plane is old and well used doesn't mean it's tuned either. The craftsman who owned it before you might not have known any more about tuning than you do. And planes don't stay in tune forever. If you're lucky, the plane just needs a thorough cleaning and its iron ground and honed. It's more likely it will need a few hours of work some rainy day.

Some planes are going to be a challenge to tune—every aspect is going to need attention. No matter what condition your plane is in, I suggest you start at the beginning and check and tune the parts as they are presented in this chapter: Tighten and shape the handles; check and flatten the sole if it needs it; take the frog apart, flatten the bed, and become familiar with adjusting the throat by moving the frog; grind, hone, and flatten the back of the iron; and fit the cap iron and lever cap to the iron. The work can be tedious, but none of it is hard, and the results will last a long time. Even a little thing like smoothing a handle will be felt every time you pick up your plane.

Pike sharpening stones, made by Pike Manufacturing Co. of Pike Station, New Hampshire, were designed to be carried in a tackle box or toolbox for touching up plane irons.

Tuning Handles

Tightening and shaping the handles is a good place to start tuning for a quick sense of accomplishment. The handles that usually need attention—the rear tote and the front knob—are those on Bailey and similar bench planes and transitional planes. Nothing is worse than a tote that wobbles around as you try to steer the plane down a board.

The loosening problem arises from the orientation of the tote's grain (parallel to the sole). Although the grain orientation does ensure a strong handle, it makes it prone to loosening as the wood shrinks. A steel rod within the tote secures it to a boss cast into the plane's body (see the photo at right). The

Handles on Bailey-type bench planes are secured to the body with threaded rods. The easiest way to tighten a loose tote or knob is to shorten the rod or to add a shim under the cap nut.

natural swelling and shrinking of the wooden tote work against the rod in much the same way that a wooden handle eventually comes loose in a hammer head. The most secure totes are attached with an extra screw through their base or have some other means of alignment besides the threaded rod.

Fortunately, the remedy for a loose tote is a simple and reasonably permanent one. The steel rod is threaded on both ends; one end screws into the body, and the other has a cap nut that screws down into a recess in the top of the tote as it threads onto the rod. You can try snugging up the nut, but chances are this won't do the trick: Usually the nut screws to the end of the threads and the tote is still loose. Instead, I either grind the steel rod $1/8$ in. or so shorter or shim the nut with a small steel, brass, or leather washer. If there is an additional screw in the tote's base, tighten this up, too. Should you ever need to repair a cracked or broken handle, disassemble the handle, clean the joint, and then glue it together with epoxy.

Handles that are cut as an extension of the infill, such as this beautiful tote on a Norris smoothing plane, never come loose. In the smaller English bullnose rabbet plane in the foreground, the wedge extends to form a secure handle.

The front knob rarely comes loose, because the grain runs along its length in a strong and stable way. If the knob loosens and tightening the bolt that secures it doesn't help, you could try shortening the bolt slightly or shimming under the nut as for the tote.

Loose handles are less of a problem on wooden bench planes. The tote is usually firmly mortised into the body and secured with a screw, a bolt, or pegs. Most wooden bench planes have no front knob. One type of wooden plane you'll never have a problem with is one where the tote and body are cut from the same stock, as on better molding planes, tongue-and-groove planes, and British smoothing planes where the tote is an extension of the infill (see the bottom photo on the facing page).

As part of the tuning process, I also recommend shaping the handles to fit your hand. Part of my love of old tools is that the handles feel wonderful—I can't resist the silky feel of polished rosewood or beech, carefully shaped and finished.

The grip is so comfortable that I forget about holding the plane and concentrate instead on using it. New totes are much squarer, rounded only ever so slightly. There's little chance that you'll weaken the tote or knob by shaping, so go at it with a rasp, file, or scraper. On new handles I always like to strip off the varnish finish while I'm at it, but this is a matter of personal taste. Round all the edges until the handles feel just right, and then wipe on a coat of tung oil or paste wax.

Flattening the Sole

There is no universal rule that planes must have perfectly flat soles to work well; in fact, there is a whole tradition that believes just the opposite. Eastern craftsmen regularly shape the soles of their planes in a very shallow, wave-like pattern with special scraping planes, by relieving some of the wood between the toe and throat and heel and throat. I am less familiar with this tradition, but I do know that relieving the sole doesn't

affect the way the plane works and makes truing the sole easier. The longer the plane, the less critical it is to have it flat along its entire length. What's important is knowing *where* the sole needs to be flat and true.

There are two aspects to the "flatness" of the sole: its truth down the length and across the width and any potential twist or winding along the length. Before you start lapping the sole, use a straightedge and feeler gauge to test how flat the sole really is. Hold the plane upside-down up to a window or bright light with an accurate straightedge against the sole and sight along the joint between the two (see the photo above). The faintest hair of light is somewhere around 0.001 in.—well within acceptable tolerances. Where there are larger gaps, try different-thickness feeler gauges to get an idea of how much of the sole you'll need to lap away. Also flip the straightedge end for end and use the opposite edge to see if there is any variation in your straightedge that might be misleading you. On used

Sight across a pair of winding sticks to detect any twist in the sole.

planes there's a good chance that the sole is worn just ahead of the throat and at the toe and heel. The area in front of the throat wears from the friction of pressing down the wood fibers as the shaving is forced through the throat.

While a totally flat sole is not absolutely necessary, having one without any twist is a must. No plane will work accurately if it rocks from side to side on a twisted sole. Check the sole for twist by sighting across a pair of winding sticks,

as shown in the photo above. (For more on using winding sticks, see the sidebar on p. 101.)

Even the soles of new planes need tuning. One explanation I've heard for the poorer quality and warped soles of modern cast-iron planes is the use of inferior cast iron—some of it recycled. Others claim that the fresh castings need to be "seasoned" just as wood does before the sole is milled flat, and more care could be taken with the milling, too. Even with virgin cast iron, I'm sure that

at the height of Stanley production some of its planes were sold without totally true soles. It's easy enough to check the sole as part of tuning each plane, and every few years to check the ones that see a lot of use. Cast iron, steel, and bronze do wear, especially when planing hardwoods.

CAST-IRON SOLES

Flattening a cast-iron sole can be tedious work. One solution is to take your planes to a machine shop, which is easier than hand lapping but a lot riskier. The biggest risk is that too much will be taken off the sole and the whole plane body will be cut unnecessarily thin around the frog or the throat will be widened. Since planes are not tools that most machine shops are familiar with, take extra care explaining what you want, or better yet work with them.

A far safer (but slower) method is to lap the sole on a lapping table, which can be as simple as a few sheets of sandpaper taped to a piece of plate glass (¼ in. thick minimum) or a flat surface like the bed of a jointer or a table-saw top. Silicon-carbide or aluminum-oxide sandpaper works well. For a sole that needs a lot of work, start with 80 grit and work up to as fine a grit (at least 220) as your patience will allow. Another alternative is to use flexible sheets of diamond abrasives (backed with pressure-sensitive adhesive) stuck to a piece of plate glass or a flat steel bed. These abrasives are available in three grits: 200, 400, and 800. Some tool catalogs sell special steel lapping plates for use with silicon-carbide powder, but these are expensive and too short for any but smaller planes.

I most often lap plane soles on a piece of scrap plate glass with silicon-carbide powder and kerosene as a lubricant. It is a little messy, but the abrasive cuts quickly. The glass eventually does wear

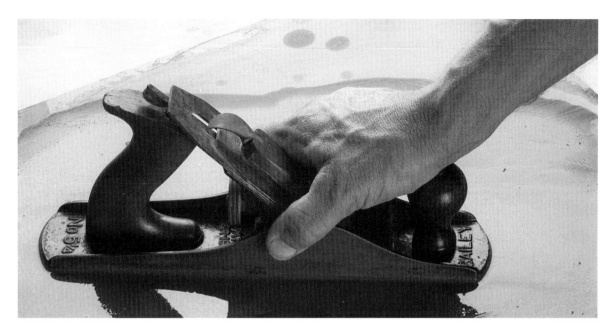

When lapping the sole of a plane, keep the plane flat on the lapping table and the pressure even.

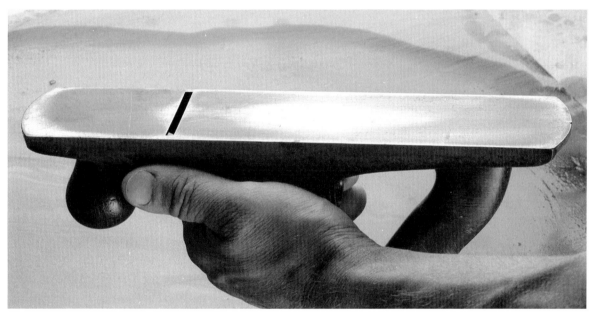

A lapped sole shows consistent lapping marks (the dull surfaces), especially at the critical areas of the toe, heel, and just ahead of the throat. This sole needs more lapping, but it's getting close.

hollow, so I either flip it over or get a new piece. I've heard that a thin sheet of hard plastic on top of the glass works even better because the abrasive particles get embedded in the plastic and are held in place.

Before you start lapping, back off the iron and tighten the frog. Don't remove the iron and the frog because they create stress on the sole that could affect its flatness if they are taken out. When lapping the sole (particularly on small planes) be especially careful to keep the plane perfectly flat on the lapping table, with the pressure about in the middle of the plane. I take a few strokes in one direction and then rotate the plane end for end and lap the sole an equal amount in the same direction. With care, you can work side to side too, first one way and then the other, making sure you keep even contact on the lapping table and don't rock the plane. After a dozen or so strokes the sole will clearly show the high areas as lighter metal or contrast against the uniform milling marks on the sole of new or little used planes.

Keep lapping until the sole is either a consistent color, or at least the areas of the toe, heel, and in front of the throat are lapped level. Check the sole often with a true straightedge. The rougher the work you expect to do with the plane, the less perfect the sole needs to be down its entire length, especially for the longer bench planes. Don't worry about small, low spots in the sole. The soles of small planes need to be flat, but flattening them should be easier considering their size. Take extra time with your smoothing planes and with planes meant to cut with a lot of accuracy, such as shoulder planes and rabbet planes.

If you intend to use a block, miter, or jack plane with shooting boards, take the time to square either or both sides of the plane body to the sole. Shooting boards are jigs for holding the work in various ways so that edges or miters can be squared or trued (see Chapter 7). Since the plane is used on its side and the sole is vertical, having the sole and sides perfectly square to one another will ensure more accurate cuts. Check the sides and sole for squareness first with a square, and then lap each side favoring the position that will bring the side and sole into square with each other.

While not the most enjoyable work, flattening the sole is rewarding—your plane will work better and with more accuracy. Moreover, once a tool is put into shape it will stay that way a long time, perhaps for many years. It is good rainy day work that you can start and come back to as the spirit moves you.

WOODEN SOLES

The soles of wooden planes are far less tedious to condition, which is convenient considering that they need attention more often. The fact that wood is softer than cast iron and more easily worn out of true is only part of the reason. Seasonal humidity changes affect the sole, as does moving the plane to a different climate (as when importing English tools) or even leaving the plane lying in the hot sun.

Take a good look at any old wooden bench plane and chances are you'll see what happens after years of reflattening

Flatten the sole of a wooden plane against a long jointer held upside-down in a vise.

Two ways to repair a worn wooden sole are to inlay a throat piece (as on the jointer at left) or to glue on a whole new sole (as on the smoother at right).

the sole. Since the greatest wear takes place ahead of the throat and the throat is well forward of the center of the sole, years of reflattening the sole cuts the toe faster than the sole and the body becomes wedge-shaped. Every shaving taken off the sole also widens the throat and the plane cuts more poorly, to the end that at some point the plane either needs a new sole or a new throat piece (explained in

the section on adjusting the throat on pp. 61-62), or must be kept for only the roughest of work.

Check the sole first with winding sticks and a true straightedge to see if you are dealing with a twisted sole as well as one worn out of flatness. Make sure the iron is wedged into place just shy of the throat opening, so that the pressure it exerts on the sole will be the same as when the plane is in use. If it is not, it could later cause the sole to bulge out just underneath the iron.

The truest way to flatten the sole is to push the plane across a jointer plane clamped upside-down in a bench vise (see the top photo on the facing page). Keep checking the sole with a straightedge and winding sticks. Small adjustments can be made with a very finely set block plane or a scraper. You could also use a lapping table and sandpaper. The sole can be scraped ever so slightly hollow in the area just forward of the heel and shy of the throat, and the same amount between the throat and toe. Chamfering the edges where the sole and sides meet will eliminate a sharp edge that could splinter or mar the planed surface if the plane should accidentally be tilted onto its edge while planing. The chamfered edges will also feel better in your hand.

Some wooden planes are worth repairing with a whole new sole when they are worn to the point that the throat is too wide or when some other defect needs correcting. I've even done this to worn molding planes when I wanted a new sole profile (see p. 194). Repairing a sole is not difficult. To add a new sole, plane the old sole flat, with the blade wedged in place as for truing it, and then glue on a new sole at least ³⁄₁₆ in. thick—even thicker is better. Dense, oily woods like rosewood, ebony, or cocobolo work very well; just take care to plane the mating surfaces before gluing for the best bond. Yellow glue or epoxy works fine. Make the new sole oversized in every dimension and later true it to the original body and carefully drill and chop out a tight throat opening. Fine-tune the throat with the iron wedged in place. Finally, chamfer all around the edges of the new sole.

Adjusting the Frog of Metal Planes

Early on in the development of the cast-iron bench plane a wide variety of different frog designs were proposed and patented. Some frogs were cast integrally with the plane body, others were a separate casting fitted to the plane later (see the photo below). Today you are likely to come across either of two adjustable frog designs: a Bailey frog common in Stanley, Record, and most bench planes, and a Bed Rock frog found in Stanley's line of Bed Rock planes (see the sidebar on p. 47).

Both frog designs are separate castings with a bed milled flat and another milled area on the frog's underside where it mates with the sole. The Bailey frog screws directly to a thickened part of the sole casting. On planes made after 1914, the frog can be adjusted forward and backward with a fine-threaded screw, once the hold-down screws are loosened. Moving the frog fine-tunes the throat opening, but the iron must be removed first to expose the screws.

The first patented cast-iron plane, Hazard Knowles' plane of 1827 (at rear), had a frog cast integrally with the body. Another early cast-iron plane, a Birdsill Holly smoothing plane of 1852 (foreground), had a frog added to the plane and connected with the tote for better support.

A Bailey frog is adjusted by loosening the two hold-down screws that secure it to the sole casting.

A Bed Rock frog has a large, accurately milled bearing surface and fits within a groove that keeps it perfectly aligned. It's secured with an ingenious system of two pins tightened with screws from behind the frog.

Good cutting performance comes from a well-secured frog. I've had only one problem with a Bailey frog over the years, but it was serious enough to make the plane useless. A previous owner had overtightened one of the screws that secure the frog to the sole and stripped some of the threads. It's easy to see how this could happen, considering the softness of cast iron and the shortness of the screws. My solution was to cut the threads slightly deeper with a bottom tap, just enough to grab hold of with a slightly longer screw. If this didn't work, I was going to try tapping the hole one size larger and use a bigger hold-down screw. I mention this problem for the lesson it tells—don't overtighten the screws that secure the frog.

The Bed Rock frog is an improvement over the Bailey design in three ways: The frog bears on the sole with a larger milled flat and thus is more stable; it fits within a groove, which keeps it perfectly aligned with the throat; and it is held to the sole with two pins that have conical dimples in their sides. Two screws with tapered ends set in the sole behind the frog secure it; as the screws engage in the dimples the pins are drawn downward and tightly lock the frog. The beauty of this system is the ability to adjust the frog without having to remove the iron and the frog's strong positive connection to the sole.

Before adjusting anything, remove the frog and lightly lap or flat-file the bed (the surface the iron lies on) to take out any burrs and check that it is reasonably true and flat. (You can also file the bed with the frog in place, as shown in the photo at left on the facing page.) The depth-adjuster lever and the screw that holds the lever cap are in the way; remove the screw and work around the lever. Check that the areas where the frog and sole mate are clean and free of

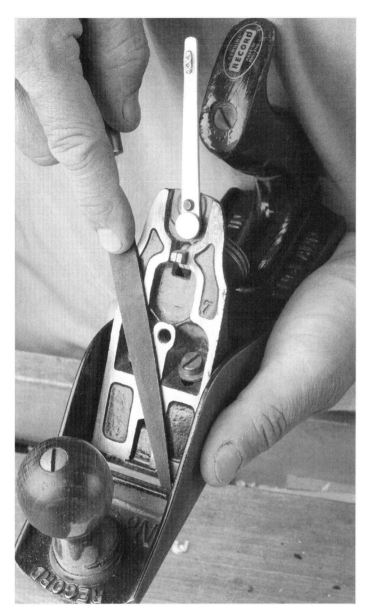

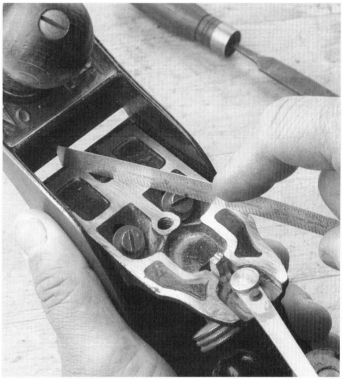

File the frog flat, after first removing the lever-cap screw. Work into the throat to true the bed to a consistent angle right to the sole.

Sight into the throat along the frog, checking that the frog and the bevel of the sole are aligned. Use a small straightedge if necessary.

burrs, too. Reassemble the frog in the plane and barely tighten the screws that secure it.

At this point, I like to run a small, fine file into the throat and check that the bed angle of the sole at the back of the throat is the same as the frog bed angle. Adjust the frog by sliding it or screwing the adjusting screw: backwards opens the throat, forwards closes it. By sighting down the bed and looking at the throat opening or the sole at the back of the throat, you can see if the frog is slightly tilted out of alignment. Get it as straight as you can (parallel with the front of the throat). Holding the flat side of a small straightedge against the bed and into the throat will help (see the photo at right above), or you can put the iron back in and look at the throat opening. Where you should set the frog depends on the work you expect to do—the section that follows will help you decide. Carefully tighten the hold-down screws when everything is aligned.

Adjusting the Throat

If you have only a few planes, you could be changing the throat opening often—a narrow throat for fine work, a wider throat for rough work and coarse shavings. If, like me, you have the luxury of owning several planes, you can set each plane with a different throat opening and choose the best plane for the work: a smoothing plane with a narrow throat, a jointer with a medium throat, and a jack with a coarse throat.

Fine-Tuning the Throat and the Frog

BAILEY PLANES

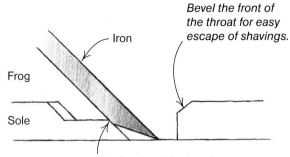

Bevel the front of the throat for easy escape of shavings.

Iron

Frog

Sole

The frog and the bevel of the sole should be in alignment.

Gap behind iron

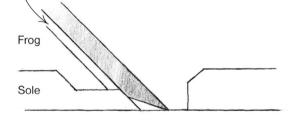

Frog

Sole

Setting the frog too far back leaves the iron unsupported, causing chatter.

Frog

Sole

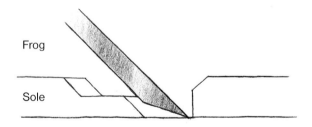

Setting the frog too far forward leaves the back of the iron unsupported, again causing chatter.

BED ROCK PLANES

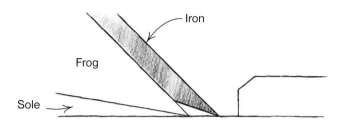

Iron

Frog

Sole

The frog extends right to the sole, giving excellent support to the iron and minimizing chatter.

WOODEN PLANES

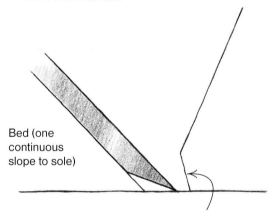

Bed (one continuous slope to sole)

The throat of most wooden planes is already beveled to help keep the throat tight as the sole is resurfaced.

With an adjustable toe piece, common on block planes and some other specialty planes (see the sidebar on p. 113), you can have an even wider range of choices.

CAST-IRON PLANES

Setting the throat width on a cast-iron plane does involve some trial and error, given the unique shape of each throat and the way the shavings curl within it. Before you adjust anything, make sure the front of the throat opening is straight and bevel it slightly to help the shavings pass smoothly out of the throat. With the Bailey-type frog, remove the iron and either slide the frog forward or backward, or move it with the adjusting screw. Retighten the screws and reassemble the iron and lever cap.

Bed Rock frogs adjust in the same way, with the added ease of not having to remove the iron. For fine smoothing work a throat opening just shy of $\frac{1}{64}$ in. is good, for general bench work between $\frac{1}{32}$ in. and $\frac{1}{16}$ in., and for rough work wider still. One rule of thumb that makes sense is to set the throat a little wider than the thickness of the shaving you expect to cut. The narrower the throat, the better it is able to support the chip as it is broken and curled and the smoother the finish in difficult grain. Just don't try to take too thick a shaving with a fine throat—the plane will quickly clog.

There is one more subtle difference between the two types of frogs that you should keep in mind when adjusting them. The front edge of the Bed Rock frog mates with a part of the sole thinned down to receive it, whereas the Bailey frog has a noticeable thickness of sole under its front edge (see the drawing on the facing page). If either frog is moved too far back the iron will bed against the beveled part of the sole and not the entire frog. Moving the frog well forward eliminates any support that the

To inlay a throat piece, position the patch on the sole and scribe around it with a knife. Chisel or rout out the recess to a depth slightly less than the thickness of the patch.

back of the iron gets from the beveled edge of the sole. Either way the iron does not get adequate support, causing it to cut unevenly, or "chatter." The design of the Bed Rock frog allows for a greater range of throat adjustment without causing a problem.

WOODEN PLANES

In keeping with their simplicity, wooden planes do not have an adjustable frog, but the throat can easily be tightened. The throat opens over time due to flattening of the sole, wear, and the slow thinning of a tapered iron. (The backward slope of the throat helps slow the rate of opening.) To close the throat, pack out the bed behind the iron with a thin sheet of copper, leather, or even

dense cardboard—whatever it takes to shim the iron enough to tune the throat. If you use a thick shim, the wedge might need some careful adjustment with a block plane.

When the throat is really worn or has grown too big, another alternative is to glue on a new sole (see p. 57) or to cut out part of the sole and fit in a throat piece (see the photo on p. 56). The same type of throat piece (only movable) is sometimes found on well-made European smoothing planes. The beauty of a throat piece is that it is replaceable and it can be made out of a dense wood that will hold up to the extra wear on this part of the sole.

To fit in a throat piece, start by cutting out a patch to inlay into the sole,

The new throat piece on this lignum-vitae smoother is secured in place with glue and screws.

an angle roughly equal to the bed angle. I can imagine that it takes some care to fit the key precisely, but otherwise the method is beautifully simple and allows for continued reflattening of the sole without widening the throat. I was lucky enough to find such a throat repair on an English miter plane—a plane that greatly benefits from a tight throat (see the photo below). I also have a Chinese plane with a variation on this theme; it has a steel dovetailed key fitted just ahead of the iron where it will hold up to maximum wear and keep the throat consistently fine.

Sharpening

If you ever want to get a heated discussion going among woodworkers, just mention the subject of sharpening. Everyone has an opinion on waterstones versus oilstones, hollow grinding, micro-bevels, and every aspect of sharpening technique. To some it almost borders on religion. So I'll jump into the fray with my opinions.

with the throat edge as wide as the throat and gently tapered toward the toe. A thickness between $1/4$ in. and $3/8$ in. works well. Square the edges with a block plane, and then lay the piece into position just ahead of the iron. Make sure to position the patch close enough to the iron so that when recutting the throat some of the patch will be cut away. Mark around the throat piece with a fine knife (see the photo on p. 61), and then chop and chisel a recess to the lines slightly shallow of the thickness of the patch. It is not vital that the fit be perfect, because the patch will be held in place with glue (and with countersunk screws, too, if you prefer). Back up the thin patch with a scrap block when gluing and clamping it in place. When the glue has set, plane the patch down to the level of the sole, either by passing the plane over an upside-down jointer clamped in a vise or by using a smaller plane.

To cut the throat, remove the iron and enlarge the opening with a fine sawblade or chisel. Keep paring it and checking with the iron in place. Err on the side of too tight and try the plane to get the best

opening. You can always enlarge the throat slightly later.

In his book *Japanese Woodworking Tools* (The Taunton Press, 1984), Toshio Odate describes a Japanese method of closing up the throat with a sliding dovetail key. The key drives through the body of the plane toward the iron and at

An ingenious way to tighten the throat on a wooden plane is with a wedge-shaped key let into the body, as on this English miter plane. Anytime the sole is jointed flat, driving the key in tightens the throat slightly.

The sharpening debate really heated up about 20 years ago when natural Japanese waterstones with their unique sharpening abilities came on the market. Now with new, synthetic waterstones, which are less expensive and very consistent, more and more woodworkers are trying waterstones and liking the results. Affordable diamond and ceramic stones have recently added more sharpening possibilities, with long-wearing surfaces of many grits that cut quickly and stay flat. Still in the debate is the more conservative crowd who learned how to sharpen with oilstones, like the results, and see no reason to change. I have to admit to falling somewhere between all of these camps—I like the rapid cutting of waterstones, I use diamond stones for some sharpening, but I'm most comfortable on my oilstones. Really it all comes down to habit: We tend to stay with the stones and techniques we learn first.

There is even more to the sharpening debate besides stones. Nearly every tool catalog would love to sell you machines and jigs to make your sharpening quicker and more accurate. You can buy motorized grinders, some of them water cooled, and a whole variety of grinding wheels. You can sharpen with narrow belt sanders and buffing wheels. And there are sharpening jigs that support the iron at a consistent bevel and gauges to check the bevel angle. However, with good sharpening technique, you can get excellent results with a minimum of gadgets.

Sharpening is one of the most basic woodworking techniques. It affects the way a tool cuts, the ease and accuracy with which it works, and how safely it is used. Naturally a sharp tool cuts with less resistance; it's the dull tool that takes more effort and is more prone to

A water-lubricated treadle grindstone was the father to modern high-speed and smaller stoned versions.

slipping, causing you injury or ruining your work. But sharpening takes time to master—no matter how long you have been at it there is always more to learn. Understanding the processes of grinding, shaping the iron, honing, polishing, and flattening the back is only part of the story. The hardest part is training your hands, arms, and eyes to work together efficiently and accurately. Relying on jigs

or gauges is one way to train your eye and get consistent results, but I feel that ultimately your body is the best jig and good results come from relying on coordination and observation.

GRINDING THE BEVEL

The first step in sharpening any iron is grinding a consistent bevel angle. The fastest method is to use a motor-driven grinding wheel—a useful tool in any shop—though the bevel can also be cut on coarse stones. My grinder is a simple shopmade affair made from an old washing-machine motor driving a pair of wheels mounted on an arbor (see the photo below). The wheels are 6-in.-dia. 60-grit and 120-grit aluminum oxide. It isn't a fancy grinder, but it does everything I need. A step up would be a $\frac{1}{2}$-hp Baldor grinder with a pair of 8-in.

The fastest and most accurate way to establish the bevel angle is to use a motor-driven grinder. In this no-frills setup, the iron rests in a simple jig that is movable backward or forward to grind different bevel angles.

You can spend a lot of money in a hurry on sharpening stones, but how do you choose the ones best suited to your skills and needs? How are oilstones different from waterstones? What about synthetic waterstones, or for that matter all man-made stones compared to natural ones? To understand some of the immediate differences between sharpening stones, the best place to start is to look at their physical qualities.

Physical qualities

Of all the many hundreds of naturally occurring stones, only a handful combine the five qualities that make them really useful for sharpening: the size of the particles, their shape, hardness, and toughness, and the strength of the bond that unites them. A Japanese master craftsman would add the more subtle qualities of color and pattern to this list.

Particle size: Most desirable for consistent sharpening abrasion is a stone of uniform grit that's free of larger particles (anomalies). Natural waterstones have an amazingly consistent particle size, graded by the ancient rivers that deposited them.

Shape: Sharp, angular particles, natural or man-

Natural waterstones are quarried sedimentary rock, each with slight differences in hardness, grit size, and color. Despite their subtle flaws, natural stones are rare and can sell for many thousands of dollars.

made, cut faster than ones that are more rounded.

Hardness: Particles need to be hard to abrade tough steel and hold up to wear.

Toughness: Particles must be tough enough to withstand the pressure and forces generated during sharpening. Yet some particle breakdown is desirable on finer stones to polish the cutting surfaces.

Bond: The "glue" that holds the particles together is one of the most important qualities of a stone. If the bond is too strong, it doesn't allow the particles to wear away and expose a fresh surface; if the bond is too weak, the stone wears hollow more quickly. Waterstones have a weak bond; oilstones and ceramic stones a strong bond.

No stone is going to be perfect for all of your sharpening needs. A coarse stone used to hone out a nick or roughly refine a bevel will have very different characteristics from a finishing stone used to polish the edge. At the very least, you'll need a few stones of different grits: a coarse stone, a medium stone, and a finishing stone. Whether you use oilstones, waterstones, or newer diamond and ceramic stones is a matter of personal choice and budget. Try out as many as you can, because once you settle on a system there is a good chance you will stick with it for a long time.

Waterstones

At one time, all waterstones were natural stones. Stones were known and named depending upon the strata they were quarried from, each with slightly different characteristics and sharpening abilities. Master blacksmiths, in a tradition that mixes science and spirituality, even went so far as to specify which stones should be used to sharpen their particular tools. Natural stones are still being quarried in Japan, but the better ones have become very expensive—sometimes costing many thousands of dollars each. Are they worth it, compared to a good man-made waterstone? Although the ones I've used gave no better edge to my tools, they certainly had a wonderful silky feel. Some believe that the cutting action of natural stones sharpens Japanese tools better than any others.

Today, the better man-made waterstones are of a quality and consistency nearly equal to natural stones at a much lower cost. Some synthetic stones are made by grinding up natural stones, mixing in some sort of binder (clay for one), and firing it. Others are made by fusing manufactured abrasives together. The resulting bond between the particles is intentionally weak, so the cutting surface is constantly being renewed and the stone cuts easily and rapidly. The drawback (for natural stones, too) is a relatively soft stone that wears rapidly and requires more frequent maintenance. Fortunately, this is not a difficult chore (see the sidebar on p. 70). A useful set of stones is 800x, 1200x, and 6000x. To see if you like waterstones, I suggest buying a couple of inexpensive combination stones with a different grit on each face.

A lubricant is necessary for any stone to wash away the worn abrasive and metal particles (called "swarf"). Using water as a lubricant with waterstones has its advantages and disadvantages. Waterstones need to be soaked in water before they can be used, which can take a few minutes. If you store your stones in water, another option, you run the risk of freezing (and ruining) them in a cold shop. While I like their fast cutting, waterstones are messy. I've never been totally comfortable with all that water around my polished tools.

Oilstones

The main difference between oilstones and waterstones is the particle bond. Oilstones are more tightly bonded and stay flat longer, but they're also more likely to glaze over and cut slowly. Using a light honing oil or kerosene as a lubricant helps flush the surface, but the stones still need routine maintenance to cut like new. I use a fine India and hard black Arkansas more than any other stones, for honing a fine edge and the back of the iron truly flat. Oilstones come in a range of grits both natural and man-made—a good set would include a coarse, medium, and finishing stone.

Diamond and ceramic stones

It's only in the last decade or so that diamond stones have shown up in woodworking catalogs and caught on as an alternative to waterstones or oilstones. The beauty of diamond stones is that they work equally well for carbide tools as for steel ones. To resurface and flatten oil- or waterstones they are unequaled. The best diamond stones are monocrystalline diamonds bonded to a flat base. They come in a range of grits, but none that are truly finishing stones for final polishing. They can be used dry or with water or kerosene. You would think that as hard as diamonds are that these stones should last forever, but in fact the diamonds can be worn down quite easily with too much honing pressure and aggressive use.

The newest sharpening stones are ceramic stones. They are similar to man-made waterstones, except that they can be used dry and need no soaking. They are extremely hard wearing, they stay flat, and they can be cleaned under running water. So far, they come in a small range of grits useful only for finishing an edge.

Ultimately it is more important how you use and maintain your stones than which ones you choose. While sharpening, keep the surface well flushed with lubricant and use only modest pressure. Regularly check your stones for flatness and maintain them. Have a range of grits, no matter if some are oilstones and others something else, and learn to use them all to get the keenest edge in the shortest time.

wheels. One thing you do need is a jig for holding the iron at a consistent angle to the grinding wheel. The jig can be shopmade, or you could spend quite a bit for one with all the bells and whistles.

More important than how you get there is that you achieve a proper bevel angle. If you read Chapter 3 on bevel angles, you'll realize that there is no "right" bevel angle. Any bevel angle is a compromise between the durability of the edge, the work required of the plane, the bed angle, whether the bevel is up or down in the plane, and whether a back bevel is used. You can get hopelessly caught up in the science to try to arrive at the best bevel, but within a modest range of bevels most planes will work just fine. You can fine-tune each plane by experimenting with the bevel angle every time you grind or hone.

For bench planes and bevel-down irons, a bevel angle of 25° is a good place to start. A good rule of thumb is to make the length of the bevel twice the thickness of the iron. Honing a 5° to 10° microbevel for an overall edge bevel of 30° to 35° gives the edge adequate durability. For bevel-up planes (block planes, low-angle planes, and some spokeshaves), 20° to 25° is a safe bevel angle. The more acute the bevel angle the lower the cutting angle, which is what you want in these planes. With modern alloy irons, this angle could be reduced 5° or more. You could also save one plane for working soft or easily worked woods and bevel its iron even lower still.

Hollow grinding

The bevel cut by a small-diameter grindstone is ground hollow, whereas the bevel shaped with a stone is not (see the drawing above). Whether to hollow-grind is part of the ongoing sharpening

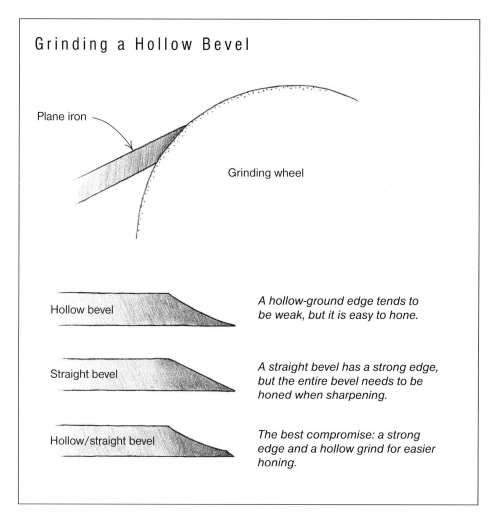

Grinding a Hollow Bevel

Plane iron

Grinding wheel

Hollow bevel

A hollow-ground edge tends to be weak, but it is easy to hone.

Straight bevel

A straight bevel has a strong edge, but the entire bevel needs to be honed when sharpening.

Hollow/straight bevel

The best compromise: a strong edge and a hollow grind for easier honing.

debate. The advantage of hollow grinding is the speed with which the actual cutting bevel can be honed, without having to remove metal across the entire bevel. Every time you resharpen, the hollow is slowly honed away or grows so small that eventually the bevel needs to be reground.

Woodworkers who don't hollow-grind believe that the cutting edge is stronger since it is fully supported by a bevel the whole thickness of the iron. This is certainly true if the hollow extends very close to the cutting edge. In practice, hollow grinding with an 8-in.-diameter or larger grinding wheel and honing the bevel 1/64 in. or more creates an edge that's adequately strong. For Japanese or

other hard irons, a slight hollow grind and then honing the bevel well back from the cutting edge will give the iron the necessary durability.

I always hollow-grind my plane irons, but I make sure to leave a thin line of polished steel where the bevel was last honed. In this way, I maintain the shape of the iron and use the grinder only to remove enough steel to make the honing process easier and quicker.

Shaping the iron

There's an old saying that a plane iron writes its name on the wood. Its signature depends a lot on how you shape the length of the cutting edge:

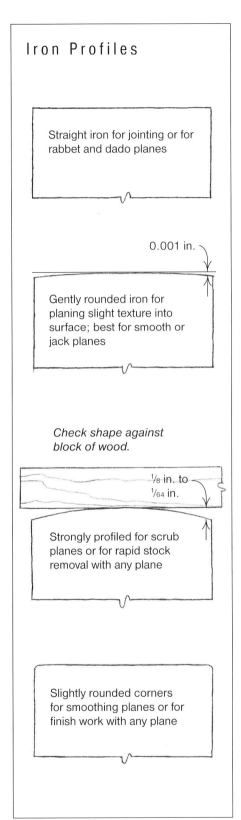

Iron Profiles

Straight iron for jointing or for rabbet and dado planes

0.001 in.

Gently rounded iron for planing slight texture into surface; best for smooth or jack planes

Check shape against block of wood.

$\frac{1}{8}$ in. to $\frac{1}{64}$ in.

Strongly profiled for scrub planes or for rapid stock removal with any plane

Slightly rounded corners for smoothing planes or for finish work with any plane

straight across, with a slight convex profile, with a pronounced convex profile, or with just the corners rounded off (see the drawing at left). Why even shape the iron at all you might ask? The usual reasons are for aesthetics (the planing marks make a nice pattern) and for improved performance. A pronounced convex profile is common on scrub planes or jack planes used to remove a lot of wood quickly. The iron cuts like a wide gouge. A slightly convex iron works well in a smoothing plane since only part of the iron is cutting and the strokes will blend together nicely with the outer edges of the iron out of contact with the wood. A convex iron will chatter less because there is less pressure upon it. Most of the time I shape the iron by only slightly rounding the corners, because this profile gives me the benefits of a shaped iron but with a maximum amount of the iron cutting. Since more of the iron is cutting, I resharpen less often than I would with a more convex shape.

To shape a convex edge, I grind more heavily on the outer edges of the iron, gently pivoting it over the grinder in a slight arc. This is where my simple grinding jig works particularly well, by keeping the iron oriented at a consistent bevel to the stone while I arc it. After grinding I hone a consistent shape. Occasionally, I check the shape by holding the iron against a straight block of wood held up to the light. Only the slightest curvature is necessary and it need not be a perfect arc. While using the iron, I can judge how I need to refine the shape next time I resharpen, either to give it a little more shape or to hone some out of it.

FLATTENING THE BACK OF THE IRON

Given that it forms half the cutting edge, a flat back on the iron is every bit as important as a well-honed bevel. Unless you are regularly going to use back bevels, the back of the iron must be polished and flat; otherwise, the iron will never be truly sharp. Of all the many plane irons I've sharpened over the years, I can remember only four that came to me with backs properly flat. Three were for new Lie-Nielsen planes, obviously carefully finished with modern technology, and the other was for a plane bought from another craftsman who had used it a great deal. Every other iron has needed from a half hour to many hours of lapping to get the back flat and polished.

There is no question that this work can be tedious. Of course, you could send your irons to a machine shop and get the backs surface-ground, but they would still need some hand lapping. Think of it in the same way as flattening the sole of the plane; the results are well worth the effort and, once done, maintaining the iron is fairly simple.

I lap the back flat on the same sharpening stones I use to hone the bevel (see the top photo on p. 68). A large diamond stone or a special lapping steel sprinkled with silicon-carbide powder also works well. More important than what you use is that the lapping surface be perfectly flat, or you will polish the back but it will not be flat. This is where I love my slow-wearing oilstones, which tend to stay very flat with little routine maintenance. The only way to find out how flat the iron is, is to start lapping. If it is really bad or slightly rust-pitted, I start on a coarse waterstone that has been recently trued. The area all behind

Lapping the back of the iron is every bit as important as honing the bevel. Lap until the back is consistently polished (like the iron to the right) and finish on a fine stone (such as the Arkansas stone in the background).

Grinding the back of the iron with a drill and a small grindstone speeds up the process of honing the back. It's an idea similar to hollow-grinding the back of a Japanese plane iron (shown at left).

the cutting edge should finish to a consistent polish.

There is one trick that helps speed along the flattening process. Looking at the hollowed backs of Japanese chisels and plane irons, I got the idea that I could do the same thing with a power drill and a small grindstone. These inexpensive stones come mounted on an arbor and are sold in many hardware stores. I use a ⅜-in. by 1½-in. stone chucked in a drill (see the bottom photo at left). Lap the iron on an oilstone a little first, and then grind the polished spots (the high areas), staying away from the cutting edge. I don't touch the dull areas because they're not contacting the oilstone yet. By grinding and honing I eventually get a back polished and flat. Often there are small grinding marks left, but these will be gradually honed out every time I resharpen.

HONING

Honing is all of the work done on benchstones to refine the bevel and bring the tool close to final sharpness. Whether you use waterstones, oilstones, diamond stones, or ceramic stones, the honing process is the same. Of all the sharpening techniques, honing probably causes the most difficulty for the inexperienced. It takes time to learn the process, and even longer to develop a feel for the subtleties.

I have five stones that I use regularly. Two are inexpensive waterstones that have a coarse grit on one side and a fine grit on the other (see the top photo on the facing page). I use them for quickly shaping an edge or for roughly flattening the back of an iron. The stone I use most often is a fine India oilstone with kerosene as a lubricant. This is a man-made stone that cuts at a moderate speed and wears slowly enough to stay true. Nearly everything passes over this stone during the sharpening process. For a final polishing of the edge I use either a hard black Arkansas (oilstone) or an *awase toishi* (a natural waterstone). For more about differences between stone types, see pp. 64-65.

Nearly all experienced sharpeners have a distinct style. It may be the way they hold the iron, the speed of the strokes, or the pattern they make across the stone. The end results are no different. Only two things are important to bear in mind: Keep the iron at a consistent angle to the stone, and use as much of the stone as possible so as to wear it evenly. My technique is to lubricate the stone and then rock the bevel upon it to feel the angle that is closest to the ground bevel angle or the old honing angle. One advantage of hollow grinding is that it is easier to feel the bevel angle because the bevel rests on the cutting edge and the back of the hollow grind. To hone a microbevel, raise the angle of the iron a few degrees.

When I feel the bevel is right I lock my hands and, moving from my arms, stroke up and down the stone in narrow figure eights (see the bottom photo at right). Light pressure is all that is needed (and it will keep your stones flat longer). Skewing the iron at about 20° feels more comfortable to me than honing straight up and down, except that the leading edge gets cut faster and the iron will hone out of square over time. I compensate for this by increasing the pressure on the trailing edge slightly.

After a dozen or so "eights" back and forth, I take the iron off the stone, wipe the edge, and look at it and feel it. If there is a slight wire edge on the back, I have cut a new edge. If not, I hone the bevel further until I do. The next step is to hone the back on the same stone. It's really important to keep the iron flat on the stone; one hand exerts pressure on the iron against the stone, while the

Effective sharpening demands using a variety of stones, such as (clockwise from top) a hard black Arkansas finishing stone, a medium and fine India, and two-sided water stones. A box keeps each stone protected and holds the stone in place while sharpening.

Using light pressure and with your arms locked to maintain a consistent bevel angle, stroke the iron up and down the stone in narrow figure eights. Use the entire surface of the stone.

Sooner or later your bench-stones are going to wear unevenly or glaze over. Ten minutes of maintenance will restore the surface as flat and sharp as when the stone was new. My oilstones need attention at most a half-dozen times a year; my waterstones about twice as often.

All stones can be renewed with the same basic procedure —the worn stone needs to be lapped against a true and abrasive surface with plenty of lubricant. A cement block, a coarse waterstone, a diamond stone, or even a sidewalk works well for waterstones. I lap my oilstones on either a diamond stone or at the same plate-glass lapping table I set up for truing plane soles (and at the same time, too). Ceramic stones can be lapped on a diamond stone.

Lap the stone back and forth with modest pressure and check it with a straight-edge occasionally. It's just like sharpening, the longer you wait to tune up your stones, the more effort it takes.

One way to renew the cutting surface and flatten oilstones is to lap them on plate glass with silicon-carbide powder and kerosene, just as for lapping a plane's sole.

other hand supports the free end (as shown in the top photo on p. 68). Honing the back up and down the stone works the wire edge back onto the bevel. Working alternately on the front and back with decreasing pressure eventually removes the wire edge and leaves a sharp cutting edge. You know that you're done when you hold the iron in a bright light and don't see any reflected light from the edge. A dull or wire edge will show as a thin shiny line.

POLISHING

Polishing is a final honing on a very fine stone that refines the edge to a mirror finish. For polishing I use either a hard black Arkansas or *awase toishi,* working first the bevel and then the back in the same manner as honing. A dozen strokes on each surface is usually all it takes. The feel of both of these stones is so smooth that it hardly seems as though they are cutting, yet the result is noticeable. Not only is the edge sharper, but it will stay sharper longer.

Another way to polish the edge is to use a leather strop. An image of a barber stropping the edge of a straight razor probably comes to mind. For plane irons you need a more rigid strop, made by gluing a piece of smooth leather (as opposed to a rough split face) to a wooden block. The length and width of a large benchstone is a good size. Rubbing a fine abrasive compound into the leather gives it the ability to polish. Polishing compounds are available in a range of grits; I recommend a fine grit such as jeweler's rouge or tripoli.

The strop is used in a similar way to honing on a benchstone, with the important difference that the strokes should all come toward you. Stropping away from you will only dig the edge into the leather. Strop the bevel a few times and then the back of the iron, again working toward you with every stroke. Just as with a fine benchstone, if the edge is not overly dulled you can bring it back to sharpness on the strop alone.

For a more complete discussion of sharpening technique and sharpening stones, refer to Leonard Lee's *The Complete Guide to Sharpening* (The Taunton Press, 1995).

Final Tuning

If you have followed the tuning procedure to this point, you should have a sharp, correctly beveled iron with a polished back, a sole that is flat, handles that are tight, and a throat that is adjusted for the work you expect to do. The plane would probably work fine as is, far better than before you started tuning, but there are a couple of final things worth checking. What you haven't tuned are the cap iron, the lever cap (or wooden wedge) that secures the iron, and the depth adjuster.

CAP IRONS

The cap iron performs at least two important functions right at the heart of the cutting action of the plane. It supports and adds rigidity to the cutting iron, which is especially important with a thin iron. The cap iron also presents a steeper "wedge" than the cutting iron and helps break and curl the shavings in the throat, thereby improving the plane's ability to handle difficult woods. In order to do

Hone the underside of the leading edge of a cap iron on a medium-grit stone, keeping the other end of the iron slightly lower than the surface of the stone.

either of these jobs, the cap iron must fit the iron exactly so that no chips can wedge between them. It must also be properly set so that it supports the cutting edge and helps curl the shavings.

When tuning the cap iron, think of it in the same way as the cutting iron. The leading edge needs to be sharp and straight, and the top of the cap iron should be polished in order to curl shavings smoothly with little friction. Fit the cap iron to the iron by first holding them together with light pressure the way they would mate in use. Looking between them toward the cutting edge you should see no light, but chances are you will. Where there is light, a shaving could wedge and clog the throat. Besides that, the cap iron cannot fully support the iron unless the two mate along the entire edge. The back of the iron should be flat, so it is the cap iron that needs truing.

To true the cap iron, hone the mating edge on a medium benchstone while keeping the upper end of the cap iron slightly lower than the stone, as shown in the photo above. Working this way trues the leading edge and hones a slight

underbevel. Polish the top of the cap iron with very fine sandpaper or steel wool, and then wipe on a coat of paste wax to help it work better and prevent rusting.

When you screw the cap iron and iron together you should feel some pressure. Sometimes you'll find that the bent part of the cap iron has lost some of its spring and it mates with the iron with little or no pressure. In this case, the cap iron simply needs a little more curvature. I clamp the cap iron vertically in a vise, with the point where the curve starts right at the top of the jaws, and then hit it a few times with a mallet (see the top photo on p. 72). The steel is soft enough to deform and hold the new shape, but go easy. Check the way the iron and cap iron mate and possibly rehone the underside of the cap iron if necessary.

The final adjustment is setting the cap iron to the iron (see the bottom photo on p. 72). Ideally, the cap iron should be as far from the cutting edge as the thickness of the shavings you expect to make. I set the cap iron and cutting iron close to this position, just

To put a little more spring into the cap iron, tap it right at the point of curvature while it is held in a vise. Only a slight amount of tension between the iron and the cap is needed.

Adjust the cap iron just back from the cutting edge for a smoothing plane and fine shavings (left) or farther back for coarse work as in a scrub plane (right).

snug up the screw between them, and then nudge the cap into final position before tightening the screw fully.

LEVER CAPS

The standard Bailey or Stanley lever cap usually needs little tuning, other than keeping it polished, waxed, and set with the proper tension against the double iron. Polish it with fine sandpaper or steel wool. As for tension, the lever cap should release easily and lock down with only modest pressure. Increase the tension by turning the screw into the bed that the lever cap locks over, or decrease it by turning the screw out. If the iron adjusts easily and stays set, the pressure is right.

Block planes and other planes with a single iron need their lever caps (or screw caps in some cases) tuned further. In these planes the lever cap does some of the work of the cap iron, mostly stabilizing the iron and assisting in curling shavings. The end of the lever cap should lie flat on the iron close to the bevel. These lever caps are cast and then chromed or painted, with little machining done to them where they mate with the iron. Flatten the underside on a coarse stone as described previously for a cap iron and shown in the top photo on the facing page. Adjust the tension against the iron in the same way as for a bench-plane lever cap.

DEPTH ADJUSTERS

Depth adjusters usually need little tuning, but a problem you may occasionally encounter is backlash, or play in the depth adjustment. As a result of wear and generous manufacturing tolerances, the "Y" adjustment lever doesn't always fit the brass adjuster wheel tightly. On older planes with a cast Y there is little you can do about it other than keep the adjuster wheel set with slight downward pressure on the iron. By this I mean if I back the iron out for a lighter cut, I then turn the adjuster the opposite way (as if to lower the iron) the quarter turn or whatever it takes to take the backlash out. This ensures that the iron will stay set.

On newer and inexpensive bench planes the Y is soft steel and appears to be made of two parts. Screw off the adjuster wheel and slightly bend one arm of the Y forward or backward. Trial-fit it in the slot of the adjuster wheel to see if it is a snug fit. For block planes, use a vise or pliers to pinch the adjuster lever where it captures the brass adjuster wheel, as shown in the bottom photo on the facing page.

WOODEN PLANES

If you've tuned your wooden plane with the same techniques explained for a metal plane, there's little else you need to do. Part of the beauty of wooden planes is their simplicity. Nevertheless, I would check two final areas to eliminate any possibility of their giving you trouble: the bed and the wedge.

Just as with a metal plane, the bed for the iron must be flat. One way to check the bed is to put the iron in position and see if it sits flat without rocking. If it doesn't, looking at the bed surface might give some clue as to high spots, which will be worn to a slight polish or show dark scrapes where the iron has rubbed against the bed. Pare the high spots carefully with a chisel, trying not to change the bed angle, or better yet use a fine file. Replace the iron to check your progress. The iron need not touch over its entire surface, but it should be fully supported.

The wedge might also need some tuning. If the plane is well used, the wedge has probably fitted itself to the grooves in the plane's cheeks that secure it. Ideally, with a light setting tap, the wedge should seat in the grooves along their entire length. Most important is that the wedge is tight against the iron (or against the cap iron in the case of double irons) close to the bottom of the throat. Tuning the wedge involves careful cuts with a block plane or file, trial-fitting it as you go. Tune the thin end the same way you would the cap on a block plane and give it a light coating of wax.

If you have taken your plane through all the tuning steps described here, you are going to be well rewarded. By understanding how the parts work together, you'll be able to fine-tune the plane for the work you want to do or troubleshoot any problems. And beyond sharpening the iron, your plane will need little maintenance to work to its best potential.

Tune a block-plane lever cap by flattening the underside of the leading edge on a coarse stone. The top edge should be polished smooth.

To take out any backlash or slop in the depth adjuster on a block plane, pinch the adjuster lever with a vise or pliers until it just fits the adjuster wheel.

5
HOW TO PLANE

A craftsman is one who understands his tools and his material and uses

them with skill and honesty. It does not matter whether his tool is a chisel or

a planing machine, it is the work that he does with it that counts.

—Thomas Hibben, *The Carpenter's Tool Chest,* 1933

For a plane to cut well, it takes more than using the right tool for the job and tuning it correctly. The way you adjust the plane, how you hold it, how you stand and balance your body through the stroke, and how you control and pressure the plane are all part of successful planing technique. Learning how to clamp or hold the work effectively and read the grain are just as important and can make all the difference between frustration and satisfaction.

The characteristics of a good bench, various clamping strategies, and ways to adjust the plane ready for work can be explained. How to hold the plane, how to stand when planing, how to vary the pressure upon the plane through each planing stroke, and how to read the grain of a board can also be taught to a point. But to plane well ultimately takes an awareness of the tool that cannot be taught—it must be felt. Fortunately, there is much pleasure in the learning, especially if you have a sturdy bench to get started on.

Holding the Work

It's hard to imagine doing good work without a sturdy bench, but it doesn't need to be elaborate to work well. Some days my bench serves as a desk and drawing table. Often it is a place to lay out parts, to mark joints, and to hold the work while cutting the joints. When I'm gluing up, its flat top is perfect for fitting parts and clamping against. It's where I hone and polish chisels and plane irons and occasionally file a saw. And every working day my bench becomes a jig to hold anything from rough planks to an assembled tabletop to small drawers as I work upon them with planes.

If a bench is a holding jig, the vises, dogs, holdfasts, and stops are what give it versatility. The beauty of these devices is

A good, sturdy workbench is essential for holding the work while planing. The bench on the facing page has a large side vise with double wooden screws and a sliding board jack with peg holes for holding the ends of long boards.

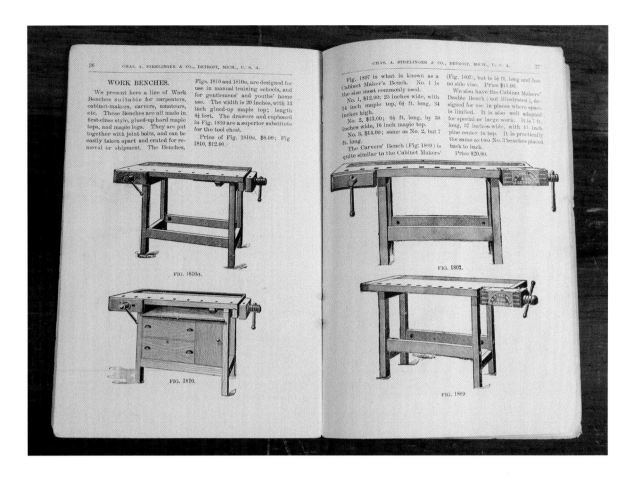

Late-19th-century catalogs, such as this one from Chas. A. Strelinger of Detroit, offered a wide variety of workbenches to suit the needs of specific trades and pocketbooks.

that they can work together or separately to hold pieces of various shapes or sizes. I rely mainly on the side and end vises, because they adjust quickly, hold positively, and give me a lot of clamping options. It's the large or oddly shaped piece that calls for more creative clamping, but with a sturdy bench and knowledge of the holding devices available, anything is possible.

BENCHES

Benches come in many shapes, sizes, types, and heights. They are as personal as each craftsman, from the bench-maker designing and building the bench to the bench-user fine-tuning each aspect to suit his way of working. Variations in bench design are most often the result of the different work performed upon them and the specific traditions they evolved from. Joiners and

carpenters building parts of houses needed flat surfaces and ways to clamp wide and long parts. Cabinetmakers needed a smaller bench and vises that could hold irregularly shaped work. Similarly, other trades adapted bench designs to suit their needs.

Bench designs have changed very slowly. A Roman workbench of well over 2,000 years ago wouldn't look a bit out of place in a modern shop. It resembles the basic bench found in many production shops, built of a wide single plank (more likely laminated solid wood or plywood today), through-mortised legs, and without any vise or clamping device except for possibly a bench stop to stop the work against. With the later addition of an L-shaped, forged iron holdfast (see p. 82), long boards could be held along the benchtop for edge jointing. Eventually side or end vises

were added to hold the work better, and workbenches were built longer and heavier and sometimes with drawers or a shelf under the top as well. By the late 17th or early 18th century, workbenches were little different from those typically found in shops today.

Bench height

When woodworking was done entirely by hand, workbenches were lower than most are today. Planing on a low bench puts more power into the stroke, through the natural gravity of more of the body driving the plane. Whereas today's benches typically range in height from about 34 in. to 38 in. or more, a bench of a few centuries ago would have been less than 30 in. high. Today's higher bench is understandable considering how much less physically demanding the work is and that a bench is just as often used for routing or cutting joints with a chisel, where strength is less important than getting the work higher and closer to your eyes for better control.

There is no perfect bench height; any height is going to be a compromise between the many ways the bench will be used. How tall you are and the kinds of work you are likely to do can help establish an optimum height. Like many craftsmen, I have a bench that is modeled on the bench that I learned on: an Ulmia bench with a single side vise, an end vise, and a row of dog holes along the length. I copied the height too—34½ in. Considering that I am just under 6 ft. tall and planing and other varied bench work feels comfortable, this height is ideal. If you're setting about building a bench and are unsure of the best height, you might want to build it an inch or two lower, especially if you are shorter than I am and expect to plane a lot by hand. It would then be a simple matter of fine-tuning the height with a board or 2-in. plank under each leg (or between the top and base), which could be secured with screws when you reach a height that feels right. In the same way, the height of a commercial bench can be fine-tuned to your height and needs.

No bench is a perfect height for all work. Sometimes I need to surface or plane an edge on a piece of furniture clamped 2 ft. or more above the bench surface. Rather than lay the work on the bench and work less efficiently and accurately with a plane on its side (if I even can), I prefer to clamp the work upright. Even though it is awkward to work at this height and use the plane with any force, I can take a light cut with a pass or two. When I need to plane extensively at this height, I pull out a 10 in. or 20 in. sawhorse to stand upon. A higher sawhorse works too, and at times I even stand on the bench itself.

The simplest bench is part sawhorse, part flat benchtop. Adding a bench stop and an L-shaped holdfast greatly increases its versatility. (From Diderot's *Encyclopédie*.)

Benches don't have to be elaborate to work well. This basic bench has everything you need to hold the work: a large, quick-acting side vise, a flat top surface, and an adjustable stop projecting through the top to plane against.

A side vise with two large wooden screws is ideal for clamping wide boards upright for planing end grain.

SIDE VISES

If your bench has only one vise, chances are that it is a side vise of some kind. A side vise is the least expensive vise option and the one most easily built or bolted on. Side vises are usually mounted at the left-hand corner of the bench, parallel with the front edge and with the jaw(s) flush with the bench top. In its simplest form this vise is nothing more than a wooden jaw with the clamping action coming from a large wood or steel screw. A small side vise opens about 8 in.; larger ones 12 in. or more. It's a useful vise for clamping work of modest size, short boards, or irregular curved shapes.

There are many variations of the side vise that add versatility or more clamping strength. The leg vise is one such design that originated in the 18th century. The movable jaw usually extends right to the floor to give the vise more stability, and sometimes reaches 6 in. or so above the benchtop. The result is a rugged vise useful for chairmakers clamping curved parts while shaping them or for wheelwrights fitting the spokes to a partially completed wheel.

Another side-vise variation has double screws through the jaw, which not only allows great clamping pressure, but also the ability to clamp work between the screws (see the bottom photo at left). This vise is as handy for clamping a board upright to plane the end grain as it is for clamping a tapered leg. The double screws also overcome a problem of the single-screw vise: It's easy to strain a single screw by clamping too heavily and racking the jaw.

Modern steel side vises such as the popular Record ED series (shown in the top photo at left) have design features that combine some of these ideas. To overcome the jaw-racking problem of a single screw, steel side vises have two steel rods parallel with the screw to help guide the jaws. Steel vises are also

An end vise and a row of dog holes down the length of the bench are useful for holding work flat on the bench surface. Built into the bench, the movable jaw also makes a powerful vise for clamping such things as curved chair parts.

available with double screws or with a quick-action screw. The quick action allows you to turn the screw part of a turn (or pull a lever) and slide the jaw freely in or out. While this is a handy feature, these vises are more expensive and more likely to wear out if stressed by heavy clamping pressure. On any metal vise, adding a bigger piece of hardwood to the movable jaw will spread the clamping pressure over a wider area, making it less likely to damage the work and easier to clamp larger pieces.

END VISES

An end vise is the real workhorse of any bench. With dog holes spaced down the length of my bench, I can clamp work on the bench surface as short as a few inches or as long as 7 ft.—boards, tabletops, doors, or round parts. My end vise is based on the Ulmia design, constructed from purchased steel mounting hardware and a large steel bench screw (see the photo at top). Turning the screw in or out moves a section of the right end of the bench with a wooden bench pin or dog in any of four dog holes. The work is clamped between this dog and another

A large end vise with two bench dogs and a double row of holes down the bench can clamp large or oddly shaped parts securely. The plane on the bench is an experimental Stanley block plane.

in a dog hole somewhere along the length of the bench. The movable jaw also creates a small but powerful vise within the thickness of the bench. Lined with thick leather, this is a stout vise for holding curved chair parts or narrow boards vertically. The entire end vise might look simple enough, yet it took me

as long to build and fit as the entire rest of the bench.

The real versatility of an end vise is the way the dogs can be positioned to hold irregularly shaped work, or any work for that matter. The dogs clamp the work-piece between two points and near the bench edge so that it is easy to position your body over the work and apply force to the plane. To hold very large work such as a tabletop securely, I often use an additional clamp somewhere along the bench, out of the way at the back edge if possible. Some benches overcome this problem by having two rows of dogs and an end vise more like an extended side vise with double screws and double dogs (see the bottom photo on p. 79).

If you don't have an end vise, it's useful to have a side vise with a bench dog in the movable jaw that can be pushed up or down. This is a common feature on many cast-iron vises, as shown in the top photo at right. Mounted in the usual position as an end vise (on the right-hand side, parallel with the end) and used in the same way, a dogged side vise can clamp long boards or parts along the bench top against another dog mortised into the bench top. With the addition of a holdfast or clamps you can probably get by, though it's still not as useful or powerful as an end vise for a wide variety of clamping jobs.

With both an end vise and a side vise, your bench will be as versatile a clamping jig as your imagination allows. While it would be impossible to explain all of the many ways you could clamp something with these two vises, some of the typical ways that work for me can be seen in the "shop" photos throughout the book. Choosing the best clamping method depends on the amount of stability desired, the effort involved with clamping and unclamping, and personal choice. Most of the best methods use bench dogs or stops of some kind for their sheer ease and simplicity.

DOGS AND STOPS

A bench dog is a wood or metal pin that slides into a dog hole or mortise in the bench. Traditional dogs are square in cross section, measuring an inch or so on

A side vise with a pop-up bench dog can serve as a versatile end vise.

Wooden bench dogs are simple to make and replace and are less likely to damage a plane iron than ones of steel or brass. An ash strip set into a saw kerf or screwed on creates a spring to hold the dog in position.

each side. Today they are just as likely to be round and fit into easily drilled round holes. A small friction spring of some type keeps the dog at any position above the bench surface or pushed out of the way below the bench top. Dogs are typically used in pairs—one fixed in an end vise and the other movable into any

dog hole along the bench surface. The photo above shows some simple wooden designs with an ash spring either screwed on or glued into a kerf.

Metal bench dogs have never appealed to me—I see only the potential of running onto one with a newly sharpened iron. When planing thin stock the tops of the

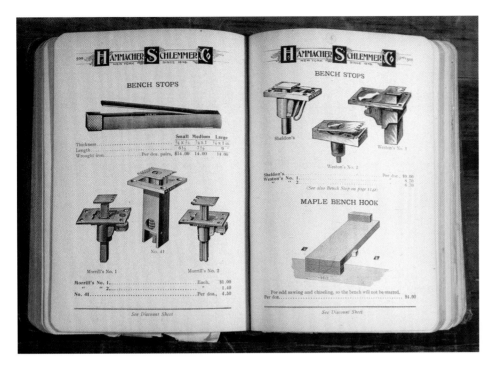

(See also Bench Stop on page 1142.)

Bench stops, such as these from an early Hammacher Schlemmer catalog, mortise into the benchtop and can be pushed up as needed. Teeth help hold the work.

dogs are close to the surface being planed, so close that occasionally my wooden ones will get an end-grain shaving or two taken off. Metal dogs stay sharp and square long after a wooden dog is worn, but, then, it only takes a few minutes to make a new pair of wooden dogs. If you insist on using metal dogs, choose softer brass over steel.

Bench stops look and work similarly to dogs, except that they are more often set in one position on the bench and are used alone. One form is a 1½-in. by 2½-in. aluminum plate set flush with the benchtop that can be flipped up to provide a secure stop to butt the work to and plane against. A toothed edge helps hold the work securely. Another form is forged like a bench dog with a flaring, toothed top. Using either type stop can be a very efficient way to hold narrow boards when planing them, since no vises need to be screwed in or out. My bench doesn't happen to have a special stop; when I want to plane against a single stable point I use either of my wooden dogs or shape one specially to fit the work. A small brad set into the dog

(with the head nipped off) helps hold the work from slipping side to side.

There is another type of bench dog worth knowing about for turning any plank into a bench for quick planing jobs on the job site. These dogs are shaped in a variety of ways, but usually with three

pointed legs—something like a trivet (see the photo below). Driving two legs into the plank stabilizes the third leg, which can be used like a stop, or another dog can be driven in to hold the other end of the board, too. These dogs are light, compact, and very handy.

WEDGING STOPS AND JIGS

Holding the end of a board on top of a bench to edge-joint it or plane upon it in some way poses a challenge that has sparked much creativity. Some designs hold the end by wedging it into a jig that has become known as a wedging stop. The most versatile ones adjust to a range of board thicknesses. Why use a wedging stop when a side vise would be more positive and maybe even easier to use? The beauty of a wedging stop is its

Forged-iron bench dogs can turn a plank into a quick planing bench.

Wedging Stops

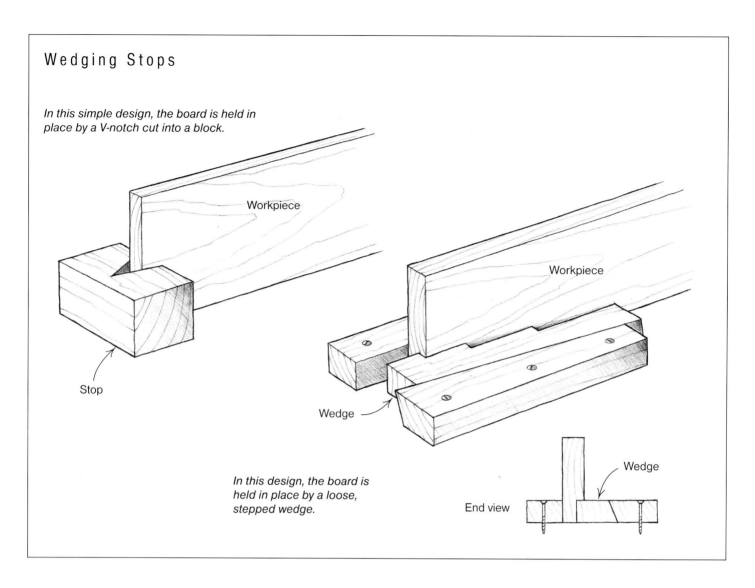

In this simple design, the board is held in place by a V-notch cut into a block.

Workpiece

Stop

Workpiece

Wedge

In this design, the board is held in place by a loose, stepped wedge.

Wedge

End view

simplicity; the work needs only to be jammed into the stop to be adequately held. Wedging stops work best for planing small parts of a uniform size where the support of a flat bench helps, for planing irregular shapes where the stop can be cut to fit the work, or for use as a temporary stop on the job site easily cut and nailed to a plank. To hold specially shaped parts such as delicate window muntins when planing against a stop, a useful addition is a planing jig to fit the individual pieces into. Used together or alone, either a wedging stop or a jig can make some planing work easier.

The simplest wedging stop is no more than a block with a V-notch cut into it. The board end is jammed into the V to hold it. Another variation uses a stepped wedge both to stop and clamp the end. Many versions were made from cast iron, most of which can be reproduced just as well in wood. The drawing above shows two very practical designs. The variations are endless, limited only by your specific needs and imagination.

HOLDFASTS

A holdfast is a hefty L-shaped steel forging that's useful for holding work on top of the bench (or along an edge in place of a board jack). One end wedges

into a hole drilled through the benchtop and the other holds against the work (see the top photo on the facing page). The beauty of holdfasts lies in their ability to be adjusted easily and to hold oddly shaped objects. A solid hit with a mallet sets the holdfast; a hit to its back releases it. Inserting a small block of wood under the clamping face will protect the work surface and can be shaped to fit it. The only limitation to a holdfast is that it can be used only where there is a hole drilled to receive it, which is not always exactly where it might be needed. Nevertheless, as a "third hand" holdfasts are very useful to help hold large surfaces such as tabletops.

A modern reincarnation of the traditional holdfast looks like half a clamp set perpendicular to the benchtop. While it might be versatile and useful, it has the same limitations as a forged holdfast—it is movable only to a point. A short bar clamp securing the work somewhere along a bench edge can be just as useful.

CLAMPING BOARDS FOR EDGE JOINTING

Short boards are fairly easy to clamp in a side vise. I have an old cast-iron side vise with a jaw about 5 in. deep that can hold boards (or thicker planks and wider parts, too) up to about 4 ft. long. The advantage of using a side vise rather than just the top of the bench with a stop is that the side vise holds the work securely regardless of whether the bottom side is shaped, rough, or uneven. The jaws merely clamp the work in position. A side vise has the added benefits of holding a board more rigidly on edge than you would be able to on top of a bench and at a good working height.

Holdfasts work as their name implies, with a long reach, secure hold, and quick release. All they require is a hole through the benchtop.

Short boards up to about 4 ft. long can be clamped in a side vise. The stronger the vise and the larger the jaws, the longer the board it can hold securely.

Long boards can be secured using both a side vise and a block of wood clamped in the end vise. A second block of wood clamped midway between the vises supports narrow and flexible stock for the most accurate jointed surface.

Longer boards are hard to clamp securely in a side vise alone. One solution is to use both the side vise and the end vise. I clamp a short board low down in the jaws of my end vise, so that it sticks out perpendicular to the front edge of my bench 4 in. or so and forms a rest for one end of the board (see the photo above). The other end of the board is clamped in the side vise. Clamped in this way, the edge of the bench lends support and the side vise holds the board in position. If the board is so narrow that it might deflect from the planing pressure, an additional block or two clamped to the face of the bench will further support the board. The same thing can be done with a short bar clamp securing the board right to the edge of the bench, but this method requires extra clamping and unclamping for every piece. Between the two vises I can comfortably joint boards about 11 ft. long, although if I were working such long lengths regularly, I would build a longer bench.

If you joint wide boards regularly, it's a good idea to incorporate a board jack into your bench (see the photo on p. 74) or build a portable one. A board jack is a

board mounted on the side of the bench (some of them slide down the bench to accommodate boards of different lengths), with spaced holes to hold a stout peg at various heights off the floor. One end of the board to be jointed rests on the peg; the other end is held in the side vise (see the drawing below). A board jack is an adjustable version of the holding method I use with a block

clamped into the jaws of the end vise. The simplest board jack need be no more than a row of peg holes down the leg near the end vise or a few larger holes for a holdfast. A portable board jack resembles a stairs cut into a board supported vertically on a base of some kind.

So far I haven't gotten around to building either a fixed or portable board jack. This has meant using extra

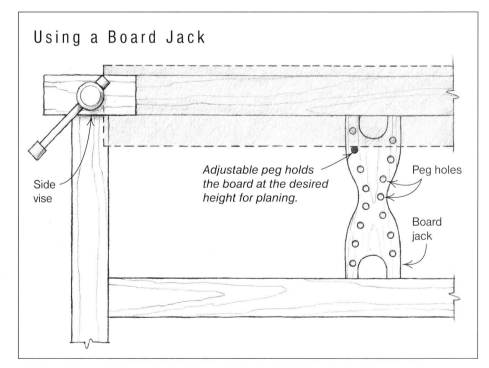

Using a Board Jack

Side vise

Adjustable peg holds the board at the desired height for planing.

Peg holes

Board jack

creativity when planing the edge of a wide tabletop or jointing a wide board. What works is to clamp one end in the side vise and prop the other end on either a short piece of plank resting flat on the floor or a 10-in. or 20-in. high sawhorse. Naturally I choose a height that puts the edge I am working on parallel with and slightly above the bench surface. A bar clamp at the tail-vise end helps stabilize the work if I need it. It's a simple solution, but sturdy and effective.

Adjusting the Plane for Work

You've got the work clamped in place at a good working height. Your plane is tuned, the iron sharp, and you're ready to start curling up those long-awaited shavings. But before you put the plane to the wood, hold on just a half-minute and check that the throat is not too tight or wide for the work you want to do, that the depth of the iron is set properly, and that the iron is parallel with the sole. It doesn't take much time working with a plane before these adjustments become second nature—a glance at the throat and a light touch with a finger to feel the iron's depth and alignment in about as much time as it takes to pick up the plane and bring it to the work.

THROAT OPENING
Chapters 3 and 4 explain in detail how the throat opening affects the physics of the cut and how to adjust the opening properly. The truth is that unless you are trying to use only a few planes for all of your planing work, the throats will rarely need to be adjusted. With a handful of planes tuned and at the ready, you'll quickly learn which one works best for what you are trying to do. The throats should range from wide for

planing coarse shavings and removing wood quickly, to very narrow for light polishing cuts.

The problem you are most likely to encounter is clogging, which occurs when the throat is tight and you try to take too heavy a cut. For day-to-day work, set the throat on your bench planes (except smoothing planes) between $\frac{1}{32}$ in. and $\frac{1}{16}$ in. An opening this wide is a fine compromise between good performance and being able to cut shavings of different thickness. Moreover, the deeper the iron is set, the more throat width it takes up. Set the throat slightly wider on a plane you expect to use just for rough work and really hogging off wood quickly. A little tearout and roughness of the surface are to be expected, and at least the plane won't clog because the throat is too small. For smoothing planes and other planes (shoulder, bullnose) tuned to cut a fine shaving, a fine throat is a must to cut with a lot of accuracy and leave a polished surface. Set these throats as fine as you can—just shy of $\frac{1}{64}$ in.

Occasionally I do change the throat width on my few adjustable-throat block planes. Used on end grain a modest throat is fine, but using the same plane to level the transition between stile and rail on a door, for example, I want the throat tight. The only other time I would change the throat opening would be if I were about to joint a number of curly-maple boards. The little time it takes to move the frog and tighten the throat on my Stanley Bed Rock #607 prevents a lot of frustration.

IRON DEPTH
Once the throat opening is checked, next adjust the iron's depth for the work you expect to do. Cast-iron planes couldn't be easier to use when it comes to making this adjustment; I'm sure it was a factor in their immediate acceptance and popularity over wooden planes. A half turn on the adjuster wheel and the iron is set deeper, or it can be backed out just as easily with a half turn the opposite way. The rotary motion of the adjuster wheel pushes or pulls the Y-adjustment

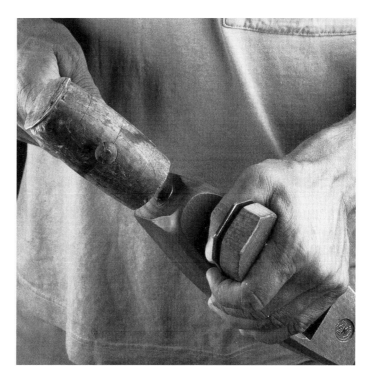

Adjust the depth of the iron in a wooden plane by tapping on the toe for a deeper cut or on the heel for a finer cut. Hit the strike button if there is one.

Moving the adjuster right or left on a Bailey-pattern bench plane tilts the iron to align it parallel with the sole. Look for an even glint of the iron or feel for its alignment with a finger.

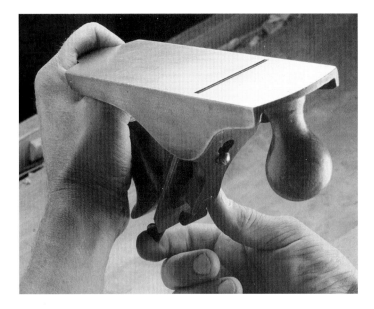

To adjust lateral alignment on a wooden plane, tap on either side of the iron to align it with the sole. Here, the author feels the alignment with his thumb as he taps the iron.

tapping on the heel raises the iron for a finer cut (and will eventually release the iron and wedge if hit hard enough). If there's a strike button on the heel, hit it there (see the photo on p. 85). On better-quality, long bench planes there is also a strike on the top of the toe end of the plane. Tapping this strike also lightens the cut. One school of thought maintains that all adjustments should be made with a wooden mallet and the iron shouldn't be hit at all, but a good look at any well-used plane will show that this is not always the case. I use light blows with a smooth-faced hammer (as the Japanese do) to tap the iron lower for a more aggressive cut.

Unfortunately, adjusting the iron depth in a wooden plane is not quite as simple as a few taps here or there. Lightening the cut of the iron also releases some of the pressure of the wedge, which will need to be tapped back snug (don't drive it too hard or you may distort the plane body or crack out the cheeks). Yet in setting the wedge, the iron is often set slightly deeper as well. Once you've gotten used to the feel of the way the plane reacts to being tapped, it's really no more difficult than adjusting a metal plane.

LATERAL ALIGNMENT
Setting the iron parallel with the sole—the lateral alignment—is just as important as setting the iron's depth. If the iron isn't parallel, one side will cut more deeply and either gouge the surface or, in the case of jointing an edge, cut the edge with a slight bevel. It's easy enough to sight down the sole from the toe and see how parallel the exposed edge of the iron and the sole are, and if need be make an adjustment. In the early development of the cast-iron plane there was no simple way to adjust the iron laterally, save for just pushing it one way or the other. After 1885, Stanley's Bailey

lever that in turns slides the iron in or out. The only aspect that is slightly confusing is that on most bench planes turning the adjuster wheel in backs out the iron. Turning the wheel out deepens the cut. Start with the iron set for a light cut and make sure to take any backlash out of the adjuster so there is slight downward pressure on the iron (see p. 72). Once you have made a shaving or two and seen how the wood behaves, you can always deepen the cut.

Adjusting the iron's depth in wooden planes takes a little more practice to develop a feel for what's happening—it is more akin to tuning a fine instrument than the purely mechanical adjustment of a metal plane. (Of course, some modern wooden planes and all transitional planes have an adjuster similar to cast-iron planes and are adjusted the same way.) For all-wood planes, tapping on the toe sets the iron for a deeper cut;

line of bench planes had a lever for lateral adjustment of the iron.

On cast-iron bench planes the lateral adjustment lever is behind the iron and attached to the frog. Moving it right or left rocks the iron slightly. The problem is that on some planes the lever tilts the iron exactly the way you predict it should, and on others the iron moves in the opposite direction. On bench planes, moving the lever to the right (sighting along the sole from the toe with the plane upside-down) generally withdraws the right corner of the iron. Moving the lever to the left withdraws the left corner of the iron (see the top photo on the facing page). This is the opposite of what intuition tells you to expect. On other bench planes and many block planes everything is reversed. It sounds more confusing than it is. Eventually you'll not even look at the iron, but feel its depth at a few places with your finger and make minor adjustments of the lateral adjuster without even thinking.

To adjust the iron laterally in a wooden plane, tap the iron to one side or the other, as shown in the bottom photo on the facing page. In this case, the iron does adjust the way you might expect—tapping the iron to the right lowers the right corner. Bear in mind that adjusting the lateral alignment might change the iron's depth setting, so give it one last check before starting to plane.

Planing Technique

Learning how to plane comfortably and efficiently is no different than learning how to master any physical activity—except that planing is more like Tai Chi or skiing than football. To plane well demands aligning yourself in a comfortable stance and balancing your body through the stroke, all the while applying pressure to and controlling the plane. Such a thing really can't be taught any more than you can teach a person to be a good skier by explaining the way to balance and move your body over your skis. Explaining the dynamics of the technique is a good first step, with sensitivity and true understanding of it coming through time. For the less experienced, your first plane strokes will feel awkward. For the more experienced, perhaps being conscious of the way you balance your body and direct force to the plane will make the work less tiring and more rewarding. As with any skill, it takes time to develop a feel for the subtleties of the tool.

READING THE GRAIN

I wish there were some easily followed rules for reading the grain of a board and knowing the best way to plane it, but unfortunately there will always be a fair measure of guesswork involved. I can look at the grain lines on the surface of a board and inspect the two edges and feel confident that I'm going to be planing "with the grain" but quickly come to find out that things aren't what they appear to be when I get deep tearouts.

The ideal technique is to plane the wood fibers in the direction that they appear to rise in front of the plane. Any splitting out of the fibers is headed toward the cut surface, rather than down into the wood, which would be the case when planing against the grain. Unfortunately, few woods are straight-grained, and on most boards the grain rises and falls in such a way that somewhere along its surface you're apt to be planing against the grain. What makes things even more difficult is irregular grain (which appears as figure), imperfections (such as knots), and the naturally inconsistent structure of some woods (such as roey, curly, or ribbon striped). The best you can hope for is to make a good guess and start in cautiously.

If you've used a machine to surface a board before hand-planing, it's a lot easier to tell which way to plane. My normal procedure is first to run a surface over a jointer after looking at the grain and picking an orientation. If the first pass leaves a smooth surface, I'll mark an arrow on the wood and go on to the planer. If not, I'll try the opposite direction. Sometimes it's a toss-up between the two, in which case I know I'll be cautious when hand-planing later. The machining arrow stays on the surface or edge right up until I remove it with a plane.

On any board, look at adjacent surfaces (a face and an edge) to get a better idea of how the grain is oriented. The more consistent the grain lines on both, the more likely the planing will be smooth and easy. Watch out for swirled or circular grain lines; these lines indicate the rising and falling grain around such areas as knots. Some boards have broad U-shaped, grain lines: plane into the Us as if the grain were a topographical map and you were working up a valley. Look at all four edges if need be and start with a light cut.

A comfortable, relaxed stance while planing, with your shoulder over the work, allows you to deliver power and control to the plane.

The most important part of the planing stance is that it feel comfortable and natural. Assuming that you are about to joint a board clamped to the bench planing from right to left, a good stance would be with your legs apart as wide as a stride, with your right foot back and left foot forward (see the photo at left). This stance puts your shoulder over the work and, if the bench is a good height, your upper body in position to be able to deliver to the plane the power and control necessary. Flexing the knees gives you the balance to rock backward when starting the cut and also to lean forward to finish the stroke.

The way you hold the plane should be comfortable, too—a tight grip is tiring. I grab the front knob on bench planes between the thumb and first one or two fingers of my left hand. The high front knob common on later Bailey-type planes is especially comfortable. This grip leaves two fingers free to wrap around the plane's side to guide the plane along the board for extra control when jointing (more on this in Chapter 6). I grip the rear tote with my thumb and three fingers, leaving my pinkie or index finger to lie along the plane's right side. This grip gives a little added control and is more comfortable than trying to jam all of my fingers around the tote. While holding the plane I can use my index finger to rotate the depth adjuster if I want to make an adjustment on the fly (see the photo at left). Wooden planes and unhandled planes are held in basically the same way, with the right hand at the heel and the left hand at the toe. Position your hands and fingers in whatever way feels most comfortable so that you can apply pressure to the plane and control its direction easily, too.

Feeling a natural start and ending to the plane stroke is the hardest part of planing technique to master. It's very

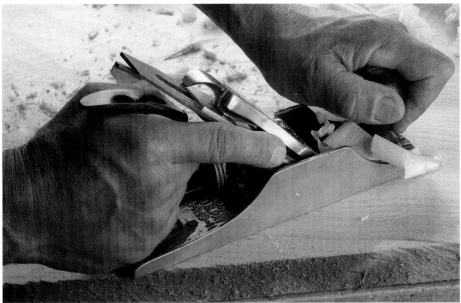

Hold the plane with a relaxed but firm grip, grasping the front knob with a few fingers and the rear tote with as many fingers as fit around it comfortably. Use your index finger to adjust the depth of the iron on the fly.

Start the cut by balancing the plane with the iron ready to cut. All of the pressure is at the front of the plane; the rear hand only helps balance the plane at the start of the cut.

Pressure the plane evenly through the cut, using both hands for balance and control.

End the cut by shifting the pressure toward the heel to avoid rounding over the end.

easy to tip the plane down at either end and cut more deeply so that before long you have a jointed edge with a slight curve, not one that's truly straight. Think of the sole in front of the iron as guiding the beginning of the cut. At the start of the cut I position the plane on the board with the iron just about to make contact (see the photo at top). My left hand on the front knob exerts firm pressure downward, as my right hand merely supports the heel of the plane. Holding the plane at a slight skew feels more comfortable and helps the cutting dynamics by slicing the iron into the cut.

As the plane starts to cut, I gradually shift pressure from the front knob to the rear tote so that by the time the sole is fully supported the pressure is equal (see the photo above left). By then the plane has a certain momentum that I try to maintain through the entire cut, not fast but steady. For long boards I have to take a step or two forward, still keeping my shoulder positioned over the work and the pressure even. It takes a bit of practice to keep the plane steady as you

RAZEE PLANES

Razee planes are interesting wooden planes that have a unique design. Part of the plane stock is cut away and lowered at the rear where the tote is joined (and sometimes at the front knob as well). This design gives the plane better balance and control by lowering its center of gravity and by aligning the pushing force right behind the iron and close to the cutting action.

The razee style has always been associated with the jack plane and longer ship planes, made of tropical hardwoods and usually narrower than conventional bench planes. Although ship carpenters didn't invent the form, they took the name from the description of a ship with an upper deck removed. Razee planes were also used in trade schools, where a slightly lighter and easier-to-control plane presumably helped students learn planing technique. Although not rare, razee planes are not common either. The reason for this is more likely their higher cost (for fitting the tote into the step in the stock) than their lack of appeal and usefulness.

Razee handles lower the plane's center of gravity and deliver the force of your hand right to the cutting action of the plane.

move your body forward, but with a heavy jointer the mass of the plane helps a lot. If for some reason the plane clogs with shavings or it feels as though greater force is needed to drive the plane, stop. Chances are the iron is set too deeply. Reading the troubleshooting section on the facing page might help, or recheck the tuning as explained in Chapter 4. The cut should feel smooth and continuous from end to end.

Ending the cut is the reverse of starting it: You need to shift the pressure toward the heel as the sole extends beyond the end of the board. By the time the iron stops cutting, all the pressure should be on the heel. Sometimes just before this point I take my hand off the front knob and let the mass and momentum of the plane finish the cut (see the bottom right photo on p. 89). Try to avoid the mistake of keeping pressure on the toe and cutting more heavily at the end of the stroke. A long plane and the design of the iron forward of center help avoid this, but it is still easy to round over the end of the cut.

A natural tendency at this point is to slide the plane back before picking it up to start another stroke. Don't, because it will unnecessarily dull the iron. Always pick up the plane at the end of the stroke. Even the heaviest plane can be picked up one-handed if the balance is right. Ending the stroke is a good time to clear the throat of any shavings to prevent clogging. Very shortly, picking up the plane to start another stroke and clearing it of shavings will become second nature.

If you're done planing or are pausing to sight the planed edge, always lay the plane on its side on the bench or rest the toe on a thin scrap of wood so that the cutting edge is off the bench. It's far too easy to nick or dull the iron by carelessly setting it on the end of a steel rule or a bit of hardware lying on your bench.

SKEWING

I've always found that it feels natural to hold the plane at a skew or an angle to the direction of the stroke while planing along (as shown in the bottom photo on p. 88). It's a good habit to get into, because skewing can noticeably improve the cut. The physical reasons for this are explained in Chapter 3: Skewing lowers the effective cutting angle of the iron, provides additional slicing force, and reduces resistance to the cut. The more extreme the skew, the easier and better the cut will often be; but the width of the cut will be a lot smaller, too.

Except when using molding planes or a jointer gauge (see pp. 108-109), I always keep the plane at a slight skew when I'm planing. I even skew a jointer plane, although with this long plane I have to be aware of keeping the entire length of the sole supported on the work. Around knots and unruly figure, skewing the plane one way or the other never fails to yield a smoother surface. When planing a tabletop or any large surface, skewing helps me smooth transitions at glue joints and areas where the grain is inconsistent. I think of skewing much the same way my workhorse thinks about hills; when he's given a choice he'd much rather skew around a hill than climb straight up it.

TROUBLESHOOTING

No matter how well you learn planing technique, at some time you are likely to encounter annoying problems. Three common problems are uneven cutting or "chatter," a clogged throat, and a misaligned iron that leaves distinct ridges. There are simple solutions for all three problems.

Chatter

Chatter shows up as ripples in the surface where the plane iron stuttered and didn't cut smoothly. It can often be as easily felt or heard as seen. Very often chatter will occur at the start of a cut, before the plane is firmly supported on the surface. The uneven cutting is caused by the buildup of pressure against the iron to the point that it starts to vibrate. As the iron springs forward and back, the cutting depth is raised or lowered slightly, enough to leave distinct parallel cuts in the surface.

The key to reducing chatter is to reduce some of the pressure on the iron, or give it more support. The simplest solution is to use a thicker, more stable iron. Alternatively, you can skew the cut to reduce pressure on the iron, or take a lighter cut. To make sure the iron is getting adequate support, check some of the tuning: Is the bed flat and even, is the cap iron fitted to the iron, is the frog adjusted too far forward so that the iron has little support near the cutting edge? It may be a combination of things. If you reread the tuning sections in Chapter 4, you should be able to solve any one of these problems.

Clogging

Clogging can sometimes be a problem even with the best tuned planes. Shavings bind up so tightly in the throat that the plane no longer cuts. The most obvious cause is that the throat is too tight. The solution is to open the throat or back off the cap iron a $1/16$ in. or so.

Nothing clogs up a plane faster than a dull iron. To compensate you take a deeper cut because the plane doesn't seem to be cutting, and then you're done for. Clogging can be caused by a poor fit of the cap iron to the iron, which allows some shavings to get under it and others to build up. The cap iron should be smooth and waxed. The wedge in a wooden plane might be somehow blocking the free escape of the shavings. Bevel the front edge of the throat forward slightly to give the shavings extra room. A lighter cut always helps, but just expect that sometimes clogging is going to be a problem.

A lot of the clogging problem can be eliminated by clearing the throat of large shavings at the end of each stroke. Often this means nothing more than pulling out the end of a long curl. Why else do you think the upper edges of the throat on wooden planes are chamfered?—to make it easier to get your fingers in to pull out the shavings.

Iron misalignment

Slight lateral misalignment of the iron is rarely much of a problem, but it can be an annoyance and is something to be aware of. If the iron isn't parallel with the sole, one side cuts more deeply and leaves pronounced ridges. If I'm rough-surfacing a board, a little unevenness isn't a problem. But for a final smoothing I want the iron parallel to the sole. I usually feel the depth of the iron projecting from the sole in a few places before starting in, and, if need be, make slight adjustments. By watching the thickness and width of the shavings while planing, I can make further adjustments as necessary. Ideally, I want to see a shaving of consistent thickness curling nearly the width of the throat.

Learning to use a plane takes practice. With the work held securely on a bench, the plane tuned and adjusted, it's just a matter of time before planing becomes a natural extension of your body motion. In time, you'll find yourself concentrating more on feeling the way the plane cuts, on the beauty of the surface, and on the texture and smell of the shavings.

6

PLANES FOR TRUING
AND SIZING STOCK

Craftsmanship is a combination of knowledge on how to use tools and

of skill with the hands.

—Stanley Rule and Level, *How to Work with Tools and Wood,* 1927

No planes are more useful or used more often than planes for truing and sizing stock, commonly known as bench planes. Before the development of woodworking machinery and its adoption in almost every shop, bench planes did much of the work that we rely on table saws, thickness planers, and jointers for today. With machines taking over the hardest tasks of working rough stock to dimension, bench planes are more often used today to refine parts at the bench. Even in a shop full of power machinery, it's hard to imagine not having a bench plane or two in your toolkit.

Types of Bench Planes

When most of us think of bench planes we think of Stanley cast-iron planes, or more exactly Bailey-pattern bench planes, since it was Leonard Bailey who patented most of the ideas over 125 years ago (see Chapter 2). But for all of the hundreds of years before Stanley and others perfected cast-iron planes, bench planes were made of wood (see the photos on p. 94) and more rarely of joined steel plates with wood infill. Most craftsmen had at least three bench planes: a jack plane for rough-dimensioning work, a jointer or try plane for shooting edges and accurately flattening panels, and a smoothing plane for finishing surfaces. They were the hardest working planes he owned. Although some modern-day craftsmen still prefer to use wooden planes, many more feel that cast iron and steel are superior materials for making bench planes.

This lid from a joiner's chest, probably made in London c. 1790, depicts the maker at his bench and shows off his considerable inlay skills and collection of bench planes. (Photo courtesy Colonial Williamsburg.)

We will probably never know why the maker of this fruitwood French try plane carved a fox head into the plane body, as well as his initials and date ("M. S. 1834"), but it is typical of early European planes.

Oriental bench planes have thick irons and white-oak bodies. Notice the sliding dovetailed "key" to tighten the throat on the plane shown upside-down.

STANLEY BENCH PLANES

Stanley cast-iron bench planes range in size from the smallest #1 to a #8 jointer, and also include scrub planes (see pp. 97-99) and block planes (see pp. 110-119). Besides these sizes there are a few odd sizes, a #4½, a #5½, and a #5¼. Then there are some specialty planes that could easily be included in this group, such as the #10, #10½, and #10¼ bench rabbet planes. For the sake of simplicity these rabbet planes are included in Chapter 7; this chapter focuses primarily on the basic bench planes used to surface and size stock.

Stanley was by no means the only manufacturer of bench planes, but it's a measure of Stanley's dominance of the market that its numbering system has almost become the standard. Lots of other manufacturers made bench planes (some were even made by Stanley and sold under other names), but no matter what their catalog numbers, we still think of them as #4s or #6s, and so on. To avoid confusion, I'll stick with the Stanley numbering system.

Despite their obvious differences in size, Bailey bench planes are nearly identical to one another in design (see the chart on p. 96 for a comparison of sizes). Of all these planes, the #1 is the least usable and the most highly sought after. To me, it's a curiosity—a miniature bench plane without any lateral adjustment. Certainly it can be used to dimension parts, but the sole is short and the handles so tiny that using it is more awkward than using a block plane the same size. One story why Stanley and its competitors made such small planes was for schoolboys and for use in woodworking schools. The #1 might have been made for small hands and fine work, but I suspect its popularity then or now has more to do with our fascination

Three early cast-iron bench planes include (from rear) a Challenge jointer sold by Tower and Lyon, patented 1883 with an interesting depth adjuster, and a #5 and a #4 Victor, a line of planes originally made by Leonard Bailey and later bought by Stanley.

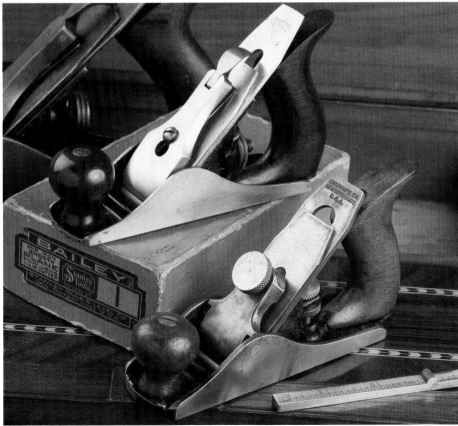

The Stanley #1 (atop the box) is the smallest and most rare of the bench planes. Competitors such as the Union Manufacturing Co., of New Britain, Connecticut, made a similar-sized plane, a #0 (foreground). The Stanley #4½ in the background gives a sense of their tiny size.

Bailey Cast-Iron Bench Planes

SIZE*	NAME	IRON WIDTH (in.)	LENGTH (in.)	WEIGHT (lb.)
#1	Smoothing	1 1/4	5 1/2	1 1/8
#2	Smoothing	1 5/8	7	2 1/4
#3	Smoothing	1 3/4	8	3 1/8
#4	Smoothing	2	9	3 3/4
#4 1/2	Smoothing	2 3/8	10	4 3/4
#5	Jack	2	14	4 3/4
#5 1/4	Junior jack	1 3/4	11 1/2	3 3/4
#5 1/2	Jack	2 1/4 to 2 3/8	15	6 3/4
#6	Fore	2 3/8	18	7 3/4
#7	Jointer	2 3/8	22	8 1/8
#8	Jointer	2 5/8	24	9 3/4
#9	Cabinetmaker's block plane	2	10 (8 1/4 after 1936)	4 1/2
#40	Scrub	1 1/4	9 1/2	2 1/8
#40 1/2	Scrub	1 1/2	10 1/2	2 1/2

*Bench planes with corrugated soles (available for all but #1) have the letter C after the number (e.g., #2C, #3C).
Adapted from Sellens, The Stanley Plane (1975).

with anything miniature. Certainly someone interested in actually using a #1 won't pay the nearly $1,000 they can trade for.

I know there are some who would disagree with me, but I find the #2 and #3 bench planes equally small and only somewhat useful. I'm sure there is fine work they are well suited for—leveling the top edges of small drawers, for example—but I find that it's just as easy to have a #4 tuned for this work and a lot more besides. For me, the #4 is the perfect size; it fits my hand, the sole is long enough to do accurate work, it has enough heft to plane well, yet I can use it one-handed if need be. It's my "odd-job" plane, used for trimming parts to size, cutting tapers or bevels, shooting small edge joints, or performing any of the varied planing work in my day.

There are four more common sizes of bench plane, each progressively longer and heavier: a #5 jack, a #6 fore, and #7 and #8 jointer planes. The odd-sized #4 1/2, #5 1/2, and #5 1/4 are just what you would expect, intermediate sizes. Which one of any of these planes you choose depends upon the work you want to do and which one has the heft and feel that most appeals to you. Often it is as much a matter of habit as which one fits the work. Some craftsmen tell me they use a #7 for everything. Such a long plane can do accurate work, but I find it too heavy for odd jobs at the bench. Instead, I use both a #7 and a #8 for jointing long edges and planing surfaces that I want very flat. I rarely use a #6, but use a #5 almost as much as a #4, for jointing

This assortment of bench planes is typical of the range of sizes once available, from the smallest #1 to a #8 jointer.

short edges, planing end-grain edges (as on a tabletop), and fitting drawers to their openings.

There are no hard-and-fast rules about which planes to use, but the design of each evolved for certain kinds of work. Use the plane that fits the scale of the work and use longer planes for greater accuracy. This goes for anything from shooting an edge joint to flattening a surface.

SCRUB PLANES

Scrub planes are the hardest working of the bench planes. Not so long ago they were part of the basic toolkit of any woodworker, used for roughing parts to size before refining them with other bench planes. You could think of a scrub plane as the plane equivalent of a thickness planer. Where parts could be left rough, such as the underside of drawer bottoms and case backs, you'll often see the strong parallel corrugations left by a scrub plane.

Three things distinguish a scrub plane from other bench planes: The throat is very large to pass coarse shavings, the iron has a very pronounced curvature or camber across the width of the edge, and the iron is usually only a single thick iron without a cap iron. All three characteristics help the plane cut aggressively without clogging, but with little refinement of the surface. This is called "hogging." With a cambered cutting edge, the iron cuts like a large gouge; in fact, the finished surface is apt to be rough and looked gouged. A single iron is easiest to set up and use, although with a minimum of tuning a double iron works fine, too. The slightly rougher surface you get with a single iron is less important than the ability to remove material quickly.

Scrub planes are used far less today than they once were. I use one when it's easier than going to the bandsaw or table

Common bench planes such as the #2, #3, and #4 shown here (from rear) have identical adjusters, rear handles, lever caps, and body shaping.

Scrub planes are the hardest-working bench planes. Shown here (from rear) are a Stanley #340 furring plane with minimal sole for "cleaning" rough boards; a Sargent #162 with two irons and cast-iron handles for a sure grip; and Ohio Tool's #040, which is nearly identical to a Stanley #40.

saw, for hogging off wood when cutting a tapered part, for beveling the underside of a drawer bottom, or for thicknessing the odd board that's too wide for my planer. A scrub plane is also useful when gathering materials for a project, for choosing boards with consistent quality, grain, or color. With a scrub plane and a minimum amount of planing through the roughsawn or weathered surface, I can get a good idea about the character of a board before sending it over the jointer and planer.

Scrub planes can be found on the used tool market, often priced quite reasonably. They are apt to be worn, but nothing that a little tuning can't remedy. Lie-Nielsen makes a new cast-iron version of the original Stanley #40 and replacement irons, too. You might consider making your own scrub plane from either a worn wooden smoothing plane or a tired #3 or #4 bench plane. Wooden-soled transitional planes work well, too. I have a couple of old wooden smoothers that have throats so wide that refashioning them as scrub planes is about all they are useful for. A cast-iron bench plane will work well as long as the throat is opened wide and the iron is cambered.

Tuning and using scrub planes

Scrub planes need a lot less tuning than most planes. Tearout and surface roughness are to be expected, so save the time you'd spend tuning a scrub plane for your smoothing or jointer planes. Stick to the basics: Make sure the handles are tight (you'll be applying a lot of force to the plane and will want a good grip), check that the sole is within the ballpark of flatness in the important areas, camber the edge of the iron, and tune the screw cap so that it holds the iron snugly in place. This is basic tuning covered in Chapter 4.

If you are going to tune a #4 or similar bench plane as a scrub plane, think about it as a dedicated plane used for this

Cambering the iron allows the scrub plane to make deep gouging cuts. If the plane has a cap iron, it can be set well back from the cutting edge (as shown) or ground to the same camber as the iron.

purpose only. Opening the throat wide enough to work well as a scrub plane and cambering the iron will make your plane useless for more refined work. Start by moving the frog well back to open up the throat (refer to pp. 59-62 for more detailed information on adjusting the throat). You'll need a throat at least $\frac{1}{8}$ in. wide—$\frac{3}{16}$ in. wide would be even better. When moving the frog, be aware of one thing: The iron still needs to be bedded well along its entire length. Move the frog so the iron just beds against the beveled sole. If the throat is still not wide enough, file the front of the throat opening.

Cambering or shaping the iron is very important to get good results. The iron's shape concentrates the cutting energy over a small arc, so it can cut more deeply than a straight iron cutting along its entire width. How much camber is a matter of choice—the more you have, the easier the tool will cut, but the smaller the width of each "gouging" cut. You'll need to resharpen more often too, since less of the edge is cutting. A good compromise is about $\frac{1}{16}$ in. relief either side of the center of the iron (see the photo above and the drawing on p. 67). I rough out the shape on the grinder, by moving the iron in an arc over the wheel. Drawing a reference line on the back of the iron with a felt-tipped pen helps you grind a more accurate shape, although

Old and worn wooden or transitional planes can be tuned as scrub planes by widening the throat and cambering the iron.

it's not vital that it be perfect. If the plane has a double iron, the cap iron can either be roughly ground to the same camber as the iron, or be moved back from the cutting edge, which will help open the throat further, too.

Stanley made what they called a furring plane (#340) that gives an idea of how unimportant a long flat sole is to a scrub plane. This tool (shown in the bottom photo on p. 97) has a sole that's flat for only about an inch either side of the throat opening, with the rest of the sole so relieved that the plane barely even rests on it. The tiny sole lets the plane follow the surface, cleaning off saw marks and the like rather than cutting it flat and true. I would lap the sole of a scrub plane only if it really needed it, otherwise consider the plane tuned and ready for work.

Few planes are easier to use than scrub planes. The very nature of the work they do is so rough that a lot less care is necessary when planing. I use a scrub plane for two different techniques: for removing mill saw marks or wood quickly to leave a finished and somewhat smoothed surface, or for hogging a surface flat enough to be more easily refined and smoothed by other bench planes (see the photo at right). The two techniques are different in so far as for the former I leave parallel plane marks with the grain, and for the latter plane marks in any direction, as long as the surface is nearly flat and true. Using a scrub plane is covered in more detail in the section on flattening stock below.

Using Bench Planes

The flat soles of bench planes cut true flat surfaces or, geometrically speaking, planes. Whether it's flattening a surface, shooting an edge straight, cutting a consistent bevel, or cutting a straight

A scrub plane is used on the diagonal to hog a panel flat before final smoothing with other bench planes. The surface is left with plane marks that look gouged, and the shavings are coarse and roughly broken.

end-grain edge, bench planes are the tools for the work. Some of this work demands careful tuning, some less so. But bear one qualification in mind: The tuning should fit the work you expect to do with the plane. Jack planes (#5) used for general work are one step above scrub planes and need only a modest amount more tuning. On the other hand, a #5 used as a jointer for short surfaces should be well tuned. A jointer (#7, #8) or fore plane (#6) used for accurate work also needs careful tuning. It's always better to err on the side of doing a more complete tuning rather than the minimum, since this makes any tool more versatile. Chapter 4 describes tuning bench planes in detail.

You can get by with only three or four well-tuned bench planes, a #4, a #5, a #7 or #8, and a low-angle block plane. It's no surprise that these are the most common sizes available on the used tool market (or new from any of the few remaining cast-iron plane makers), as generations of

craftsmen have found that they vary just enough in length and heft to work well for a wide range of bench work. You won't use each one every day, but in the course of a week or month you will use them for everything from flattening rough stock to thicknessing it, leveling glued-up panels, and jointing long-grain and end-grain edges.

FLATTENING STOCK

Hardly any board dries flat across its width and straight along its length. Instead, due to the very nature of wood and sawing a log into boards, most of those boards will warp in some way. The three most common defects are twist, cup, and bow (see the drawing on p. 100). Twist is what the name suggests, a gradual twist of the board's face down its length. Cup is a warping across the width of the board, and bow down its length. Fortunately, these are just the sort of problems bench planes were designed to resolve.

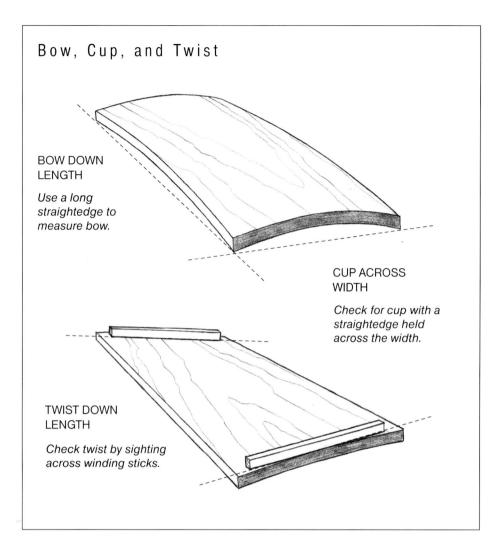

Bow, Cup, and Twist

BOW DOWN LENGTH

Use a long straightedge to measure bow.

CUP ACROSS WIDTH

Check for cup with a straightedge held across the width.

TWIST DOWN LENGTH

Check twist by sighting across winding sticks.

Let's say I want to flatten a board a few feet long and 14 in. wide that has all three of these defects. First, I saw the board close to final dimension so I'm not planing wood that will just be waste later. The most secure way to hold the board is clamped between dogs on a bench (for more on holding the work, see Chapter 5). Chances are good that it might rock or otherwise not lie steady, which can be remedied by tucking a few wedges under the board at the high spots (see the photo on the facing page). Checking the warp with winding sticks and a straightedge gives me a good idea of where wood needs to come off (see the sidebar on the facing page).

There is no rule of thumb for which plane to start with, either a scrub plane or one of the longer bench planes tuned with a slightly cambered iron. If the board is quite warped, I start surfacing by hogging off the high spots with a scrub plane. Think of a scrub plane as one step above a hatchet and a jack plane as one step above that. No matter what plane I start with, the technique is the same: I plane on the diagonal, with the plane at a skew. Planing diagonally end to end cuts out the twist and cup by working more heavily on the corners that are high.

While flattening the surface, I find it useful to turn the board end for end at least once. Planing diagonally in the opposite direction evens out a natural

tendency to pressure the plane to cut more heavily in a certain direction or at the beginning or ending of a stroke. I stop occasionally and sight along the surface for a quick check on my progress. You can use straightedges and winding sticks, but, to save time, it's really good practice to train your eye to see the plane your tools are cutting. You'll still need to check with winding sticks for final accuracy.

Planing across the grain at a skew is efficient for another reason: It lessens the tearout likely when cutting along the grain. With the iron set for a hefty cut, the throat wide to pass large shavings, and the iron less than perfectly sharp (as it will quickly become with this hard cutting), it's easy to imagine that the plane won't cut perfectly smoothly along the grain. The aim is to cut a flat surface, with some roughness to be expected, especially if you start with a scrub plane. The planes that follow will refine and smooth the surface.

As the surface gets flatter, I lighten up on the cuts. Once the bulk of the waste is removed, it's also a good time to resharpen or switch to a plane with a finer throat and less cambered iron. Sometimes a slightly rough but flat surface is all that I need, say for the underside of a drawer bottom. In this case, I leave a smoother surface by overlapping the final strokes across the width and planing with the grain from end to end.

For a very true panel, it's best to finish with a long plane. With the plane set for a light cut and slightly skewed, I continue to plane on the diagonal, as shown in the top photo on p. 102. The final strokes should be down the length of the panel to leave a surface ready for final polishing with a well-tuned smoothing plane and scraper. I like to delay finish-planing the parts until just

MAKING AND USING WINDING STICKS

A pair of winding sticks is one of those shopmade tools that you can either lavish time and attention on making or grab out of the scrap pile. I've seen them made of boxwood with laminated edges of holly and ebony, or of just two pieces of plywood. Either works well.

Traditional winding sticks (or "winking" sticks, as they're sometimes known) are made from a stable wood such as mahogany, rosewood, or teak, about 2 ft. long, 2 in. wide, and tapered in cross section with a wide base. Laminating contrasting woods to the top edges makes it easier to read one edge against another, although you can simply run a dark pencil line along the top edge of one for contrast. More important is that each stick have top and bottom edges parallel with each other and that the sticks are not warped. It doesn't matter if the sticks are different heights.

The way winding sticks work is simple enough. One stick is laid across one end of a surface, the other stick across the other end. Sighting across their top edges shows any twist or winding (hence the name). If the top edges are parallel, then the surface is "out of winding," or not twisted. The farther they are out of parallel, the more twist there is. Long sticks accentuate any winding and make it easier to see. Considering their simplicity and accuracy, winding sticks are a quick way to check the flatness of plane soles, boards, or glued-up panels.

Sighting across the top edges of a pair of winding sticks reveals any twist or winding in a roughly flattened panel.

A long jointer is used to bring the board to flatness, removing the scrub or jack plane marks before a final polish with a smoothing plane.

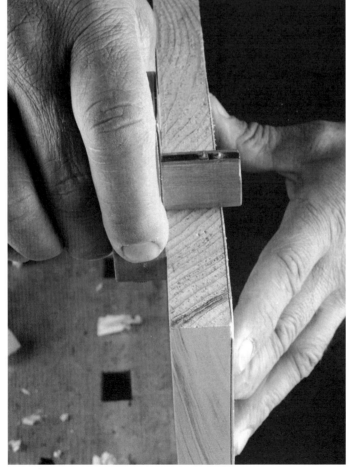

To plane a board to consistent thickness, first scribe around all four edges with a marking gauge, using the flattened face of the board as a reference surface.

before assembly and after all fitting and joinery are completed (with the potential for dings and other mishaps). Techniques used for final smoothing are covered in Chapter 8.

THICKNESSING STOCK

Once one face is flattened it becomes a reference surface for thicknessing the reverse face. To thickness the 14-in. rough board that was flattened in the previous step, set a marking gauge to the desired thickness and, bearing against the true face, scribe around all four edges of the board, as shown in the bottom photo at left. (It's easier to see the line if all four edges are smoothed with a plane beforehand.) By planing right up to these reference lines the board will finish to a consistent thickness and be as flat as the face first trued.

The flattening technique is the same as for the face already completed, except that it should be easier knowing where you need to end up. Start with a scrub plane if you like or with a longer bench plane. Either way, work the surface at the diagonal and stop just shy of the reference lines. I like to plane the lines away with a finely set jointer, held at a slight skew and planing down the length of the board with overlapping strokes. A final once-over with a smoothing plane will take off so little wood that the thickness should be virtually unchanged. With two true faces and consistent thickness, the next step is to joint parallel edges and ends.

JOINTING SQUARE EDGES

Only occasionally do I joint roughsawn (as opposed to table-sawn) edges with a plane, rather than go straight to the jointer. In my small shop it's usually those boards longer than about 9 ft. or the ones too heavy or awkward to pass over

Working the surface on the diagonal, plane just to the gauge lines.

the jointer. More commonly, I use a plane to refine edges that have already been straightened with a jointer or table saw, say for trimming straight parts to size or for edge-gluing boards for wider parts.

Jointing technique is harder to master than flattening, mostly because it takes time to learn how to balance the plane on an edge where it is only partially supported—quite different from having the entire sole resting flat on a board when surfacing it. And if the forces on the plane through the stroke are not even, it's more likely that you'll cut a crown or high point along the edge by cutting the ends more heavily. Fortunately, there are a few tricks that will help.

To joint short boards, I hold them in a side vise. Longer boards can be clamped along the front face of the bench with one end held in the side vise and the other supported in some way. I use a short board clamped in the jaws of my end vise, but a portable board jack or one fixed to the bench works well, too (see pp. 83-85). However you hold the board,

set the edge you are going to joint at a comfortable height, get it as stable as you can, and orient it so that you are cutting with the grain.

Choose a plane that fits the work you're doing. The longer the plane, the easier it is to get a straight edge, but with more weight to balance and control. For

edges under a few feet long I use a #5 or #6; any longer than that a #7 or #8. The better the tuning for any of these planes, the finer shaving you can cut and the better the jointed edge.

The key to getting good results is to concentrate on each stroke. Initially flattening a surface is very different in

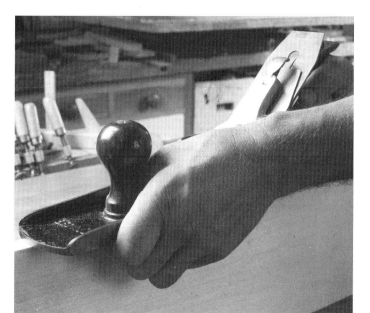

While jointing an edge, use your front hand to steady the plane, with your thumb against the front knob and your fingers wrapped around the sole against the board face.

Today we take it for granted that you can buy materials thicknessed and planed smooth by machine, in whatever dimension or quantity you desire. But the amount of labor it once took to work roughsawn boards to finished dimension was enormous. Just think of the thousands of feet of planed lumber in a building: for trim and moldings inside and out, windows, doors, floors, wainscoting, stairs, cupboards, and clapboards. And the only machine the 18th-century carpenter had was himself.

While the work took considerable energy, the tools and skills of the carpenter made the work as efficient as possible. Benches were low so that the whole upper body could apply force to the plane. Holding devices were simple—a toothed stop at one end of the bench and a large forged holdfast. The planes were simple, too: wooden jack or fore planes, jointers, and smooth planes.

Flattening and thicknessing a rough board was a straight-forward process. First, one face was flattened and smoothed. Any warp or twist was planed out with a jack or fore plane (so named because it was used "before"). With a wide throat, a convex shape to the edge of the iron, and sometimes even a sole with the same convex shape, the plane could cut quickly and take coarse shavings. A jointer, with its long sole and square iron, refined and trued the surface. A smooth plane gave a final polishing.

Once one face was flattened, the carpenter used a jointer to shoot one edge straight. He then used that edge to guide a panel gauge in marking the opposite edge parallel and to the board width. This second edge was either ripped with a saw, chopped close to the line with a hatchet, or hogged straight with a jack plane and then trued with a jointer. Often the carpenter stopped here, with a board surfaced on one side and cut to width. For boards exposed on one side only, to plane the back only added unnecessary labor.

To cut a board of consistent thickness, the carpenter used a marking gauge set to the desired thickness and, guiding it against the flat face, scribed a line along each edge. With the same jack and jointer, he cut the back to this line. In a day a man could plane perhaps 300 surface feet.

An 18th-century carpenter's bench was low, enabling the carpenter to deliver optimum power to the plane. (From *The Little Book of Early American Crafts and Trades;* courtesy Dover Publications.)

this way—strokes can stop and start where they will as long as wood is coming off where needed. To joint accurately you need to think about both balancing the plane and pressuring it evenly, especially at the start and end of the stroke (see pp. 88-90). Long even strokes give the best results.

I hold the front knob in a particular way to give me extra control guiding the plane. Instead of grabbing the knob with a few fingers as for flattening, I wrap my fingers around the side of the plane and rest my thumb either against or around the front knob (see the bottom photo on p. 103). My fingers under the sole act like a fence to steady the plane. At the end of the stroke I can still pick up the plane with both hands or take most of the weight with the rear handle.

There are other things to concentrate on that will help. Think about keeping the plane at right angles to the face of the board. When you become sensitive to it, you can actually feel when the plane is tilted a few degrees to one side or the other. Watching the shaving will help,

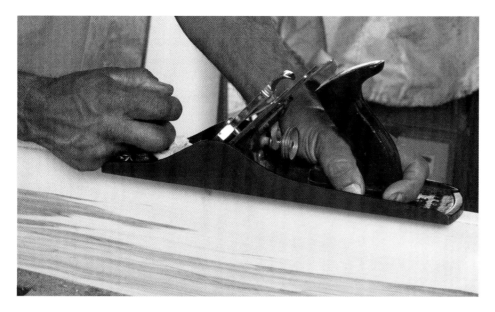

Turning the jointer around and planing backwards takes out any crown at the starting end of the board.

To joint boards for edge gluing, lay them out in order, mark the joints, and then joint each edge.

occasionally to check that the edge is square by holding a square against the face of the board and across the edge. Sighting down the length of the edge will give a good idea of your progress, too. One thing to watch out for is if the edge is crowned—even the longest plane will follow it somewhat. On the other hand, a plane will eventually cut a hollowed edge straight.

To straighten crowned edges, think of it as taking off the high spots one shaving at a time. Start the cut in from the end, plane along, and lift off the plane before reaching the other end. Look down the edge and keep on cutting partial strokes where the edge is high and eventually the crown will be gone or will be a lot smaller.

Sometimes it's still hard to straighten a crown at the starting end of the cut. Even on the longest jointer the length of sole in front of the iron is only 8 in.—hardly enough to guide the plane straight when the edge is gently crowned. At the end of the stroke the entire sole is guiding the plane straight, so it's easier to cut away a crown there. The solution is to plane the starting end the same way; turn the plane around, start the cut a plane length or so from the end, and pull it toward you, as shown in the top photo at left. Used this way the whole sole is guiding the cut and cutting off the crown. You'll be planing against the grain, but with a light cut any tearout should be very fine. Repeat this a few times, and then plane the edge along its entire length to straighten it completely.

Jointing boards for gluing edge to edge

Of all the edge jointing I do, more than half of it is for fitting butt joints for edge gluing. It has always amazed me how often I hear of other woodworkers gluing up edge joints right off of a machine. I've never had the same success. Gluing two

too. If the iron cuts more deeply on one side than the other, the shaving will be more opaque along that side. The thinner edge of the shaving might be frayed. If the shaving is inconsistent across its width, either the iron is out of parallel with the sole or the plane is tilted and cutting more heavily on one side.

With the first few jointing strokes, the shaving will come out in pieces as the

high spots are planed off. On a really rough edge, I set the iron quite deep and hog away—sometimes even using a scrub plane to start. Jointing an edge off the jointer or table saw, I start with a light cut to see how the grain behaves. In either case, use the entire width of the iron (not just the center) by shifting the plane right or left with each stroke; it will mean fewer sharpenings. Stop

boards edge to edge jointed on even a sharp jointer can be risky. Under a magnifying glass the machined surface is a pattern of fine ripples. Two such surfaces put together will never mate well, because they touch only along the tops of the ripples. It's even worse when the jointer is slightly dull—the wood fibers are beaten down or so abraded that they become a poor glue surface. And, as accurate as I like to think my jointer is, the edges it cuts are never truly straight. It's no wonder then that gluing up machine-jointed edges takes a lot of clamps and glue.

Run a jointer plane over the edges before gluing and the story is very different. The edge will be flat and straight (or you can plane in a slight hollow if you like, as explained on p. 107). The cleanly cut fibers will give the best glue surface there is. The joint will go together more easily, and it will be strong and as invisible as it can possibly be. Better yet, such joints will stay together long after the limited glue bond of the machined edges has failed.

Edge-jointing boards meant to be glued to each other is more difficult than merely jointing an edge straight. Mating edges must be straight and square along their entire length. There are several ways to joint them. One method is to joint the two edges together as they are held side by side in a vise. Special shooting boards or jigs can also help. I prefer to joint each edge singly and, if need be, adjust it slightly to fit its mate.

I begin by laying out the sequence of boards for the best grain match (or for other criteria such as color) and mark each joint. Then I joint the edges of each butt joint in order. For the sake of clarity the edges of each joint can be identified as A and A^1, B and B^1, and so on (see the bottom photo on p. 105). Once A is jointed and laid aside, I put A^1 in the vise and shoot it straight. Keeping A^1 in the vise, I turn A upside-down onto it as if gluing them together. I check for two things: that there are no gaps between the boards (particularly at the ends) and that their faces lie in the same plane. If there are any gaps in the joint, I take another shaving or two from A^1 (still in the vise) until the two edges mate perfectly. To check that the faces lie in the same plane, I hold a straightedge across the width of both boards resting

When edge-jointing two boards, check the dry joint with a straightedge and look for gaps between them.

To joint boards in pairs, fold the boards together, line up the edges to be jointed, and clamp securely.

Making wider panels from edge-glued boards is probably the most common woodworking joint there is, used for everything from case sides to tabletops. Thickness planers that can flatten such wide panels are expensive. The two or three planes it takes to do the work by hand can be bought for under $200—and you'll have them for a lot of other work besides.

No matter how carefully the joints were made and assembled, there's bound to be slight variation between each. Start surfacing with a long jointer for the truest finished surface, using the same diagonal technique described on p. 100 and cutting with the grain as much as possible. Use a light cut to avoid tearout, or you risk having to plane the whole surface lower. The best results

depend on being aware of the direction that you machined the individual boards initially. I always mark each surface with an arrow, indicating the direction it passed through the planer or over the jointer, and try to align all the arrows in the glued-up panel. If I then plane against the arrows, I get the least tearout.

The iron needs only a very slight camber or none at all; I generally relieve only the corners. Work in an overlapping pattern along the panel and be aware of trying to cut to a consistent depth so the overall thickness doesn't change. Stop when the surface is covered with an even pattern of planing marks. If it's easier, draw some random pencil scribbles on the surface to plane away. Use a smoothing plane and a very fine cut for the final finish.

Surface a glued-up panel by flattening out the transitions between pieces. Plane on the diagonal just as with a wide board.

edge to edge (see the top photo on the facing page). If they do not lie in the same plane, I'll apply slightly more pressure to the plane or tip it to cut a minute bevel to adjust the edge of A¹ and tip its face into alignment. The better the dry joint is, the easier they will go together with glue and the stronger the joint. And so it goes down the row of joints.

Some woodworkers like to hollow-joint the edge slightly. The theory is that a slight hollow between the pieces will create more pressure upon the ends as the hollow is clamped together. The

pressure helps keep the joint together as the end grain gains and loses moisture, potentially cracking open the same way the end of a board seasons and checks. I use hollow jointing for long edge joints. The technique requires one extra step: I take an extra shaving or two off the center of the board and then make one more pass from end to end. With A and A¹ edge to edge, the hollow appears as the faintest hair of light between them.

It might sound tedious or a matter of chance to joint edges singly, but it's surprisingly easy when you get the feel

for it. An alternative is to shoot the edges in pairs, as shown in the bottom photo on the facing page. The theory is that as long as the edge is straight, any minute bevel planed into the edges will balance out. This technique works best for jointing short boards (under about 4 ft.) and thin stock, for such things as drawer bottoms. The double thickness of the two boards together gives that much more support to the plane's sole. Fold the two boards together, clamp them in the side vise, making sure the edges are

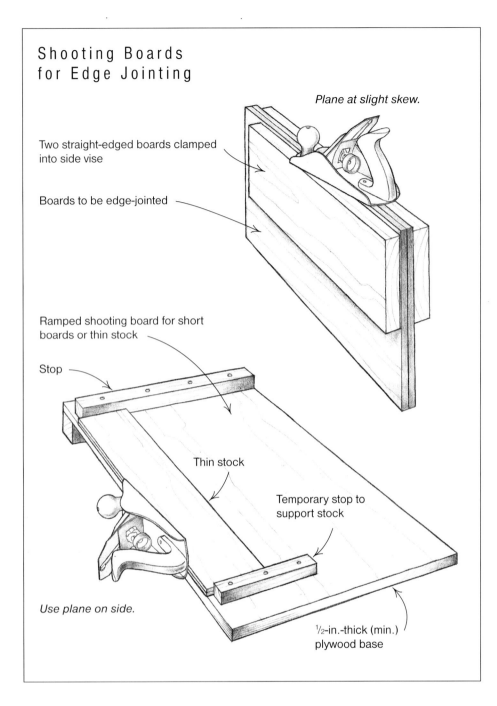

Shooting Boards for Edge Jointing

Plane at slight skew.

Two straight-edged boards clamped into side vise

Boards to be edge-jointed

Ramped shooting board for short boards or thin stock

Stop

Thin stock

Temporary stop to support stock

Use plane on side.

½-in.-thick (min.) plywood base

JOINTING BEVELED EDGES

There is no doubt that cutting a lot of boards to a consistent bevel is faster on a table saw or jointer than with a plane. But for one or two bevels, especially ones cut on tapered pieces, it's easier to pick up a plane than make a jig for holding the work safely on a machine. And when it comes to adjusting bevels, say for coopered work, a plane has no equal.

A jointer gauge is a useful aid in learning to guide and balance a plane upon an edge, for shooting both straight and beveled edges. I usually don't have much time for jigs and gimmicks, but this is one tool that is invaluable. Essentially it's a guide that clamps to either side of a Bailey-pattern bench plane with an adjustable fence against the sole (see the top photo on the facing page). With the fence held against the face of the board the plane is supported to cut any bevel from 30° to 90°. It's not a foolproof jig and it takes some skill to use, but it's the best way I know to cut bevels consistently with a plane. Mine was made by E. C. Stearns Company and dates from about the turn of the century. There are fancier versions; Stanley made a jointer gauge that was nickel-plated, with a rosewood knob on the clamp to the plane to allow more control. Although I've never seen new ones for sale, jointer gauges can be found at tool sales. It's also easy enough to fashion a wooden version to cut a specific bevel (see the bottom left photo on the facing page).

I use two beveling techniques: cutting a specific bevel on an edge or refining or adjusting a bevel cut on a machine. For either technique, a jointer gauge helps you work easily and with more accuracy, but it's not essential. To cut a bevel without one, mark out the bevel angle on the end grain at both ends to give you reference lines to plane to. Use your forward hand much like a jointer gauge

tight to one another, joint the edges straight, and trial-fit them. Check for gaps and that the faces lie in the same plane as described previously.

Another alternative is to use some sort of jig or shooting board. A shooting board is a good aid for getting a feel for jointing or for jointing really thin pieces; otherwise, I find that it's more trouble setting everything up than it's worth.

The simplest setup is to clamp two boards together as in the method described previously, but slightly above and sandwiched between another pair of shooting boards with true edges. Plane down until the plane just starts to ride on the edges of the shooting boards and stop before cutting into them. The drawing above shows this setup and another shooting board useful for shooting the edges of small, thin pieces.

A beveled block of wood clamped to a bench plane serves as a simple jointer gauge.

You can joint a bevel freehand by using your outstretched hand to steady and orient the plane.

to steady the plane on the bevel (see the bottom right photo above). To use a jointer gauge, set the fence with a bevel gauge to the desired angle and make sure the fence is tight to the work. Just as with edge jointing, it's very important to think about each stroke, feel the position of the plane, and watch the shavings to see where the plane is actually cutting.

Refining a bevel means planing it straight and true, free of machine marks, and ready for gluing or other joinery. It's awkward only because the plane is tipped at an angle and it's harder to balance (a jointer gauge helps); otherwise, the strokes are the same as if shooting the edge square. It's helpful to set a bevel gauge to the angle and check often along

the edge. Where the bevel is low I'll make a pencil line, so I can cut more heavily on the opposite edge (saving the line) and correct the bevel. An alternative is to pressure the plane more heavily to cut the high side or to adjust the lateral alignment of the iron out of parallel. Either way, I watch the shavings and finish with a continuous pass from end to end.

Inspired by low-angle British miter planes, this rare Stanley #9 cabinet-maker's block plane has a ball-tail handle and a "hot dog" for holding the plane when it's used on its side for shooting miters or planing end grain.

Planes for Dimensioning End Grain

When it comes to dimensioning end grain, the techniques are basically the same as for planing long grain. Even the same bench planes can be used. What is different is that end-grain fibers are a lot more tenacious than long grain. The physics of block planes, with their low-pitched irons, can be a definite advantage in cutting end grain easily.

The first block plane that Stanley offered (a #9 in 1870) was squarish and heavy, a little longer than a smoothing plane, and with an iron bedded bevel up at 20° (see the photo above). It was the most expensive bench plane Stanley offered, to be "used by Piano Forte Makers, Cabinet Makers and kindred trades, where an extra-fine Tool is required in finishing hardwoods." Stanley didn't advertise it to cut end grain specifically, although the plane's mass and low-pitched iron helped. The

design came from earlier British miter planes made from a block of hard-wearing wood (see the bottom photo on p. 35) or of the metal-and-wood construction typical of these and other high-quality British planes.

Within a few years Stanley came out with a new line of block planes for general-purpose work and some for special tasks. The name "block" plane, so the story goes, comes from the plane's use to resurface the end-grain tops of butcher blocks. Stanley offered the #64 specifically for surfacing butcher blocks.

It was a low-angle plane with a toothed cutter for initial leveling and a straight cutter for finishing the surface (see the bottom photo on p. 117). For the cabinetmaker, Stanley made a similar plane, a low-angle jack (#62). It was really just an oversized block plane, much longer and with larger handles to allow a good grip while working stubborn end grain.

It wasn't very long before Stanley and other manufacturers were offering a wide range of block planes for use throughout the woodworking trades. The variety was huge—with adjustable throats, very low bed angles, skewed irons, ball-tail handles, fancy lever caps, double ends (one end was for bullnose

work), and different sizes and qualities. Today there are maybe 10 new block planes available, all nearly the same as the basic planes offered 100 years ago.

TUNING BLOCK PLANES

Three things set block planes apart from other bench planes: They have a single iron without a cap iron, the iron is bedded at a low pitch, and the bevel of the iron faces upward. Each characteristic can improve the dynamics of cutting end grain, which is quite different from planing long grain. Long-grain cutting curls up a shaving, cut (and split) from the surface along the plane of the wood's natural weakness. The steeper the angle

the iron makes with the surface, the more abruptly the shaving is curled and generally the smoother the surface the plane cuts. Cap irons stiffen the iron and accentuate this curling action. End grain, by contrast, is best cut with an iron more like a knife than with the wedging cut of a higher pitched iron. The best end-grain cut slices the end of each resilient fiber.

The lower the pitch of the iron and the finer its bevel, the better it can cut the fibers. Ideally zero pitch, cutting like a chisel, would be best. But to make a plane like this would be impossible; at even a low pitch the thinly tapered bed is fragile. As it is, end grain is tough to cut and wears on the sole more than long grain.

The lowest practical bed angle turns out to be about 12°. Cutting with the iron bevel up, the effective pitch (the pitch of the actual cutting edge) is the total of the bed angle and bevel angle, something about 32° (see the drawing on p. 49). Most block planes have a bed angle closer to 20°, which, interestingly, makes their effective pitch not much different from that of a jack or smooth plane. It might look as though the iron is cutting at a lot lower angle, but the physics is actually quite similar. Herein lies the crux of the tuning question: Should you tune the plane to work like a small smoothing plane—which it will do very well—or take advantage of its low bed angle and potential to shave end

Block planes once came in a variety of qualities and sizes from many manufacturers. Shown here (from top) are planes from Metallic Plane Co. of Auburn, New York, c. 1873; O. R. Chaplin (with a corrugated sole and adjustable throat), 1888; Foss (patent #3 with adjustable throat), c. 1878; and Davis Level Co. of Springfield, Massachusetts, 1892.

A block plane disassembled shows its single iron, adjuster, cam-locking lever cap, adjustable toe piece and the knob that secures it, and low bed angle. Too low a bed angle is fragile, as shown by the skewed block plane in the background whose bed has cracked away.

the sole so there is no chance of any burrs or sharp edges marring your work. Then turn your attention to the lever cap. This part of the plane is doing a few jobs—securing the iron, stiffening it, and supporting your palm at the rear of the plane. To do the first two jobs it needs to lie against the iron completely, just as a cap iron would. Sand off any paint on the underside where it mates with the iron, and then lap it on a coarse stone by holding the lever cap slightly below the level of the stone along one side (see the photo on p. 73). Polish the top edge so the shavings will pass smoothly from the throat. Anything more you do with the lever cap won't really affect the plane's performance, although you might want to smooth the area where your palm rests.

Next in importance is a smooth and consistent bed for the iron. If you have just bought a new Stanley or a Record #9½ or #60½, classic block planes that are nearly unchanged from over a century ago, the bed will probably need some work. First, remove the lever-cap retainer screw and the adjustable toe piece if there is one, so neither is in the way. With a small flat file, file the bed flat right to the bottom of the sole (see the photo at left on p. 59). Applying a thin coating of wax to the bed helps the iron adjust smoothly.

The way the iron is ground and honed will really determine how your plane performs. Ground at a normal 25° bevel, with a bedding angle of 20°, the plane will work like a small smoothing plane. Hone a microbevel of another 5° (a 50° cutting angle) and it will work even better for difficult grain. A 10° micro-bevel (a 55° cutting angle) will give you about the best performance you can expect with long grain, but you're way off the mark to plane end grain easily.

grain? But, before we get into this issue, there are other characteristics of the plane worth understanding.

Having a low bed angle means the iron has to be used bevel up; if it were down, the bevel would have to be smaller than the bed angle and impossibly fine and fragile. But this also means there is no way to have an effective cap iron. For a few reasons it really isn't needed anyway. The low bedding angle puts the cutting forces more in line with the iron (the knife vs. the wedge again), and as a result the iron is able to resist them without a

cap iron. The lever cap (or screw cap) that secures the iron helps to stabilize it, too. Block planes can cut well without a cap iron for one more reason: There is little need to curl the shavings. End-grain shavings are so weak that they break apart easily. If you do cut a long end-grain shaving, you'll know your plane is properly tuned.

The basic tuning is the same as for any plane, described in Chapter 4. Take extra care lapping the sole, because this is a plane you'll want to get accurate work from, and the sole is small anyway. Smoothly bevel all around the edges of

The width of the throat has a major effect on the way a plane cuts, yet adjusting the throat opening is not always quick and easy. On most bench planes you first have to remove the iron and lever cap, and then loosen the frog and slide it forward or backward.

For real ease and versatility in throat adjustment, nothing beats the few planes manufactured with a separate toe piece. By loosening a screw or the front knob, a piece of the sole (or the entire sole) ahead of the iron can be moved forward or backward. In a matter of seconds, the throat can be widened from as thin as a hair to as coarse as a jack plane. This is the design Stanley and others used for a modest number of planes: block planes, a low-angle jack, a bench rabbet (similar to the #4 in size), the #9 miter plane, and a few other specialty planes. A few modern wooden planes have the same feature.

Given the benefits, you might wonder why more planes are not made with an easily adjustable throat. One reason is that milling the toe piece, the recess for it, and the front knob that secures it takes careful manufacture, adding to the cost. Another reason this design doesn't suit all planes is that it makes them more fragile. No longer is the plane one solid casting, but a milled-down main casting and a thin attached toe piece. And, finally, not all planes need that much range of adjustment or need to be adjusted all that often. They are tuned for certain work and are used for just that.

The adjustable toe piece is secured to the plane body with a knurled knob.

To cut end grain you want the lowest cutting angle. Choose a plane with a bed angle of 12°, hone the bevel to 20°, and then hone a back bevel of 5°. The effective cutting angle is 32°—quite a bit lower than a bench plane. The overall bevel angle is 25° and sturdy enough to plane hardwood end grain. But you could get a little more from the plane if you regularly planed only softwoods. A 15° bevel and 5° back bevel yield a cutting angle of only 27°. Work this plane on the skew and you'll be amazed at how easily it cuts and how smooth a surface it leaves.

DIMENSIONING END GRAIN

If the biggest challenge with block planes is tuning them, actually using them is easy. Most fit your hand so comfortably and can do such a variety of small planing jobs that a block plane will quickly become the first plane you reach for. I have three block planes at the ready on my bench at all times. Two are about a hundred years old, with adjustable throats and castings beautifully designed so they are comfortable in my hand for long periods of planing. One is a Stanley #9½, the other a Sargent #1317 (basically the same plane only a little longer) with a ball-tail handle that makes the plane more comfortable to use two-handed (see the photo on p. 114). The third plane is only a few years old; it's a Lie-Nielsen low-angle bronze plane based on an old Stanley design, which I love for its compact beauty and the way it can handle the work of a plane many times its size and weight.

It would be difficult to list everything these planes can do. Certainly they square or bevel end-grain edges, or any

Four of the author's favorite block planes include (from top) a low-angle Stanley #60½, a Sargent #1317 with a ball-tail handle for a comfortable two-handed grip, a Stanley #9½, and a Lie-Nielsen bronze low-angle block plane.

edge for that matter; cut miters, chamfers, and bevels across or with the grain; and true up joints such as rabbets or the face of a tenon. The Stanley I have tuned to work more like a small smoothing plane, so I use it to level transitions at joints (for example, between stiles and rails on a door), to fair curves, and to do the job wherever a small plane seems to fit the work best.

Squaring or trimming end-grain edges is the work block planes do much of the time. This might be in fitting a piece, taking a shaving or two off its length, or truing the edges of a glued-up panel such as a small tabletop. The technique is easy to learn, but as with any plane, it takes sensitivity to the way the plane cuts. You want a sharp iron for any planing task, but especially for planing end grain. Use a light cut, too; end grain is tough stuff.

Clamp end-grain edges upright in a side or end vise to work on them most

comfortably. Keep the piece low in the vise so that it's as well supported as possible; end-grain planing takes a fair bit of force. Large end-grain surfaces are easier to plane, only because there is more to rest the sole on. To plane small surfaces like the end of a table leg, I often just lay the item flat on my bench with the end projecting beyond the edge. I can then comfortably look down on the work as I plane, and turn the leg to work from all four sides.

One way to plane end grain is with the workpiece securely clamped in a vise, your rear palm around the plane supplying the force and the control, and your fingers in front stabilizing the cut.

Clamp a scrap block to the workpiece to prevent the end-grain fibers from splitting out.

You can hold block planes with one or two hands. Grasping the plane one-handed, I rest my palm against the lever cap and wrap my fingers around the sides for a firm grip. Holding a block plane two-handed, I have the palm of one hand against the round lever cap and grab the toe with the thumb and index finger of my other hand (see the photo at left above). My free fingers on my front hand help guide the cut and stabilize the plane in the same way they do when jointing a long-grain edge. The ball-tail handle on the Sargent makes holding it two-handed even more comfortable and

secure. With any block plane the control and force come mostly from the rear hand, although I steer with the front hand, too. Both are keeping the plane firmly engaged with the cut. More so than with long-grain cuts, where the curling shaving holds the edge of the iron in the cut, end-grain cuts rely on firm and consistent pressure on the plane.

It's important not to overshoot the edge as you plane, because the end grain will split away quite easily. One strategy to prevent splitting is to clamp a waste block to the work to support the edge, as shown in the photo at right above. When I'm working quickly, I usually

don't want to take the time to go through all this, so instead I chamfer the edges and plane with a light cut. This works fine on things like tenons, which get a small chamfer anyway, but it isn't always a detail I want. Another tactic is to plane in from each edge, skew the plane heavily, and go easily. With a light cut at a skew I can often cut very close to the edge.

A shooting board is a particularly useful aid for truing the ends of parts. It not only helps you cut a perfectly square edge (or a beveled edge if you want), but it also holds the work and supports the

Shooting Board for End Grain

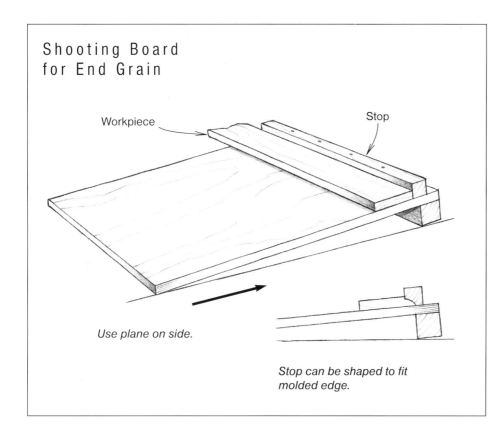

Workpiece

Stop

Use plane on side.

Stop can be shaped to fit molded edge.

end-grain fibers. The drawing at left shows a simple ramped design for planing square ends; another design for planing beveled ends is included in Chapter 7 (see the drawing on p. 143). The photo below shows a bench hook that works as a shooting board. Any of these ideas can be customized to fit a particular need, such as with a molded stop to fit the molded profile on a door stile. The technique is straightforward—hold the work firmly and guide the plane along the fence. Block planes work fine for this work, but they are small and harder to hold lying on their side. For long edges I prefer to use an old #9, a #4, or a #5.

If I'm planing a long end-grain edge, on a tabletop, for example, I almost always use a #4 or #5 (see the top photo

A bench hook works as a quick shooting board. The Stanley #9 was designed for use as a shooting plane, with sides accurately milled square with the sole.

at right). The longer sole gives me the same advantages on end grain as it does when shooting long-grain edges—ease of cutting and greater accuracy. But the main reason I use a larger plane is for the handles that give me a good grip. It's less tiring using both hands to deliver the necessary force to the plane, especially when both have large handles to bear against. The 45° pitch of the iron is not a problem; in fact, I can cut more continuously and smoothly with a heavier bench plane than with a block plane just because I can hold and push it better. At that pitch the iron scrapes somewhat as it cuts, so it dulls more quickly, but it's still worth it.

The alternative is to use a low-angle jack plane, a Stanley #62 (similar to the #64 in the photo below), or Lie-Nielsen's version, which is basically the same plane. An original #62 is fairly rare and sells for at least a few hundred dollars.

Shooting a long end-grain edge with a #5 or longer bench plane works well. A #5 cuts a true edge and is easier to hold and use than a smaller block plane.

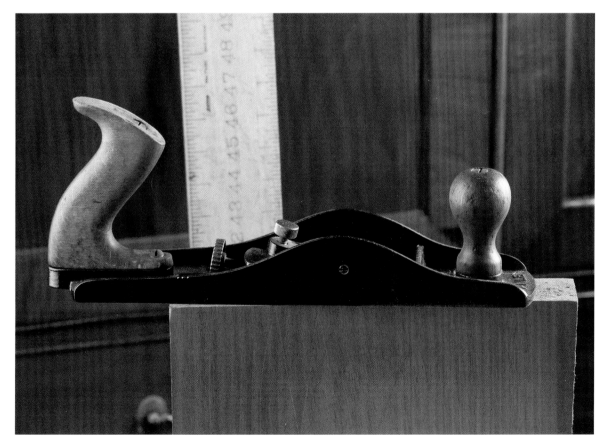

The Stanley #64 low-angle jack plane shown at left was designed for truing butcher blocks. The #62, a similar plane for furniture makers, is slightly shorter with an adjustable throat and rosewood handles.

Three unique planes for truing surfaces: (foreground) a Stanley #95 for trimming end grain, with its 90° fence cast into the body; (left) a Millers Falls skew block plane (nearly identical to a Stanley #140), with one whole side removable for rabbeting work; and (right) a Sargent rabbet block plane #507 useful for rabbet work in tight places.

I owned and used one for a few years and finally gave up on it. It worked no better than my #5, despite its low-angle physics and the comfortable handles. I suspect the #62 is uncommon because it was double the cost of smaller block planes that readily served the needs of most craftsmen.

SPECIALTY END-GRAIN PLANES

I'll admit it, I have a fascination for odd-ball planes. A number were designed specifically for cutting end grain. Some I use once in a while for work I know they do well. Sometimes I pick one up just for the experience, to learn the range of what it can do. Few planes came with instruction manuals—certainly none of these did—and it's not always obvious how and where they should be used. But what is certain is that they represent part of the incredible variety of planes once available, the fruit of some fertile minds. Others must think there is value to these planes, because a few of the old patterns have reappeared in recent years, cast in bronze, with thick irons and smooth adjusters.

One of these planes is the Stanley #95. It's a block plane with a skewed iron and a 90° fence cast as part of the plane body (see the photo on the facing page). The low angle of the iron makes it handy for cutting end grain, and in fact the original purpose was for carpenters trimming the ends of boards. The fence holds the plane square to the cut, so it's a snap to get square ends. The original Stanley version has two holes in the body to attach a beveled wooden fence with screws, to guide the plane in cutting end-grain bevels. It's a little like a shooting board and plane rolled into one.

Another curious plane is a low-angle skewed rabbet, the Stanley #140. The design is like that of any other low-angle block plane, except for two important differences: The iron is strongly skewed, and one whole side is removable so the plane can be used for rabbeting. A new model has an adjustable fence as well. In theory, this should be an incredible tool, but mine has always fallen well short of expectations. The throat is very wide, so it cuts poorly. This is less of a problem with end grain, but a big problem when I happen to want to plane long grain. For cutting rabbets, I prefer the heft and precision of a shoulder rabbet instead. Maybe I just haven't found the best work for this plane yet.

Sargent was one of Stanley's competitors who made some unique and very fine planes. Long before I knew who Sargent was, or knew much about planes for that matter, I was given a Sargent rabbet block plane by an old man who had built water-powered mills and all types of heavy wooden buildings throughout Vermont. This was one of his favorite planes. What makes it so handy is that the iron extends flush with both sides of the plane. I use it one-handed, to clean up wide rabbets or to work in tight places, and think of my old friend every time.

All of my bench planes have their own stories. Parts of some of them I know—about the Sargent inherited from my grandfather or about the new Record #5 discovered at a barn sale for $3. The rest are old enough to have had a few lives and the dings and scratches to prove it. Who knows how many miles of edges they've planed or thousands of board feet they've surfaced. What I do know is that there's always going to be a place for them in any shop; a well-tuned plane is too handy to be easily replaced by any machine. They'll be just as valuable to my children as they have been to me. Meanwhile, I'm adding to their stories every day.

7
PLANES FOR JOINERY

Joinery, is an art manual, whereby several pieces of wood are so fitted and join'd together by straight-line, squares, miters or any bevel, that they shall seem one entire piece.

—Joseph Moxon, *Mechanick Exercises* (3rd. ed.), 1703

Good joinery is basic to good work—work that will survive the wear and tear of many years, and the stresses of wood movement brought on by swings in temperature and climate. I trust traditional joints, mortise and tenons, dovetails, rabbets, and dadoes that have proved their strength over the centuries. While it would be nice to cut them as they were cut traditionally with chisel, saw, and plane, today machines are more likely to do most of the work. Yet when you have only a few joints to cut, planes can be an efficient alternative.

When it comes to fitting joints precisely, no tools are more useful than planes. Although I rarely cut a joint with just a plane, I use many planes in fitting joints, which allows me a flexibility impossible with machines alone. No longer must I design the perfect router jig or table-saw setup to cut a complex joint; instead, I can rough it out with either machine and more quickly get to where I enjoy being—working quietly with hand tools. With a plane, I can adjust the joint one shaving at a time, make fewer mistakes, and do the best work I'm able.

Once you learn the skills and gain the confidence, fitting joints is easy, fast, and accurately done with planes. In an age when every joint was cut by hand, the sensitivity that generations of craftsmen had for their tools slowly improved them. The tools we have inherited are every bit as energy- and time-efficient in a shop today. Not only are planes the best tools for cutting some joints and fitting many, but they will encourage you to work in ways or use details difficult or nearly impossible to create with machines. And if that isn't enough, you'll get a lot more satisfaction besides.

One of the most beautiful joint-cutting planes, a center-wheel plow plane by Ohio Tool Company of solid boxwood with ivory tips, is used for plowing grooves of various widths. Turning the large brass center wheel positions the fence.

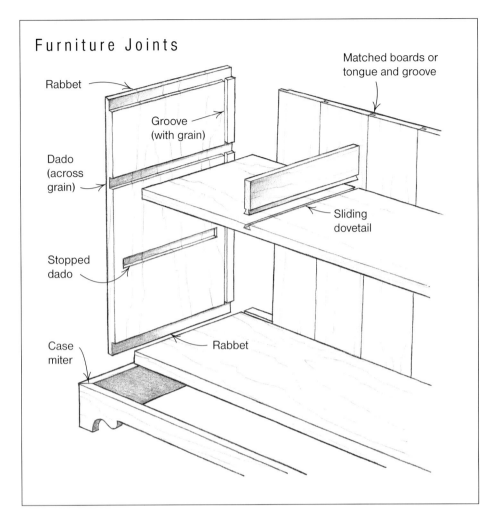

Furniture Joints

Rabbet

Groove
(with grain)

Dado
(across
grain)

Stopped
dado

Case
miter

Rabbet

Matched boards or
tongue and groove

Sliding
dovetail

Planes
for Cutting Joints

No matter how complicated a joint seems, it can be reduced to a few basic elements, such as rabbets, dadoes, grooves, and miters. A rabbet is a step cut into the side of a board, cut either with the grain or across the grain. A dado is a groove of any width cut across the grain; with the grain it's called a groove. A miter is a joint between two angled edges. Usually the sides of these joints are at right angles to one another, but not always. In the case of a joint like a sliding dovetail, the sides are angled toward one another. Rabbets and dadoes can be tapered as well. It's easy to imagine that there are nearly unlimited variations in the ways these basic elements can be cut

or combined to create joints from the simple to the complex. It's no wonder then that there are numerous planes to help cut them.

As Moxon states, joints are a way of joining parts together to make a whole. It's not quite so simple. As wood slowly gains and loses moisture seasonally, it expands and contracts as if it were still a living material. Any joints that unite the parts must be flexible enough to allow this movement; otherwise, the joint will eventually fail or something will crack open. Rabbets, dadoes, and grooves are three of the most basic joints that allow parts to move yet still stay joined and supporting one another. Miters can be used to strengthen or conceal a joint.

There are at least a few steps to cutting any of these joints and planes for each step. First, the parts are dimensioned and trued, which is the work of bench planes. Once the joint is designed and laid out, it's cut by machine, hand tools, or both. Of the many different planes that help with this work, some more easily cut the actual joint, others adjust it. And once the joint is assembled and glued, any minor differences at the transitions can be smoothed with another set of planes or scrapers. The first section of this chapter discusses those planes that cut joints most easily, the second those designed to refine and fit them.

RABBET PLANES

Rabbet planes are among the most basic joint-cutting planes. They all share one distinct characteristic: The iron extends flush with the sides of the plane body (see the photo on the facing page). Sometimes the iron is "rabbet-mouthed" on only one side, although it's more usual for it to be flush with the body on both sides. The full-width iron allows the plane to cut right up into the corner of the rabbet. If the iron were not flush with the side of the plane—for example, if you tried to cut a rabbet with a bench plane—it would cut only a shaving or two before the sole to either side of the iron contacted the wood and stopped the cut.

Some rabbet planes have another characteristic that they share with their cousins the dado planes: a nicker or small knife-like cutter flush with the side of the plane (see the photo on p. 124). Its main purpose is to score the end grain ahead of the iron, for cutting sharp rabbets across the grain. Without the nicker the iron would tear the fibers, unless it was very sharp and the cut was light. A sharp nicker also helps to guide the plane and keep it engaged with the

The iron of a rabbet plane extends flush with the side, forming a "rabbet mouth" for working right up to the shoulder of a rabbet. Note the unusual adjustable throat on the plane at center.

cut. It's one more idea that originated in an age of hand tools when craftsmen needed to sink a sharp, square rabbet as quickly and efficiently as possible.

Another common characteristic of rabbet planes is a skewed iron. As discussed in earlier chapters, skewing the plane improves the cut with any plane. In a rabbet plane confined to cutting along a shoulder where the plane cannot be skewed, skewing the iron gives the same result. There are additional benefits besides. As long as the plane is cutting with the leading edge of the iron against the shoulder of the rabbet, the sideways pressure on the skewed iron helps keep the plane tight into the corner. And by slicing into the cut gradually, a skewed iron is easier to get started.

A skewed iron not only improves the cut but also makes ejecting the shavings easier. With the leading edge of the iron cutting along the shoulder, the shavings curl out of the way. In some rabbet planes (see the bottom photo on p. 125) the shavings are ejected up through the throat and out the top in what is known as a bench throat (because it's common to bench planes). For other rabbet planes without a bench throat, the shavings curled up along either side of the iron spill out the sides of the plane. Sometimes a bevel on the end of the wedge helps direct the shavings. For shallow rabbets ejecting the shavings is usually no problem, but for deeper rabbets the shavings can clog up or get

Nickers score the fibers on cross grain ahead of the iron for a clean sharp rabbet. Shown here are a Stanley "wheel" type nicker with individual spurs and a wooden rabbet with a knife-like nicker dovetailed into the side of the plane. The notch filed into the side of the nicker is used to adjust its depth.

lodged along the side of the plane. The solution is both functional and elegant; one side of the throat is opened up in a snail-shaped escapement that widens toward the outside, encouraging the shavings to move that way (see the photo above).

For the hundreds of years before cast iron became the material of choice for planes, most rabbet planes were made of wood and had this distinctive throat shape. Less common, and far more expensive, were British rabbet (or "rebate" in Britain) planes made by the same makers and with the same methods

as their better-known smoothing planes: Spiers, Mathiesons, and Norrises of joined steel soles and sides, with exotic wood filling the space within.

The average carpenter or cabinetmaker of the 18th and early 19th century had only a few styles and sizes of wooden rabbets to choose from. They were used for a wide range of tasks, everything from cutting rabbets to join boards for wainscoting, wall sheathing, and cabinet backs, to fitting or cutting tenons and cutting rabbets in door and window frames for securing glass or wooden panels. As might be expected with such a

useful plane, each trade adapted the rabbet to its particular needs. The housewright and bridge builder had heavy rabbet planes for fitting large timbers and trimming tenons and shoulders; the coachmaker had a different set of smaller curved rabbets that suited his work cutting rabbets for curved doors, windows, and panels (see the photos on p. 217).

As machines became more and more sophisticated and capable of many of the tasks formerly done by hand, the uses for rabbet planes changed, too. A table saw or shaper could cut any size rabbet far more rapidly and accurately than any plane. It was a familiar story for many planes, yet rabbet planes were too useful to disappear entirely. Instead, wooden versions were replaced by cast iron, in similar patterns and styles and, typical of the inventive spirit of the last half of the 19th century, in many more designs besides. If machines were doing the bulk of the hard work, planes were still necessary to refine the work. Eventually, Stanley and other manufacturers offered wide and narrow rabbets, bullnose rabbets with the iron very close to the toe of the plane for working in tight places, low-angle and bench rabbets, rabbet planes with single irons bevel up and others with double irons, heavy shoulder rabbets, and specialty rabbet planes for coachmakers and others.

The very nature of cast iron lends itself to a variety of rabbet-plane designs that are difficult to make in wood. The design of the rabbet mouth means that at least one if not both sides of the plane and sole are partially cut away. What remains of the plane body has to be strong enough to support the sole ahead of the iron. Cutting away part of the sole, sides, and bed for the iron in a wooden plane can weaken it and make it more prone to warping out of true. Cast-iron rabbet planes could be light yet still stable and strong, although generally these planes are more fragile than similar bench planes. And because the material could be cast and worked so easily, a lot of new designs were tried that would have been impossible in wood (see the photo at right).

It's an understatement to say that there was once an enormous variety of rabbet planes available. Although there are subtle differences between each, they are similar enough to be discussed in two broad groups: those designed to cut a rabbet, and those better suited to fine-tuning rabbets and other joints. Shoulder rabbet planes—heavy, very fine mouthed, and low angle—represent this second group and are discussed later in this chapter along with other planes that adjust joints.

The use of cast iron allowed rabbet-plane designs that would have been difficult or impossible to make with wood alone. One such design is this extremely rare Stanley #196, for cutting a rabbet along a curved edge.

The first group designed to cut rabbets includes bench planes with rabbet mouths, common wooden and metal rabbets, and fillisters—rabbet planes fitted with fences, depth stops, and nickers. Stanley designs such as #10, #10½, #10¼, #78, and #289 fall within this group (as do combination planes like the #45, #55, #46, and #141 dealt with in Chapter 10). Within this broad group of rabbet planes there are unique American styles and planes offered by one manufacturer that are different from another. For example, in 1872, at the height and glory of wooden planes,

Bench-mouthed rabbet planes were designed for cutting wide rabbets. The rare, early Leonard Bailey's Victor #11½ (foreground) has a fence and depth stop (secured with screw eyes); the equally scarce Stanley #10¼ has tilting handles (to avoid skinning your knuckles in tight spots) and two nickers.

Greenfield Tool Company, one of many wooden plane manufacturers, offered nearly 100 sizes and types of rabbet planes and 38 different models of fillisters, some with screw arms, some with wedged arms, and one made of ebony with ivory trim (and for 17 times the price of a simple fillister).

Tuning rabbet planes

There are enough subtleties between rabbet-cutting planes that no general explanation of tuning can adequately cover them all. Some of the more sophisticated planes clearly need special tuning attention. Nevertheless, once you understand the concept of tuning any plane, and in this case a rabbet iron and mouth, you'll know the basics for getting any rabbet plane working well.

The key to tuning a rabbet plane is to adjust the iron so that it is parallel with the sole and just barely proud of the side (see the photo at left on the facing page). Fine-tuning the iron is one of those things that's easier said than done. Experiment with different settings to see how far the iron should project to cut well. To align the iron parallel with the sole, tip it laterally to one side or the other. Most irons can't be tilted much, but there should be a small range of motion. Check that the corner of the cutting edge still projects beyond the side; the rest of the iron should be back behind the line of the side so that it won't drag on the shoulder of the rabbet. Most irons have a shape that makes this easy; they narrow down in width about 1 in. or less from the cutting edge. Usually the iron is also slightly wider than the width of the sole, so that it's possible to cut a rabbet the full width of the plane.

If by tilting the iron you still can't get it parallel with the sole (and proud of the side), the only remedy is to grind and hone the edge. I do this mostly by eye, grinding a little and checking with the iron back in place. If it's really off (as might be the case with a flea-market plane I'm tuning for the first time), it might take a few tries. The alternative is to paint the back of the iron with layout dye and scribe a fine line with a scratch awl using the throat as a guide, and then grind to this line. The cutting edge should be straight across. Once the iron is tuned, careful honing should keep everything in alignment. I always check before removing the iron for sharpening to see if working a little more heavily on one side or the other might improve it.

Skewed irons require an additional tuning step: The back of the iron along the shoulder side has to be beveled at least as much as the skew angle and preferably more (see photo at right below). If the iron isn't beveled, the shoulder corner of the edge can't project beyond the side without the back of the iron projecting even further. Actually, beveling the iron can work to your advantage. I bevel the side of the iron slightly more than necessary and hone it sharp, so that if I choose, it will scrape the face of the shoulder ever so slightly as the cutting edge sinks the rabbet.

The nicker should be sharpened along with the iron. Nickers are of two types, either an actual knife-like iron dovetailed and wedged into the side of the plane or, in the case of Stanley planes, a small wheel with one, two, or three individual spurs (see the photo on p. 124). The wheel is set into the side of the plane and can be loosened and rotated to expose a spur. The beauty of this design is that one spur can be reserved for finish work, another for roughing out, or no spur used at all. The outside of the nicker or spur should be aligned with the cutting edge and should be razor-sharp. Hone it on the inside edge only. If the corner of the iron projects beyond the side more than just a hair, the nicker or spur wheel might have to be shimmed with a washer or bent slightly (like the set in a saw tooth).

The rest of the tuning steps are similar to those for any plane: Check and lap the sole; tighten the handles if there are any; for double irons fit the cap iron to the iron; hone the underside of the

To tune a rabbet plane, here a #78 fillister, adjust the iron so that it is parallel with the sole and just proud of the side.

To tune a skewed rabbet iron, the back of the iron along the shoulder edge should be beveled at least as much as the skew angle.

This Japanese fillister has an adjustable fence, a hollow-ground knife nicker, and a rosewood sole to hold up to hard use and wear.

cally as the #4 and #5, with a double iron at the same pitch, an adjuster, and a lever cap. Of these only the #10, a so-called carriage-maker's rabbet, is common. This plane is a favorite of timber framers for truing the faces of tenons and over-sized joints. The #10½ is just a smaller version, and the #10¼ the same size as the #10, only far more rare and with the handy feature that the knob and rear handle can tip to one side or the other to avoid the problem of scraping your knuckles when working close to a wall or in tight quarters (see the bottom photo on p. 125). I would use any of these three for working large rabbets for something like a door or large window frame.

To explain how to cut a rabbet along the long-grain edge of a board, I'll use the example of a #289, which is one of my favorite rabbet planes. The fence makes it easy to cut a rabbet of consistent width, and the depth stop ensures a uniform depth. The skewed iron helps where the grain isn't totally consistent. Planing with the grain the spur isn't necessary, unless the grain is very irregular. Even then the nicker can get in the way by causing the plane to follow the grain rather than the fence.

lever or screw cap so that the iron is held snugly (or in wooden planes check that the wedge holds the iron tightly against the bed); and check that the bed for the iron is flat and true. A light coating of wax on the parts will make adjustments smoother. (Look back at Chapter 4 if you have any questions about this tuning.) One word of caution: With your plane sharp and ready for work, handle it carefully because the iron is so exposed it can really give you a nasty cut.

Cutting rabbets with the grain

The simplest rabbet to cut is along the long-grain edge of a board. You can use a basic wooden rabbet plane to cut this joint, but it's easier and more accurate to use a fillister.

The Stanley #289 and #78 cast-iron fillisters are just two of about a dozen fillisters that Stanley made. Both have spurs, depth stops, and fences. The #289 is slightly more versatile, with spurs on both sides of the plane, a depth stop that

fits either side, and a wide, heavily skewed iron. The #78 has a bullnose position useful for working up tight to a corner. Both are accurate planes useful for all but the heaviest rabbeting work.

For heavy work, the bench rabbet planes #10, #10½, and #10¼ are ideal. They are called bench rabbets because they are essentially the same mechani-

To cut a long-grain rabbet with a #289, keep the fence pressed against the guiding edge and plane until the depth stop prevents cutting any deeper.

With the iron tuned, planing the rabbet is not difficult. I set the fence for the width of the rabbet—the distance between the cutting corner of the iron and the face of the fence. The depth stop is set measured from the cutting edge. With the iron set for a modest cut and using long, even strokes, I plane down the length of the board. My right hand supplies the force and orients the plane square with the cut; my left hand applies consistent pressure to the fence to keep the plane cutting squarely into the rabbet (see the bottom photo on the facing page). The rabbet is cut when the depth stop just touches the surface all along the board, or, working without a depth stop, when I've planed to a scribed depth line.

There are three problems you might encounter when cutting a rabbet. The most common is that the inside corner of the rabbet steps outward with each cut, making the rabbet progressively narrower, as shown in the drawing at right. What's happening is that the iron doesn't project far enough from the side to cut right up to the shoulder. The solution is to tap the iron farther out until it cuts a clean corner. A second problem might be that the rabbet is not parallel with the outside edge of the board (not a consistent width), particularly at the ends. All this means is that you're not being careful enough about keeping the fence tight to the guiding edge. There is less fence to guide the plane at the start and end of the cut, so be particularly careful there. The third problem is that the rabbet is not parallel with the surface of the board, which is caused by tipping the plane off plumb. I check this periodically while cutting the rabbet, with a straightedge on edge along the surface of the board and extending over the rabbet.

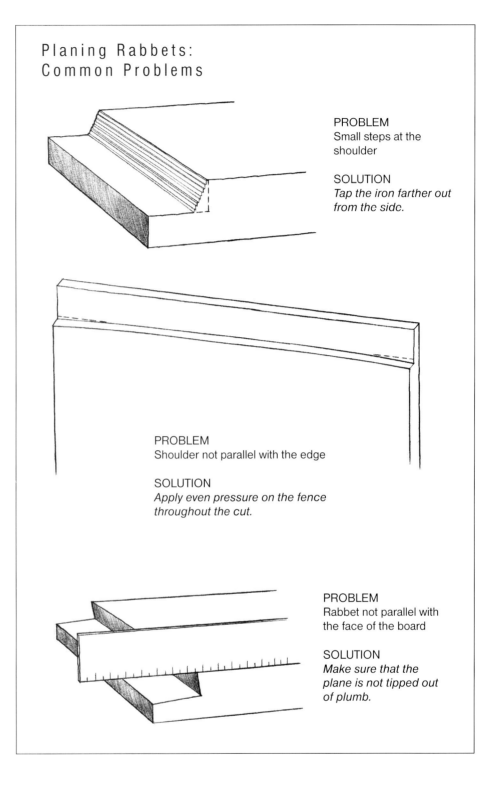

Planing Rabbets: Common Problems

PROBLEM
Small steps at the shoulder

SOLUTION
Tap the iron farther out from the side.

PROBLEM
Shoulder not parallel with the edge

SOLUTION
Apply even pressure on the fence throughout the cut.

PROBLEM
Rabbet not parallel with the face of the board

SOLUTION
Make sure that the plane is not tipped out of plumb.

Cutting the same rabbet with a #78 without a fence or with a wooden rabbet plane involves a somewhat different technique. First, I mark out the depth and width of the rabbet with a marking gauge or pencil. To guide the plane I either tack a cleat onto the surface in line with the shoulder of the rabbet, tack a temporary fence onto the side of the wooden rabbet, or start the cut by tipping the plane onto the shoulder corner of the cutting edge and use my palm or fingers as a guide along the

A quick way to start the cut when using a wooden rabbet plane is to tip the plane onto its corner so that it cuts along the shoulder line first. The shoulder then guides the rest of the cut.

Use a wooden fence to guide the plane when cutting a cross-grain rabbet, here for the tenons and continuous stub tenon for joining a breadboard end. Set the nicker slightly lower than the iron to score the fibers and cut a clean shoulder.

board edge (as shown in the top photo at left). This last method might seem a little crude, but it is surprisingly accurate and quick. Even if the initial cut isn't perfectly straight, after a few strokes it will be close; to make it really straight I turn the plane on its side and cut along the shoulder to the line. With no fences in the way this is easy to do.

All of the same problems can occur with a wooden rabbet plane or a #78 as when using the fenced #289. With these planes, the side of the plane is guiding the cut, so it's even more important that the iron be ever so slightly proud of the side and the plane be held tight to the shoulder. It seems that no matter how careful I am the inside corner still has a little bit of a step. To remedy this I turn the plane on its side and plane the shoulder a few times to bring it back to square.

Cutting rabbets across the grain

Cutting a rabbet across the grain is nearly the same technique as cutting one with the grain. The main difference is that you have to use a spur or nicker to cut a sharp clean rabbet. The nicker need not be set very deep, perhaps $1/32$ in. for softwoods and half that for hardwoods. If you're cutting rabbets on adjoining edges, always cut any end-grain rabbets first, so that any chipping of the end-grain fibers at the ends of the cut can be planed away when cutting the long-grain rabbet. There are three different methods to help reduce or avoid this chipping. One is to cut a fine saw kerf a few strokes deep into the shoulder line at the end of the rabbet. Another is to scribe along the entire shoulder line (down the edges, too) with a marking gauge or knife against a straightedge. The third method is to draw the plane backwards from the end of the cut a few times. The nicker scores the shoulder line when you pull the plane back.

You might run into any of the same problems cutting a rabbet cross grain as when cutting long grain. Because most end-grain rabbets are relatively short, it's easy to cut out of parallel with the edge. One thing I find that helps is to undercut the size of the rabbet slightly and then true up the shoulder by using the plane on its side and working from the far end toward me. This puts the tuned side of the plane (the one with the iron adjusted perfectly) riding along the bottom of the rabbet. And when you work backwards like this there's no fear of chipping the end grain. It's also the same technique more fully explained for shoulder planes later in this chapter (see pp. 146-148).

Cutting tenons

Cut a cross-grain rabbet on both sides of a part and you've cut a tenon. These might be tenons on parts as narrow as window-sash muntins or as long as the stub tenon along a wide tabletop for joining on a breadboard end (see the bottom photo on the facing page). On parts that are awkward to bring to the table saw (where I cut most tenons), cutting the tenon with a rabbet plane is about as fast as setting up a router. I mark out the shoulder line on both faces first and then set the fence on my #289 to cut just shy of the line. Scribing the shoulder line with a knife or sawing into it at the far end helps avoid chipping. I cut close to the final depth on both faces and finish the cut with a heavy shoulder plane—the best tool for the job—working up to the shoulder line and final depth.

Cutting a series of narrow tenons (such as for window muntins) can be done in a similar way if the parts are ganged together on the benchtop. I clamp the work between dogs at right angles to the front of my bench and line up the shoulder lines. I work the

The best planes for cutting stopped rabbets are of a bullnose design, with the iron set close to the toe. At rear is a craftsman-made boxwood and brass bullnose plane; in the center, a shapely English bullnose with ebony wedge; and at bottom an E. Preston English bullnose similar to a Stanley design.

rabbet down on one side, cutting one face and shoulder of the tenon, and then flip the pieces and cut the other face and shoulder.

Cutting a stopped rabbet

A stopped rabbet is a rabbet that is cut along only part of an edge; it can be stopped either along the grain or across the grain. Stopped rabbets are used where you don't want the rabbet to show or as part of the joint design. The first step in cutting a stopped rabbet is to

chisel away the corner of the stop and an inch or two of the rabbet to create a place for the toe of the plane to plane into. I either use a marking gauge to lay out the shoulder to chop to or plane right up to the stop, in which case the plane (or nicker) defines the shoulder. Once the wood is removed from the corner, I can plane right into it as I cut the rest of the rabbet. A bullnose rabbet plane (such as the #78 or #90) is handy for cutting the rabbet because the forward position of

Dado planes are specialized rabbet planes with a nicker with double spurs for scoring both shoulders of the dado ahead of the iron.

This experimental Stanley dado plane, similar to the #239, cuts a groove across the grain, in this case for an inlay band. There are two irons; one acts as a nicker and the other actually cuts the shaving.

the iron lets the plane cut close into the corner. Using a chisel plane (described on pp. 148-149) is another alternative for working the rabbet into the corner.

DADO PLANES

A dado is a groove cut within the surface of a board across the grain. It has two shoulders and a flat bottom. It's the kind of joint used for housing shelves into the sides of a bookcase, for joining the back into the sides of a drawer, or for inlaying a band into a surface. A sliding dovetail with sloping shoulders is also a dado.

Dado planes are specialized rabbet planes. They look very similar to rabbet planes, with a few small differences; the most obvious is a variation of the nicker design. On wooden dado planes the nicker can be a separate iron wedged ahead of the cutting iron, vertical or canted slightly forward, with two knife-like spurs. The spurs are filed into the outside edges of the nicker iron and align with the outside edges of the cutting iron. On cast-iron planes there are separate nickers on either side of the plane, also in line with the outer edges of the iron. Dado planes usually have depth stops and skewed irons to work cross grain most easily. They do not have fences, so the plane can be used anywhere on a surface. Another common characteristic is a working sole that's narrower than the width of the plane body; in the case of the #39 dado planes, Stanley made soles varying from 1/4 in. to 1 in. wide (see the top photo on the facing page).

Tuning and using dado planes

Dado planes need all of the same tuning as skewed rabbet planes, with one additional step: The nickers or spurs and the cutting width of the iron need to be adjusted to one another. The iron should be set so that it's just peeking out from either side of the plane and in line with the nicker. In theory, the nickers score the fibers ahead of the cut and the iron lifts out the waste. Working cross grain, as a dado plane normally would, it's not important if the iron is slightly narrower as long as the nicker is scoring the desired width of the dado. The grain is weak enough in this direction to break away and leave a smooth-bottomed dado. Sighting down the sole will give you an idea of whether the nickers and iron are aligned; actually using the plane tells you a lot more.

If the iron cuts a dado that's wider than the nicker, I very carefully spread the nicker spurs apart. It's the same idea as putting set into the teeth of a handsaw. Hold the iron on its edge against a hardwood block and lightly tap the spurs out with a small faced hammer. On the Stanley line of #39 dado planes, however, adjusting the spurs is not possible. But because of the ingenious way the spurs are set into the sides at an angle, exposing more of them widens the cut they take. This allows for a small amount of adjustment. To cut a clean-bottomed dado, set the spurs (or nicker) to cut slightly deeper than the iron. Once everything is adjusted it's likely to stay that way for years, that is, unless you decide to start cutting all of your dadoes with planes.

Traditionally, dadoes are cut by sawing the shoulders and chopping out the waste. A plane is a lot handier to use out in the middle of a wide board where it's awkward to saw. The cut is started much the same way as for cutting a cross-grain rabbet: along a tacked-on fence and either by scoring the end of the cut with a knife, by drawing the plane backwards a time or two (against a fence), or by sawing the ends of the shoulders. Once the plane starts cutting it guides itself. For a stopped dado, saw and chisel out the corner as for a stopped rabbet. A

Stanley made a series of dado planes, with skewed irons, depth stops, adjustable nickers, and sole widths from ¼ in. to 1 in. (#39¼, #39⅜, and so on). The simple wooden rabbet plane in the background has a nicker iron wedged ahead of the main iron.

These unusual curved wooden dado planes were made for cutting dadoes of a specific radius for architectural work.

A tongue-and-groove joint is cut with a pair of wooden match planes, each designed for a specific thickness of stock. The plane on top with a steel skate cuts the groove; the other plane cuts the tongue.

Match planes came in a wide variety of styles and sizes. This hard-working pair has rear handles formed from the plane stock and steel "plated" fences to resist wear.

MATCH PLANES

A tongue and groove is used to join the edges of two boards just as the name suggests: A groove is cut near the middle of one edge, and the mating edge is cut to form a tongue to fit this groove. This joint is used throughout the woodworking trades whenever an airtight, watertight, or simple and strong joint between two boards is called for. Popularly, the boards so joined are known as matched boards and the planes that cut the joint as match planes.

Wooden match planes usually come as pairs tuned to each other for a tight fit between the tongue and groove. Each pair is made for a specific thickness, from $\frac{1}{4}$-in. boards to $1\frac{1}{2}$-in. planks (or larger). The lighter of these planes (as shown in the top photo at left) resemble rabbet and molding planes—they have no handles and are side-mouthed. Match planes for working thicker stock can have large, adjustable screw or wedge arms, or a heavy body and rear tote more like a jack plane (see the bottom photo at left). Somewhat less common are single planes, so called double-ended match planes, that look like a pair of tongue-and-groove planes joined together. They have two irons—part of the sole cuts the groove, another part the tongue.

On all match planes, steel plates are used for the sole of the plane that cuts the groove. A wooden sole alone would likely break off in no time or wear quickly. Fitting the plane with a steel "skate," as it's known, allows the plane to cut a deep and narrow groove, gives stable support to the iron, holds up to wear, and stays true. Steel is also used to reinforce and reduce wear on the face of the fence of both planes (so-called "plated" planes).

The grooving iron is similar to the iron on a plow plane, tapered and thickened toward the cutting edge. On

bullnose dado plane would be handy, but I've never seen one. A router plane (discussed later in this chapter) is a good tool for working into the corner.

I use dado planes mostly for cleaning up the bottom of long dadoes cut with a table saw or a router. If I want an

accurate, smooth, and flat bottom, a dado plane is the best tool for the job. I use a narrower width plane so it fits comfortably in the dado and I can see what I am doing. I have no doubt that a couple of dado planes of different widths would be handy in any shop.

Innovative cast-iron match planes combine the functions of two planes in one. From the top, a Stanley #148 double-end match plane with two irons and shared fence; a Stanley #48 swing-fence match plane, and an early Miller's patent match plane, also by Stanley, with a bronze wash on cast iron.

better-quality planes the iron has a small groove ground into its back where it beds against the skate. In quite an ingenious design that keeps the iron in line with the skate, the bedding edge of the skate is sharpened to seat into this groove. The wedge then holds the iron tightly in place.

The tonguing iron is the reverse of the groove, with a long rectangular slot cut out of the middle. The cutting edges to either side of the slot cut the surface to leave the tongue. Most

matched-plane irons are bedded at York pitch (50°) for a slight advantage when cutting hardwoods.

Cast iron considerably simplified the construction of match planes and allowed for some innovative designs. The skate could now be made as part of the casting of the plane body, along with a strong and long-wearing fence and a comfortable handle. And instead of two planes, an early Stanley pattern (#48 and #49) has an ingenious swing fence and two irons that cut both the tongue and

groove (see the photo above). In one position the irons cut the tongue. Swing the fence 180° and lock it in position, and one iron cuts the groove. A later pattern is known as a double-end plane; it resembles a pair of match planes joined side-by-side and sharing a common fence. Planing in one direction cuts the tongue, planing in the other the groove. The combination planes #45 and #55 also cut various tongues and grooves. (For more on these planes, see pp. 202-204.)

Tuning and using match planes

Match planes are rarely used today, except in restoration work, though I'll sometimes use them just to enjoy the feel of cutting a tongue-and-groove joint by hand. I have a pair of wooden match planes that are the right size for joining boards for cabinet backs. If I have only a few joints to make, it's just as quick to joint the edges and cut the tongue and groove with these planes as it is to set up the table saw or router. I use them like any other plane, with continuous strokes and pressure against the fence that rides against the face of the stock. Both sides of the joint are cut relative to the face so that any inconsistency in their thickness will be less noticeable and at the back side. With a fence and depth stop cut as part of the sole, it's rather easy to match boards with these planes. Tuning them is a little bit more challenging.

There are two things to watch out for. The irons have to match one another for size, and they need to be accurately positioned relative to the fence so that the faces of the boards in the assembled joint will be flush. The tongue and groove should make a neat fit—so that the joint can be "tapped together with your hat" as the saying goes. A little loose is better than too tight. Adjust the fit by honing the irons: Honing the sides of the grooving iron will make it cut a narrower groove; widening the rectangular cutout in the tongue-cutting iron will make it cut a wider tongue. As for positioning the irons, a little trial and error works as

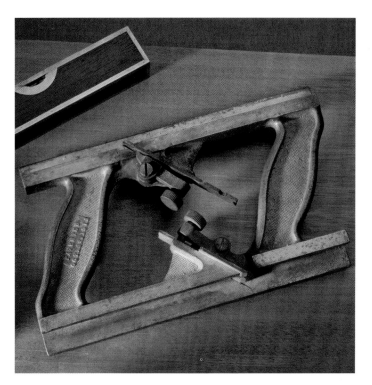

This unusual match plane by one of Stanley's competitors, a Sargent VBM ("Very Best Made") #1068, cuts the tongue with one sole and, when the plane is turned over, the groove with the opposite sole.

One of the earliest metal combination planes, this Phillips patent plow plane is cast of bronze, with a rosewood handle and fence. It included a set of irons and nickers for plowing various-sized grooves, dadoes, rabbets, and matching tongues.

well as anything. I've tried cutting a scrap of wood whose width equals the distance from the board face to the groove or tongue. I use it like a gauge to adjust the irons away from or closer to the fence. Trying both planes on a scrap to see how the joint goes together is the best test. This tuning might be a little fussy, but once the irons are set, the only maintenance they will need is a little honing once in awhile.

PLOW PLANES

Plow planes are simply grooving planes with various-sized irons to plow grooves of specific widths. They are the earliest combination planes, used for cutting grooves for such things as securing panels in a frame, holding drawer bottoms in drawer sides, or roughing out the profile of a large molding before refining it with molding planes. Although they might do basic work, as plows evolved they became anything but simple.

Early plows are no different from the grooving plane of a matched pair, with a single-width iron, steel skate, and fence. By replacing the fixed fence cut from the sole with an adjustable fence, the plane was more versatile and useful. Adapting the plane to fit various-sized irons made it more useful still. Most planes were supplied with a standard set of eight irons from ⅛ in. to ⅝ in. wide. Eventually the fence was made as a separate piece with two arms connecting and securing it to the plane body. With a widely adjustable fence, grooves could be accurately cut parallel to an edge any-where within a board up to about a foot wide. These fences are often lavishly molded on the long-grain and end-grain edges, both for decoration and for a more comfortable handhold.

Although most wooden planes were slowly improved from one generation to the next, few tools caught the interest of

Screw-arm plows adjust slowly but positively. A nut on either side of the plane body locks the boxwood threads.

inventive minds as did the plow. It wasn't so much the body of the plane that attracted them—it was improved, too—but the fence and arms, which posed unique challenges. How could they be secured to the plane, be adjustable, and be held so that the fence accurately guided the plow? And how to make the fence and arms easily adjustable and parallel with the plane body?

Early on, British plane makers came up with one solution and Continental makers came up with another. Continental makers secured the arms in the plane body and slid the fence along them, with wedges to hold the fence in

position. British makers took the opposite approach and fixed the arms to the fence, which could be adjusted toward and away from the plane body as a unit. To hold the fence parallel to the body, the arms were wedged into place with keys or secured with brass or wood thumbscrews tightened down from the top of the plane. Both designs were prone to binding or not staying in adjustment. Given our shared heritage and the influence of British tools, it's not surprising that American plane makers initially followed British prototypes.

Every woodworker who used a plow plane experienced the same frustration of having to set and then hold the fence once it was in position. To adjust the fence meant either tapping on the fence or the tips of the arms, which if done enough damaged their ends. One solution was to tip the arms with brass. Another was to find an easier way to adjust the arms. Many possibilities were tried, including going back to Continental designs of fixed arms. Threading the arms (often fine-grained boxwood) and locking them in place with large nuts against the plane body was one idea that worked well (see the photo on p. 137). Adjustment was positive but slow. Another solution was to have sliding arms (or fixed arms) and thread a third arm to screw the fence in

and out with. On some designs threaded rods were put inside the arms or they were fitted with rack-and-pinion gears.

Arguably the best solution was one of the last: the center-wheel plow made by Ohio Tool and Sandusky Tool in the last quarter of the 19th century (see the photo on p. 120). The fence has three arms, two for support and the center one to adjust the fence with a large brass or boxwood wheel—the center wheel. It wasn't that simple, though. In order to adjust the fence, the center-wheel arm had to be threaded in opposite directions to either side of the wheel. If it wasn't, the center wheel would move in and out but the fence would stay put.

While these designs were suitable for a carpenter or a furniture maker, coachmakers needed a tool that could plow curved grooves. This took some real invention. Two variations of the coachmaker's plow were made. In one, the body of the plane was radiused (concave or convex), with a straight fence for such work as plowing a groove in a flat door for a curved panel. In another, the fence was curved and the plane body was quite short to plow along a radius (for examples of both, see the top photo on p. 218).

By the mid-1870s the catalog of any of the larger wooden-plane manufacturers offered perhaps as many as 50 plows, of different woods, qualities, and styles. They ranged in price from a basic beech plow selling for about $4.00 to ebony and rosewood models with ivory or silver tips for $25.00 or more. Clearly the sheer numbers of plows available, all doing the same basic work, gives some idea of the degree to which these planes captured the imagination of all wood-workers. The quality of a craftsman's plow spoke of his status, so it's no wonder that craftsmen traded up as they could afford a fancier tool (even though it worked no better). In a final act of acknowledgment, examples of the finest plows were often given as retirement gifts.

The concept and utility of the plow plane did not disappear with the passing of beautiful wooden planes. They might

English cast-iron plow planes are uncommon, but none is more unusual than this Howkins model C, made c. 1920 and designed to cut curved grooves, at angles, or even with dovetailed sides. So few were made that the original label and instructions were hand-written at the factory.

not be made of the same beautiful woods, but in terms of a practical tool the plow lived on in cast-iron designs and later in the combination plane. Stanley made at least four different combination planes that used between seven and ten plow irons of various widths, including the #45 and #55 (see the photos on pgs. 184 and 203). And just as wooden plows were beautiful beyond their utilitarian needs, early cast-irons plows were decorated with fancy filigree (see the photo at right); the fences, skates, and arms were gracefully curved or ended in curves; and the planes were cast of beautiful gunmetal or were nickel-plated. They couldn't help but catch the eye and aspiration of any craftsman.

Tuning and using plow planes

I've used a plow plane but little—just enough to get a feel for the tool. Unless you want to do things in a traditional 18th-century manner, a router or a table saw is a more efficient (though noisier) alternative. Still, no tool quite symbolizes planes and hand tools as does a finely made and beautiful plow. The best are functional sculpture, from the delicately shaped and polished thumbscrews to the ornately molded edges of the fence. Despite what might look like a complicated plane, a plow is quite easy to use.

Three adjustments are necessary. The fence needs to be set parallel to the plane body and the required distance from the iron; the iron must be set for the depth of the cut; and the depth stop needs to be set for the depth of the groove. The width of the iron determines the size of the groove. Odd-size grooves are cut with two passes of a smaller iron (with a lot more difficulty, since an iron the same width as the groove helps the plane track). The iron wedges into place as in any wooden plane, but to make setting

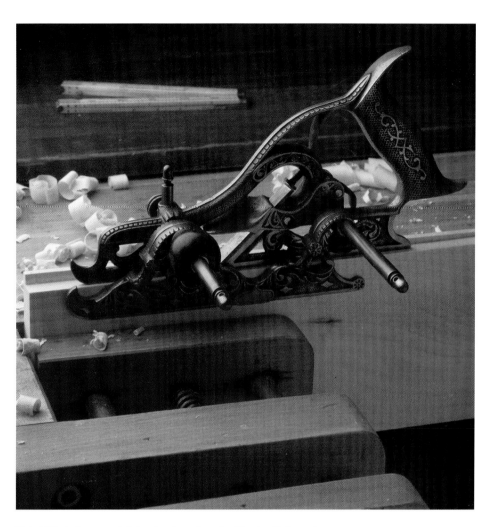

This Miller's Improved Joiner's plow plane by Stanley Rule and Level, 1872, is an extremely rare early combination plane. The castings were adorned with beautiful floral decoration to increase the appeal.

it easier it has a "sneck," or small offset, at its top (see the photo on p. 120). Tapping upward on the sneck removes the iron or reduces its cutting depth; hitting downward on the end of the iron sets it deeper. The iron can be set for a coarse cut, since any roughness at the bottom of the groove will likely be hidden. The final adjustment is the depth stop. Simpler plows have a wooden stop held in a groove by either friction or a thumbscrew; fancier versions have a brass thumbscrew and a stop along the skate.

Plows don't cut as smoothly as many other planes. For one thing, although the iron is supported well enough from behind, the skate in front doesn't form much of a throat. With a wider iron, the skate in front does little or nothing. Still, if the iron is sharp and the grain is not too unruly, you can plow a satisfactory groove. Keep steady pressure on the fence, hold the plane square with the work, and take continuous strokes. Not surprisingly, it's a captivating tool.

DOVETAIL PLANES

For me, dovetail planes have some of the same allure as plow planes. A number of years ago I was at one of Richard Crane's special fall auctions (see pp. 246-248). I had my eye on a few tools—one of them a Stanley #444 dovetail plane. It was right about lunch time and the crowd was getting fidgety when Richard started the bidding. "Where to start this plane, boys? Do I hear $100?" Now this was a plane I rarely saw come up for sale, but when one did it sold for closer to four figures than three. As a dedicated plane user, I had always imagined that this would be the tool for cutting sliding dovetails or accurate tapered ones. When the bidding got up around $150 I jumped in, just about the time the few bidders either paying attention or interested dropped out. With hardly any more bidding, the plane was mine.

The #444 is one of the most daring and complicated planes that Stanley ever made. No other manufacturer even attempted to make such a plane, although wooden versions were available (though uncommon) for at least a few hundred years before. Wooden dovetail planes were more common in Europe, where the joint they cut is known as a "French" dovetail. My #444 is a beautiful tool, all nickel-plated and nicely detailed and finished. For reasons I now understand, it has seen little if any wear. It has three main parts—a main body, a square fence, and a beveled fence—and four cutters. It cuts a sliding dovetail $\frac{1}{4}$ in. wide or wider, and as deep as $\frac{3}{4}$ in. Despite its range, more than one craftsman has disparagingly described it to me as a "boat anchor." An expensive one at that.

Over the years I have owned it I've used it a little and would have to agree somewhat with these sentiments. It's an awkward tool to use, no matter how versatile. Just setting it up is a challenge—all those angled parts to align—to say nothing of tuning everything into harmony. Using a router for all of the same work is a snap in comparison. But what I have to keep in mind is that this tool predates routers by quite a few years and for a long time it was the best tool for cutting a complicated and very useful joint. Yet I suspect that even 75 or more years ago craftsmen who had the #444 available chose to use other tools, or make other joints. This is why they are somewhat rare and few show much sign of use. I don't expect my #444 to see much wear in my lifetime either.

PLANES FOR CUTTING MITERS

Miters are the angled cuts made along edges to form a neat joint between parts, to hide some part of the joinery (such as a set of dovetails), to add to the joint's strength, or to cover end grain. Miters are of three basic types: frame miters, case

Stanley's unique dovetail plane #444 cuts sliding dovetails of various widths. Before the days of mechanical routers, it was the best tool to cut this difficult joint accurately, but it required two separate fences and setups to cut the mating parts.

Miter Joints

FRAME MITER

CASE MITER

EDGE MITER

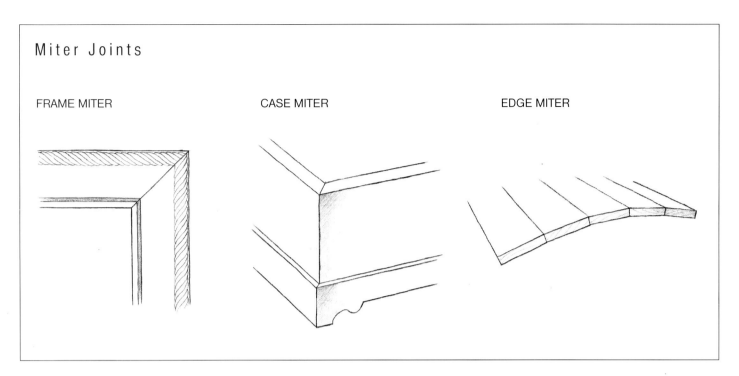

miters, and edge miters (see the drawing above). A frame miter is the typical corner joint of a picture frame. A case miter is cut along the end-grain edge, as for a case of some kind or to join the ends of boards for a blanket chest. Edge miters are cut with the grain along an edge for such things as coopered work. While any of these miters can be cut freehand, shooting boards greatly improve accuracy and speed the work.

Frame miters

A frame miter is not particularly strong without some other means, such as nails, screws, or splines, to strengthen the joint. And where the frame members are wide, as on a door or window casing, the miters will open and close as the humidity levels change no matter how well they are fit. Nevertheless, the frame miter is a useful joint and in some cases the only joint to unite parts neatly. In the case of joining two parts with a molded surface (a picture molding, for example), a miter is the only practical way to join the two and maintain a continuous flow of the profile.

Miter Shooting Board

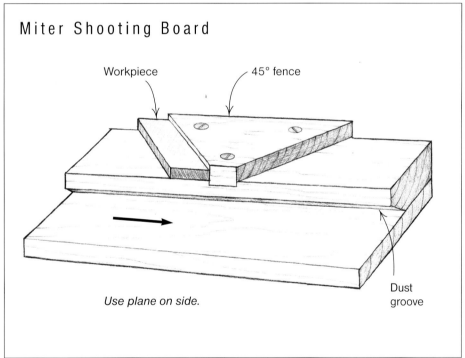

Workpiece · 45° fence · Dust groove

Use plane on side.

Most miters are cut at 45°, so the parts join together and form a square corner. A shooting board made at this angle will suit most of your needs. For odd-angled miters, working freehand will probably suffice.

To cut a clean and sharp miter that meets at 90° is quite a bit harder than it might seem. I have a number of different-size shooting boards for mitering anything from small stops to secure glass in a frame to wider moldings. Each is made with a 45° fence, as shown in the drawing above. The fence is actually two fences in one, with two positions for the

A miter shooting clamp is a jig for trimming miters; as the name suggests, it is part shooting board and part clamp. The two large jaws of the clamp are cut at 45°; one is fixed and the other slides in a slot, with a wooden screw applying the clamping force. With the work clamped securely between the jaws, their bevel orients the plane, making it fairly easy to cut an accurate miter. Miter shooting clamps work best for frame and case miters of modest size or for cutting miters on any parts with edges square enough to be clamped securely.

In shops of a century ago, when all miters were cut and trued by hand, a miter shooting clamp was a common sight. While it might be nice to have one, unless you are

going to be doing a large amount of this sort of mitering, such as making picture frames for a living, I would save the considerable time needed to build such a clamp and make simpler ones that suit each situation. Old miter clamps are not that common or inexpensive either. Another alternative is to use a Stanley shoot board and plane (see the sidebar on p. 144).

A miter shooting clamp guides a plane to cut accurate miters on any work that can be clamped between the jaws.

work so that I can always plane toward the long point of the miter for a clean and accurate cut.

In planing miters with any shooting board and a bench plane on its side, it's important that the plane's sole and side be perfectly square. The iron must be parallel with the sole, too. The plane's length is not that important, since most miters are short, so tune up a #4 or #5 for the work or use a miter plane made just for this purpose (see the photo on p. 110).

Actually cutting the miter is no different than shooting an end-grain edge—in fact, it's easier. The cut is partially long grain, partially end grain. I position the work to plane from the inside of the miter toward the point, supported against the fence so there is little chance of splintering it as the plane cuts by. If I'm cutting the miter freehand, I mark it out with a pencil line, saw close to it, hold the part in a side vise with the miter level, and plane toward the point, as shown in the photo on the facing page. Light cuts and a slight skew prevent splintering. As I work, I check the miter

with a small square to make sure that the edge is square to the face; as I get close to the miter line, I check the angle with a bevel square set to the desired angle.

Case miters

A case miter is cut where two end-grain edges meet, as, for example, at the corners of a box or crown molding. The miter is typically 45°, but with something like a multisided box or an irregular corner, it can be any angle. By itself, the miter is weak (just as a frame miter is), but it can be strengthened with nails, screws, wooden splines, or even a set of hidden dovetails set into a mortise cut into each miter. Shrinkage across the grain is not a problem, because the grain is oriented in the same direction for both pieces and they move together.

To cut the neatest case miter, the parts must be flat and accurately thicknessed. Even if the parts are thicknessed by machine, check for and plane out any cup with a bench plane. (Otherwise, the miter may be neat but the cup will be noticeable against the mating piece at the corner.) If the parts are molded, cut the profile before mitering. If you have only a few miters to cut, you can cut them freehand, although the wider the piece the more difficult it is to do. If I am cutting a number of miters, I build a shooting board known as a donkey's ear for the easiest and most consistent results. This shooting board is constructed so that the work rests at the proper angle against a stop and is oriented to the plane cutting on its side. I've got one built at 45° that clamps into my side vise (see the drawing below).

With a stop in the middle of the shooting board I can hold the work on either side and plane into the stop to prevent splintering. For parts with molded edges, the side with the straightest profile bears against the stop. If you have a lot of similar parts to cut, the stop could even be profiled to a mirror image of a molded part (see the drawing on p. 116). I mark out and saw the miter and then place it on the shooting board slightly proud of the edge. When the plane iron just contacts the edge of the shooting board I stop.

Working freehand, I mark out the miter carefully along the top and bottom edges and both faces, saw the waste, and then plane up to the line using light cuts. I check the miter angle with a long straightedge and a bevel gauge set to the miter angle.

Frame miters can be planed quickly by clamping the piece in a vise and planing toward the point with a low-angle block plane.

Donkey's-Ear Shooting Board

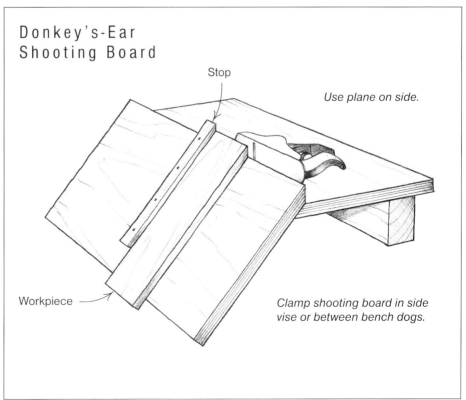

Stop

Use plane on side.

Workpiece

Clamp shooting board in side vise or between bench dogs.

Where there was a need for a special tool, in this case for cutting accurate miters, Stanley was happy to supply it. The Stanley #52 shoot board and plane was just such a tool—a universal shooting board and plane adjustable for a wide range of miters. In 1915, when a #4 Bailey bench plane cost $2.20 or the complete #45 $7.00, the #52 cost $10.00. Even today, these tools are relatively rare and sell for a few times the cost of a good chopsaw—their modern replacement.

The shoot board is a ribbed casting, carefully made for strength and lightness. The plane, slightly longer than a jack, rides in a wide groove down the length of the shoot board. The groove is adjustable to allow for wear. The plane has an accurately machined side that rides in this groove, a skew iron for a shear cut, and a rear tote comfortably angled for using the plane on its side.

The real beauty of this tool is the adjustable stop that swivels like a table-saw miter gauge and locks in any

A Stanley shoot board and plane is a very accurate tool for cutting miters. The heavily skewed iron gives a clean shearing cut on work held against a stop that adjusts over a wide range of angles.

position. It has two additional features: a clamp for holding the work and a sliding back that can be adjusted right up to the cut to support the work and prevent splintering. For irregularly shaped work a custom wooden fence can be made and attached to the adjustable stop.

There is no doubt that this is an expensive tool, especially for a craftsman who doesn't cut a lot of miters. Although it would be time-consuming and challenging to make as fine a tool yourself, there are plans and instructions available (see Kingshott's *Making and Modifying Woodworking Tools*, listed in the bibliography).

Another alternative is to make a hardwood version and attach different fences to suit the work. For the plane, you can often find orphaned shoot-board planes at tool sales or through old tool dealers. Some of these planes are manufactured, others are craftsman made, but most are priced quite reasonably.

Edge miters

An edge miter, the last of the three miter types, is cut along the grain, for example, where two stiles meet at the corner of a case or where coopered parts are joined together. It's a strong and stable joint

that doesn't require additional fastenings such as splines, though driving a few ⅛-in.-long brads (with heads snipped off) into the inside of the miter makes aligning the joint easier when gluing.

A donkey's-ear shooting board can be helpful for cutting an edge miter if the

parts are short. In this case, the piece butts against a stop and is held along the shooting board with clamps. If it's important that the parts be finished to a consistent width, I add a second stop along the length of the shooting board to butt the opposite long edge against. The stop should be parallel with the front edge (or skewed for tapered parts).

If I'm cutting only a few miters or parts that are too long for the shooting board, I prefer to work freehand or with a jointer gauge attached to the sole of my #5 or #7 bench plane (see pp. 108-109). This way, I can see the cut a lot better to adjust the pressure on the plane to fine-tune the bevel, and I can save the time it takes to make the jig. With some oddly shaped parts this is often the only way to cut a bevel easily. The jointing technique was described in Chapter 6. Quite simply, I mark out the bevel on the end grain and plane close to it with a coarsely set plane. I refine the bevel with a fine cut, checking the angle occasionally with a bevel gauge. The longer the edge, the longer the plane I use.

Planes for Adjusting Joints

Cutting strong joints involves more than just sizing the parts and sawing, chiseling, and planing them to fit. Take a simple mortise and tenon, for example. Your first thought might be that the tenon is doing most of the work, securing the joint from pulling apart and giving it rigidity. Actually the shoulders of the tenon and the face of the mortise are doing every bit as much. Any stress on the joint presses these parts together, so they need to be large enough and mate well to give the joint real strength. The best way to fit these parts is with a sharp shoulder plane and a block plane.

There is another aspect of good joinery and fine work that I like to call clarity. Not only do the parts of a joint need to fit well internally, but what's visible should be sharp and concise. This isn't to say that transitions and edges need be square, far from it, but that each element should have distinct definition. In just the same way that it's hard to get a really good edge joint between two boards straight off a jointer, joints with the most clarity have shoulders and faces cut with a sharp plane.

Just as there are planes designed to cut joints, there is a whole range of planes for fitting them. Sometimes one plane can do both jobs, but more often a tool is better suited to one task or the other. Four joint-adjusting planes that I use often are shoulder planes, chisel planes, router planes, and side rabbet planes. All of these planes work best when they take light paring cuts. Shoulder planes are heavy rabbet planes with a fine mouth and an iron bedded at a low angle. A chisel plane has its iron at the toe of the plane to cut into a corner or tight place. Router planes deepen a groove or cut it to a consistent depth. And, lastly, unusual side rabbet planes cut along the shoulder line to widen or adjust a dado or rabbet.

Stanley shoulder rabbet planes #90 (foreground), #92, #93, and #94 (a #91 was never made) are accurate and heavy planes, with irons bedded at a low angle, adjustable throats, handy milled depressions for a comfortable grip, and chrome or nickel plating.

SHOULDER PLANES

Shoulder planes are among my favorite planes. They are some of the most beautiful shop tools ever produced, made from rich materials such as gunmetal, rosewood, ebony, polished steel, and nickel-plated cast iron. They have a heft and size that feels good in my hands. I use various sizes for truing the shoulder of a tenon or rabbet (hence the name shoulder plane), but they work equally well wherever I need to make fine and precise adjustments of a part and require a rabbet mouth.

Shoulder planes look like any rabbet plane, with a rabbet mouth and an iron that peeks through the side. Traditionally, they are metal planes, either wholly of cast iron or gunmetal or fabricated from dovetailed-together steel plates with exotic wood infill (see the photo below). Generally, they are a lot smaller than rabbet-cutting planes, although there are some British shoulder planes that are quite large. The sole and sides are machined or lapped precisely square so that the plane can be used on its side to accurately shoot the shoulder while guided along the tenon or the bottom of the rabbet. A nicker isn't needed, because these planes cut cleanly with light paring cuts.

Most of the work of shoulder planes is cross grain. For this, the iron is bedded at about 20°, with the bevel up as for block planes. With the iron sharpened to a bevel of 25°, shoulder planes have the same basic cutting dynamics as a bench plane. (I have one plane with an iron beveled closer to 20° for softwood end grain.) The only difference is that in this configuration the sole supports the iron right to the cutting edge, preventing the chatter more likely when cutting tough end grain. Although not typical, some planes have skewed irons. Some shoulder planes have the iron close to the toe of the plane, a design known as a bullnose. I've got a Scottish plane by Spiers that has both the bullnose and normal position for the iron, as do the new Clifton "three-in-one" planes made in England.

The traditional British shoulder plane at top has gunmetal sides and mahogany infill, combining beauty and adequate mass to work exceptionally well. The two smaller bullnose planes are solid metal and have shapely wedges.

Use a shoulder plane, here a Spiers plane with rose-wood infill, to adjust and true a tenon's shoulder.

The classic shoulder plane is the British "stuffed" pattern (see the photo on the facing page). These are heavy, fine-mouthed planes, carefully made to last many, many generations. None of these planes have adjusters. The most common shoulder planes are the Stanley designs, the #90, #92, #93, and #94 (a #91 was never made for some reason). The #90 is a bullnose rabbet, the #92 to #94 gradually larger versions of the same plane (see the photo on p. 145). All have adjusters. The Stanley cast-iron design is basically similar to the British pattern. Recently available are a few of the beautiful and heavy Preston designs, once made by Stanley's biggest English competitor. And for those wanting the challenge, kits can be bought to make your own classic shoulder plane.

If I could own only one shoulder plane, I would choose the #93. It's simple to use, accurate, and the right size for a wide range of work. A nicely knurled knob on fine threads adjusts the iron's depth easily, and the throat can be brought up very fine. It has another nice feature, which it shares with the #92 and #94, namely that the whole front of the plane is removable to convert the plane to a small chisel plane. This gives me the versatility of two planes in one.

Tuning shoulder planes

Shoulder planes are used for precise work, and the more careful the tuning, the better they will perform. These are some of the planes worth spending all of the time that you saved not completely tuning your jack, scrub, or other coarse-cutting planes. But since shoulder planes are made for fine work and are more carefully manufactured and finished because of it, most will need only minor tuning.

All of the same characteristics that make any precise plane cut well apply to shoulder planes. Take special care with three areas: the sole, which should be flat and square with both sides of the plane; the bed for the iron, which should be flat; and the iron, which should be carefully sharpened and parallel with the sole. Before buying an old plane, check that the sides are accurately machined flat and square with the sole, because lapping the three faces square with one another is a real chore. None of this tuning is different from that already explained for rabbet planes in particular and tuning in general in Chapter 4.

Using shoulder planes

I use shoulder planes by far the most for fitting the shoulders of tenons, and sometimes for sizing the tenon itself. Considering how many tenons there are in a set of cabinet doors or a table, this can be quite a bit of work. And the fact that even the slightest misfit of the joint shows up as a dark gap at the shoulder line makes these tools invaluable for cutting strong and tight-fitting joints.

To adjust the shoulder of a joint I lay the part flat on my bench, butted up against either a bench hook or one of my wooden bench dogs (see the photo above). Even though I take paring cuts and use the plane one-handed, it still takes enough force that I can do better work if I help support the part against something. I could just as easily clamp the part, but I like to be able to pick it up for trial fitting, to shift it to a new position, or to pare it with a chisel. I lay the plane on its side on the tenon and plane along the shoulder line. All of the same problems can occur as with a rabbet plane, with the same solutions (see p. 129). And planing by the end can splinter out the fibers. To prevent splintering I often stop just shy of the end and pare the last ¼ in. with a chisel, or flip the plane around and plane toward me for a short distance.

A shoulder plane cuts a straight and square shoulder. I use one after either chopping the shoulder or cutting it with a table saw. Neither method gets it quite as true as a pass or two with a shoulder plane. As I plane I can look down and see any gaps between the sole and the shoulder line. When the sole lies flat along it over the whole length, I stop planing. The only drawback is that it's useful only for square shoulders or where the angle between tenon and shoulder is greater than 90°.

The beauty of these tools is that they can cut just the thinnest of shavings in fitting a joint. Don't think of them as limited to cutting shoulders, though. Anytime I need a small and precise rabbet plane, this is the tool I reach for.

CHISEL PLANES

Chisel planes are unusual in that they have no sole in front of the iron. They look like a chisel iron held in the back half of a plane body (see the top photo at right). This design makes the tool challenging to use because, with no sole out front, the iron wants to dive into the cut, making the plane hard to control.

Early chisel planes were simply wooden bodies with a plane iron wedged or screwed into place. I have a European chisel plane that looks like a wooden

With the cutting edge right at the toe, this craftsman-made wooden chisel plane is ideal for working into tight corners or into areas inaccessible with other planes.

Stanley made a single-size chisel plane, a #97, for "Piano Makers and all Cabinet Workers" (center). Today, Lie-Nielsen makes a smaller version in cast bronze (foreground).

molding plane cut in half. Even the iron is bedded at the same angle—a far too steep 50°. Stanley made a rather large cast-iron pattern they called a "cabinet-maker's edge plane" (#97). The iron is at a much lower angle (15°), making it more of a paring tool. But like a lot of antique specialty planes, it's rare and expensive. I had my eye on one for a long time, but I couldn't justify spending that much on a plane that might not earn its keep, especially when a chisel by itself is often just as handy. So when Lie-Nielsen came out with two sizes of their version of the #97 for a lot less money, I bought the smaller one.

A chisel plane isn't a tool that you are apt to use a lot, but there are times when it's the only plane for the job. Even though catalogs describe it as the perfect tool for removing glue and for trimming dovetails or plugs, I use it mostly for cleaning into tight places, for such things as stopped rabbets and chamfers. The sole helps me to cut a smooth and consistent surface right up to where the cut ends—better than I can do with a chisel. As long as I keep the cut light, tear-out is only a minor problem. The iron has to be very sharp, too, so I wouldn't recommend planing much glue.

Chisel planes need only the usual tuning. Since they are essentially a form of rabbet plane, they should be tuned the same way. For the best control, the iron should be parallel with the sole. To adjust the cutting depth, I slowly lower the iron, all the while trying the plane on a scrap. When it starts to cut the finest shaving, I start in. The only other trick is to keep pressure well back from the cutting edge, with your palm centered over the knob at the heel of the plane. At least in this position I'm able to balance out most of the natural tendency of the iron to dive into the wood and lift the toe of the plane.

Router planes for working in grooves were often craftsman-made to suit some specific need, so they can be found in a wide assortment of styles and materials. The single iron cranked at a right angle worked at a low cutting angle for a smooth finish.

ROUTER PLANES

Today the motorized namesake of router planes is far more likely to be used for both cutting and fine-tuning grooves and recesses. While I'm far from a purist and not against routers, there are still a lot of places where a router plane works better—and certainly a lot more quietly. I use one for deepening and smoothing the bottom of grooves and shallow mortises and for cutting a consistent-depth recess for an inlay.

It might not be the most politically correct name, but one of the oldest router patterns is known as an Old Woman's Tooth (OWT). Like all routers, the sole and bed of the plane have many forms, but the iron is usually small and square and it projects below the sole—

resembling an old hag's single tooth. The iron can even have a slight flare toward the cutting edge as a tooth does. One trait all router planes share is a throat open enough to see down into the recess or groove that the iron is cutting. Stanley and others perfected a cast-iron design with two large knobs to grasp and control the plane, a large throat (sometimes open) to see into the work, and a cutter that could be adjusted up or down (#71 and #71½).

The Stanley router has a different iron design from many traditional routers, not like the iron in an OWT router, but bent at right angles so that part of the iron acts as a sole of sorts. Dynamically, this orients the iron at a much lower angle and gives a smoother finish

A Stanley router #71½ came with two different irons, an adjuster to set their depth, and large maple handles for a good grip. The smaller router, a Stanley #271, is an extremely useful tool in tight places.

because of it. For heavy work, the #71 or #71½ is an excellent tool. Where router planes surpass mechanical routers is in working a convex or concave groove to a consistent depth, in finishing the end of a stopped dado or groove, or in working in a tight place. My #71½ came with an additional beveled and sharply pointed iron that works like a "V" snowplow and cuts with little resistance. It's good for cleaning into tight corners, whereas the square iron is best for working long grooves. The sole has two holes for attaching a custom wooden sole—for instance, one beveled or shaped to support it against a molded workpiece.

I have a small router plane made by Record (the Stanley #271) that is gem of a tool. It has two iron positions, either normal or bullnose, and an iron narrow enough to work in the smallest places. I use it for stopped grooves for drawer bottoms, case backs, or anywhere it fits the work better or more comfortably than my larger router plane.

None of these router planes are hard to tune or to use. The only challenge is in sharpening the bent irons. They can't be ground or honed easily in the normal way, so I end up bringing a fine slipstone or the edge of a square stone to the iron. Hone the "sole" or back of the iron as you would a bench-plane iron. Take care to work the heel a little more than the cutting edge to create a slight relief angle; otherwise, the iron will ride along on the heel and won't cut. I always use a modest to light cut, since any tearout will likely be hidden at the bottom of a groove. For the neatest job deepening a groove, I cut with a knife along the shoulder, using

the shoulder to guide the knife edge. It's the same thing a nicker would do if there was one.

SIDE RABBET PLANES

Side rabbets are as interesting, unusual, and useful as the other joint-adjusting planes. They almost always come in "handed" pairs, that is, two planes, one of which works left to right, the other right to left. This way you can always be working with the grain in any situation. Even in patterns that are one plane, there are two cutters facing in opposite directions, or in the case of some English patterns, coming out opposite sides of the plane. Another unusual feature is that the side of the plane usually guides the cut (hence the name) and sometimes even the side of the iron does the cutting. These unusual traits let the plane trim and widen grooves, dadoes, and sliding dovetails or tune tight molding profiles.

One of my favorite planes of this group is the wooden version known as a snipe bill. It looks like any other molding plane with a profiled sole, except that there is no throat and no iron projecting through it. Instead, the iron is quite vertical and peeks out from the side, which acts as the sole. The narrow curved point of the sole is reinforced with boxwood and resembles the snipe bill of the name. More common and easier to tune and use are the Stanley pattern #98 and #99 (a pair) or the #79, a two-in-one plane. On any of the three, the toe piece comes off for working right into a corner or tight place. The #79 is available new, complete with a fence. My only problem with this tool is that no matter which direction I cut with it, one of the irons is dragging and dulling. The irons are hard enough to sharpen and adjust as it is.

I'll use the #98 as an example to explain tuning and adjusting the iron.

Side rabbet planes cut along the shoulder of rabbets and dadoes to widen them to fit other parts. These two planes with crisscrossed iron patterns are by Stanley competitors: The upright plane in the background (#81) is by Sargent of New Haven, Connecticut; the other fancier version with adjustable irons is by E. Preston of Birmingham, England.

Side rabbet planes either have two irons or come in "handed" pairs, such as the Stanley #98 and #99 shown here. Both planes have depth stops and a removable toe piece for working into a corner.

The iron is angled across the side, downward toward the throat. Two things must happen at the throat: The cutting edge must be parallel with the side (acting as the sole), and the lower point of the iron should barely peek out the bottom (the true sole) of the plane. With the iron slightly below the bottom, it acts as a nicker for cross-grain planing. The trick is to adjust everything together. Tapping the iron deeper brings the point further below the bottom, which isn't a problem as long as it's not too far below. If the iron is above the bottom, the shoulder won't be cut its full depth. And if the iron is not parallel with the side, the shoulder will be cut at a bevel.

Trial and error seems to work as well as anything. Sometimes I have to hone the iron to bring everything into adjustment. But once side rabbet planes are tuned, they are the only planes that can work in a narrow groove or dado and, fine shaving after fine shaving, widen it to fit a tenon. Since the sole is so narrow and the plane short (at least the #98 and #99 are), these planes can work in the tightest places. With a light cut, they work as well cross grain as with the grain.

Cutting strong, precise joints with any of these planes takes patience, sometimes creativity, and certainly an understanding of the specific characteristics of each tool. But it doesn't require a lot of different planes. With a simple rabbet plane, a shoulder rabbet (that separates into a chisel and bullnose plane), a narrow dado, a router, and a side rabbet plane, you can cut and fit almost any joint, with or without the help of machines. When you see the clarity of the joints cut with planes, you'll likely want to add a few more planes to your toolbox. Even if your shop is equipped with all the latest machinery, there are times when a plane and skilled hands are still the best tools.

8
PLANES FOR SURFACING

Spiers planes...are not only a luxury but a necessity to every superior

woodworker. No journeyman can be without one, and it is the ambition

of every apprentice to possess one.

—c. 1930 catalog for Spiers planes, a competitor of Norris

Nothing really finishes the surface of a board as well as a smoothing plane. Not a planer, which mars the surface with machine marks, nor a sander, which leaves behind an abraded surface that's smooth but without real clarity. To get a surface that unveils the wood's figure, its subtle depth of color, and its texture, you have to shear the wood cleanly. The heavy iron of a smoothing plane provides this shearing cut as nothing else can—leaving a surface that's smooth and polished.

A lot of woodworkers probably think that smooth-planing is tough work, inefficient at best, grueling labor with dubious reward at worst. But, in fact, smoothing planes do their job quickly and efficiently. In the time it takes to change belts on your belt sander, you can surface a few square feet of even highly figured wood. In well-behaved wood, it would be easy to surface a modest tabletop in less than 10 minutes—about as long as it takes sanding with a single grit on a random-orbit sander. But, when you are finished planing, you are done. And, yes, you may have worked up a sweat in the process.

There are many tools that will smooth wood surfaces, but unfortunately no one tool can efficiently handle all possible situations. A well-tuned smoothing plane comes close; it will perform much of this work, smoothing every surface from a large curly-maple tabletop to the table leg. For challenging woods where the grain is particularly prone to tearing out or for veneered surfaces, even a perfectly tuned smoothing plane has limitations. In these situations, a scraper is an alternative; it will smooth the most difficult grain, though more slowly than a plane. Whether held in a plane-like body, a cabinet scraper, or by hand,

No tool can match a well-tuned smoothing plane for clarity, smoothness, and polish of the cut surface. The machine-planed surface visible at rear might appear smooth, but close inspection reveals that it's covered with a network of fine ripples.

It's not totally correct to say that no machine cuts a surface like a smoothing plane; there is one. Hitachi, Makita, and others make a machine called a super-surfacer that cuts more like a plane than a conventional rotary planer. The wood is carried along on a powered belt and forced against a heavy fixed knife that shears the surface exactly like a big inverted plane. The iron is adjustable to cut on the skew—for all the same reasons that skewing is a useful technique with a handplane.

Shearing the wood surface by pushing the wood over a fixed iron is not exactly a new idea. Coopers have been pushing barrel staves over long, inverted jointer planes for a couple of hundred years or more (see the photo on p. 212). And a tool similar to the cooper's jointer has been used in Japan for a century to cut thin, wide shavings for use as wrapping paper. The physics of shearing the surface with a heavy iron has been known since the plane first appeared.

In its modern, motor-driven form, the super-surfacer might not look like a handplane, but in principle it works the same. On one model the iron is a 10-in.-long, $\frac{5}{16}$-in.-thick knife tipped with high-speed steel, bolted to a similarly shaped knife that acts as a chip breaker. The knife is held in a heavy fixture that can be rotated up to 60° to skew the cut. A movable plate ahead of the iron adjusts the throat—a fine throat for hardwoods and a more open throat to reduce clogging with softwoods. To cut the best surface the feed rate should be high and the iron very sharp, which really means surfacing only about 300 lineal feet between sharpenings. It's no wonder that this machine can nearly match the polished surface of a handplane—the mechanics of the cut are so similar.

scrapers allow for a variable angle of attack and a steep cutting angle. The problem is that scrapers don't work well in very soft woods. The best strategy is to use both planes and scrapers to smooth surfaces. In this chapter, I'll explain the advantages and limitations of smoothing planes, how to choose the right ones for different surfaces, how to tune and sharpen them for the best work, and how to use them for the best results. Scrapers are discussed at length in Chapter 9.

Smoothing Planes

If I could imagine the perfect smoothing plane, it would be only about 8 in. long, widest at the iron and tapered at the ends, and it would be heavy—very heavy, as massive as if it were cast of pure lead. The iron would be thicker and wider than those of common bench planes, and it would be firmly bedded against a solid frog. What I'd really like is to be able to adjust the iron's bedding angle,

Some of the most beautiful and effective smoothing planes ever produced were made in Britain up until early in this century. Both the A6 Norris (rear) and #6 Spiers are massive, with thick irons and tight throats.

Bailey-pattern smoothing planes include the #2 and #3 (foreground). The Bed Rocks #604 and #604½ at rear are ideal for smoothing all but the most highly figured woods.

and low-angle block planes, which are not even technically smoothing planes but smooth nonetheless with good results. Each type has advantages and disadvantages.

CHARACTERISTICS OF SMOOTHING PLANES

Most smoothing planes are quite small, commonly only from 7 in. to 10 in. long, which is a real advantage for smoothing a surface already flattened by longer bench planes or machines. Smoothing planes can also smooth surfaces that are not absolutely flat. Their compact size makes the plane comfortable to hold with both hands and easy to control, and it concentrates the forces of your upper body, through your hands, close to the cutting action of the iron.

Whatever their size or shape, the best smoothing planes have one thing in common: mass. They have a thick massive iron, a heavy cap iron and lever cap or wedge, and a heavy body—whatever it takes to add weight to the plane. Greater overall mass translates into greater stability of the plane and better support of the iron, which will chatter less and give a smoother cut. A heavy plane will also tend to maintain its momentum through a stroke, especially as the iron encounters contrary grain. To imagine the difference mass can mean to cutting quality, compare a lightweight table saw to a much heavier cast-iron machine. The heavy machine dampens the cutting vibration more fully and gives a far smoother cut. Adding blade stabilizers improves the cut even more and is analogous to using a thick iron in a smoothing plane.

Plane makers have chosen many ways to add mass to their planes to improve performance. This partially accounts for some of the many different plane designs that have evolved. Traditional wood-

especially for nasty woods where a steeper angle is more effective. My imaginary plane would have a fine throat, so fine that the thinnest of shavings could be planed and not clog. So far, no such plane exists, though some come close to my ideal. British (Norris-type) smoothers, as shown in the photo on the facing page, combine the massiveness, thick iron, and tight throat necessary for really effective smoothing. Unfortunately, these antique tools are so expensive and so rare that most woodworkers will never even see one, let alone have one to use. So most of us have to make do with what we can find. Fortunately, new and antique

smoothing planes are widely available and can be easily tuned.

More so than any other class of planes, smoothing-plane designs vary widely—from traditional wood-bodied smoothers, to the Stanley bench planes #1, #2, #3, #4, and #4½, to the highly evolved designs of Norris planes. Until recently, every furniture maker and carpenter had at least one smoothing plane in his tool chest, and since these planes were often craftsman-made, it's natural that many styles evolved due to personal choice and regional differences. As a result, smoothing planes differ in size, materials, iron width, and ways they are meant to be held. And there are other planes, such as the longer bench planes

One way that plane makers add mass to their smoothing planes to improve performance is to cast them of heavy bronze.

bodied smoothers are made from the heaviest and densest woods available, such as rosewood, lignum vitae, and ebony, which hold up well to the wear on the sole, too. For bench planes, heavier castings add mass. The Stanley #4½ is a pound heavier (and an inch longer) than the #4 and performs a lot better because of it. At one time Stanley made a #4½H, which was even heavier still and meant to appeal to British craftsmen used to the mass of Norris and similar planes. The greater mass of longer bench planes accounts for why they often work well at smoothing.

Contemporary plane maker Tom Lie-Nielsen increases the weight of his planes by casting them of a bronze alloy heavier than traditional cast iron (see pp. 236-239). Heaviest of all smoothing planes, British smoothers have a heavy steel or cast-iron body, and the space within it is "stuffed" or infilled with a dense hardwood, such as rosewood, ebony, or beech. These massive planes are slightly smaller than a Stanley #4, but they weigh nearly twice as much and work a lot better, too.

The best and quickest way to add mass and improve the performance of an ordinary bench plane is to replace its thin iron with a thicker one. It will chatter less and give a smoother cut (as explained further in Chapter 4). Old irons on traditional planes are always quite thick. It wasn't until the development of the Stanley-Bailey bench planes that thin irons became standard, presumably because sharpening them was easier. These thin irons are simply too thin to resist the high stresses of smoothing all but soft and more easily worked woods (which the planes were really designed for). Under great cutting pressure the thin iron deflects and vibrates or chatters. No amount of tuning or adjustment can really prevent this problem in difficult woods.

In the mid-1920s, Stanley took the idea of thin irons one step further, with the development of quickly replaceable cutting edges that it named "ready edge" blades. This #4 smoothing plane with "T" lever cap is another innovative Stanley idea.

To work efficiently, a smoothing plane should cut a shaving nearly the width of the iron, without chattering or hesitating as the grain direction changes. Only a thick iron that is well bedded against a solid frog is able to do this. Equally important is seating and locking the iron securely close to the throat of the plane where vibration originates; a stout lever cap or wedge provides the necessary locking force.

In all other ways, smoothing planes are similar to other bench planes, with the iron bedded at a common pitch of 45°. Since the mechanics of the cut are really no different from jointing or other planing operations, this bed angle is a good compromise. A steeper angle would be an advantage only in very hard or figured wood, where the iron would begin to act more like a scraper. But this comes at the cost of dulling the iron more quickly and creating greater resistance to its cutting the wood fibers. I have a Chinese smoothing plane with a bed angle of 58° that for many years has been my plane of last resort when smoothing particularly challenging bird's-eye maple or some other densely figured hardwood. Even if you can't change the bed angle of your plane, you can alter the effective cutting angle with microbevels and back bevels, which are explained fully in Chapter 3.

CHOOSING THE RIGHT PLANE

Hardly a surface leaves my shop that is not touched by a plane. Most of this work is smoothing, for which I turn to any of perhaps seven planes: a #4 and a #604½ bench plane, a lignum-vitae coffin-shaped smoother, a high-angle Chinese rosewood smoother, a low-angle block plane, and my favorites, two Norris rosewood and cast-steel heavyweights. While each plane performs slightly

Traditional wood-bodied smoothers feel wonderful in your hands, are easy to tune, and can work exceptionally well. From rear are a lignum-vitae, coffin-shaped smoother; a small but heavy ebony smoother; and a distinctive cocobolo plane by James Krenov.

differently—some handle difficult woods better than others—they have all proved to be dependable and consistent as I have come to understand how and when to use each of them.

No one plane is going to do it all. Two different craftsmen could easily get different results from the same plane depending upon the way it is tuned, held, and used. I recommend that you experiment for yourself, try different planes, and don't be discouraged if your new Record #4 isn't the perfect smoother you imagined—maybe it just needs a good tuning.

Wood-bodied smoothers

Wood-bodied smoothing planes include traditional coffin-shaped smoothers made of hard tropical wood (lignum vitae, rosewood, ebony), as well as transitional planes with a wood body (usually beech) and metal frog and iron adjuster. Old wooden smoothers almost always have a thick iron and cap iron that are sometimes bedded at a steep angle— an advantage in hardwoods. The wooden body can easily be cut to bed the iron more completely against the frog, to add a throat piece to tighten the throat, or to flatten the sole. Traditional smoothers

Eastern wood smoothers are simple, low-profile planes with three basic parts: an iron, a sub-blade, and a wooden body (usually dense white oak). A heavy iron and stable low center of gravity help them cut smoothly and consistently.

are comfortable to hold and use and generally work well for any size surface. To some craftsmen, nothing matches the feel of a wooden plane planing wood. Transitional planes closely resemble cast-iron bench planes and have the same limitations: The iron is too thin and will tend to chatter when overstressed, and overall the plane is a little light.

Eastern smoothing planes

Eastern smoothers, distant cousins of traditional smoothing planes, have a solid-wood body (usually white oak, rosewood, or a similar hardwood) and work extremely well. The iron is short, thick, and massive; the sub-blade (or cap iron), if there is one, wedges against the iron rather than screwing to it (see the plane in the foreground in the photo above); and the throat is fine. The low profile and lack of handles make for a low center of gravity and wood-hugging stability.

These planes are commonly available with a bed angle of 40° (better for soft woods), 45°, or 47½° (better for hard woods) and with enough variation in size and style to be extremely versatile in all smoothing situations. The sole and iron of any of these Eastern planes demand special tuning and sharpening with special tools—to some as much tradition as science. Toshio Odate's *Japanese Woodworking Tools: Their Tradition, Spirit and Use* (The Taunton Press, 1984) is an excellent source of information on this subject.

Bench planes

All of the bench planes from #1 through #4½ are called smoothing planes, but some give better results and are easier to use than others. The larger sizes are widely available, either used or new. For general bench work it is hard to beat a #4 with a thick replacement iron. It adjusts easily, is comfortable to hold, and will handle most well-behaved woods. A #4½ is more useful as a smoother, because it is wider and heavier. It works well for any size surface, but less so for difficult woods. I find that the smaller sizes are too small to smooth anything but the smallest surfaces efficiently or to hold comfortably for very long.

Longer bench planes, such as a #5 or #5½, are useful for special smoothing work. I use one where I want a very flat and smooth surface, for example, to smooth the underside of a small case of drawers and a desk top so that they will mate together well. Some craftsmen prefer to smooth with a #7, which might not be the most efficient tool for the work, but the large mass of the plane helps it do a good job. The performance of any of the bench planes can be improved by replacing the standard thin iron with a thicker one.

British smoothers

Undoubtedly the most handsome and consistent in smoothing many different woods, British smoothing planes combine massiveness, a thick iron and cap iron, a stout lever cap locking the iron, and a tight throat—all of the virtues of a good smoothing plane. Early planes of this type had a steel sole with rosewood or ebony infilling and no means to adjust the iron, other than tapping it as one would a wood-bodied plane. Norris improved the design by adding a threaded adjuster to control the depth and lateral

EASTERN PLANE IRONS

Eastern plane makers have taken the idea of a heavy plane iron one step further than any of our Western designs. In some of the many variations of their smoothing planes, a short and extremely massive laminated iron is secured by a sub-blade or cap iron and solidly bedded in an oak or hardwood plane body. These irons are easily four or more times thicker than a standard Stanley bench-plane iron and double that of the very heavy irons of Norris-type smoothing planes.

Thickening the plane iron is the simplest way to reduce cutting vibration or chatter and get a smooth finishing cut. Similar irons are common in other Eastern tools such as spokeshaves, and even their chisels have the same distinctive short, thick form.

The short length of Eastern plane irons is a further advantage when they are set into an oak plane body quite low compared to its width. With the heavy iron in place, the plane has a low center of gravity that hugs the wood surface. The performance of one plane I own (shown in the photo below) is further enhanced by a very fine throat formed between the iron and a dovetailed steel insert driven into the body just ahead of the iron. The combination of a heavy iron, fine throat, and a solid body makes this an extremely effective plane for all smoothing work.

An Eastern plane iron (foreground) is considerably thicker than a standard Stanley bench-plane iron.

Block planes are useful for smoothing small surfaces and working in tight places. Shown here (from top) are a Leonard Bailey Victor #12½ with a decorative front and depth-adjusting knob and two English planes by Marples.

Relieving the outer edges of a smoothing plane sole with a fine file helps to prevent marring the finished surface with a sharp edge.

alignment of the iron (see the photo on p. 169). British smoothers are easy to adjust, hold, and control for the best smoothing work; they are ideal, except that they are getting rare and are incredibly expensive. Fortunately, new Norris-type planes are available. (For more on British smoothers, see pp. 167-169.)

Block planes

Block planes might not be considered smoothing planes, but they are useful for truing small surfaces and handy for working in tight places. I use a Sargent #1317 with an adjustable throat and a ball-tail handle for smoothing transitions, such as where stile and rail meet on a door, or for smoothing gently convex surfaces (see the photo on p. 166). Bedding the iron at a low angle creates a shear cut with little resistance, but the low angle can also become a problem— where the grain direction changes, the iron tends to lift and tear out the fibers. A microbevel on the iron and a very fine throat help.

Tuning Smoothing Planes

To do the best possible work, smoothing planes have to be tuned carefully. Whether they're old Stanleys or new planes right out of the box, they all need the same step-by-step attention. This is the basic tuning explained and illustrated more fully in Chapter 4. Considering the work expected of a smoothing plane, I am particularly careful about flattening the sole, adjusting the throat, and checking that the iron is well bedded against the frog and that the cap iron lies flat against the iron close to the cutting edge. And just as scrub and jointer planes have different cutting edge profiles, smoothing planes can have a shaped iron, too.

FLATTENING THE SOLE

To smooth well, the plane's sole must be really flat. A plane with a distorted sole is hard to get started smoothly in a cut, since it will rock. The distorted sole also makes it hard to end the cut neatly. Through the cutting stroke, any rocking can either disengage the iron slightly or cause it to cut more deeply and leave a gouged surface. The sole of most smoothing planes is relatively small anyway, so flattening it is no great chore. Wooden-soled planes can be trued with another plane, such as a jointer. Metal-soled smoothers can be lapped on a lapping table of abrasive paper laid end to end on a piece of plate glass or with silicon-carbide powder and kerosene on the same glass surface. For more explanation of flattening the sole, refer to pp. 53-57.

The flattened sole should be smooth and polished, with no burrs that could mar a finished wood surface. On used planes it's common to have a few deep scratches or other sole defects, but these are usually of no consequence as long as the sole is still flat and smooth. I always finish tuning the sole of smoothing planes by relieving all of the outer edges with a fine file to eliminate any chance of a sharp edge gouging the wood (see the bottom photo on the facing page). Lightly sanding the sole with 320-grit or finer silicon-carbide paper brings it to a smooth polish.

ADJUSTING THE THROAT

Not all smoothers allow for throat adjustment, but it's an area to check and fine-tune if necessary. The throat should be set as tight as possible—as wide as the thickness of four sheets of office paper is ideal for a light finish cut and slightly wider for heavier smoothing cuts. The throat opening noticeably affects the

These three planes tuned for smoothing have flat soles and throats to suit the work. The lignum-vitae smoother with an added throat plate (left) and the #4 (center) have medium throats for preliminary smoothing and general bench work. The Norris at right has a very narrow throat for the finest smoothing cuts.

plane's performance. As the chip is cut from the surface it is forced through the throat and curled up against the iron bevel and cap iron. The front of the throat acts like a fulcrum, breaking the chip and limiting the amount of tearout of the fibers ahead of the cut. A tight throat is especially important in figured or difficult woods where, as the grain direction changes, the plane is often cutting against the fibers.

Using a thick replacement iron is one way to tighten the throat and get better performance, whether the frog is adjustable or not. If the frog is adjustable, such as on all of the Stanley-pattern bench planes, moving it forward tightens the throat. But be aware that adjusting the frog can sometimes cause another problem, especially on cheaper, mass-produced planes not designed to have tight throats. If the frog is moved too far forward, the back of the iron near the cutting edge will be left unsupported, rather than bedding against a beveled portion of the sole (see the drawing on p. 60). This allows the iron to vibrate and chatter more easily in the cut. You could try shimming behind the iron as described below for wooden planes, or keep your plane for general bench work and find a better plane to tune as a smoother.

Adjusting the throat on wooden smoothers is easy. The throat can be finely tuned by adding a throat piece just ahead of the iron, by replacing the existing throat piece with one slightly larger (or sliding it toward the iron as on some contemporary European planes), or by shimming behind the iron. Leather, thin sheet metal, or dense cardboard all work well as shims; just make sure to adjust the wedge to compensate for the added thickness. For more help with tuning the throat, see pp. 59-62.

TUNING THE CAP IRON AND FROG

There are two final things to check while tuning a smoothing plane: First, that the cap iron lies flat against the iron close to the cutting edge, and second, that the iron is well bedded against the frog. Tuning both of these parts is important to give stability to the iron under cutting pressure, which makes for a smoother cut.

Screwed to the iron, the cap iron adds mass, supports the cutting edge, and curls and breaks the chips (that's why it's also known as a chip breaker)—three important functions right at the heart of the cutting action of the plane. The better the cap iron mates with the iron, the more help it can give. Hone the underside of the cap iron as described on p. 71 and set it very close to the cutting edge (see the bottom photo on p. 72). Similarly, bedding the iron firmly against a solid frog will dampen out cutting vibration more effectively. I run a fine file over the bedding surface to leave it smooth and flat (see pp. 58-59). Before finally putting your tuned smoother to work, hone and shape the iron.

SHAPING THE IRON

One of the beautiful characteristics of wood planed by hand is the subtle surface left behind by the iron. Since the iron of a smoothing plane can be shaped from modestly convex to square with relieved corners, the texture it leaves on the wood can vary from a wave-like pattern across the grain to a smooth, flat surface.

How do you decide the right iron profile? Partly it's a matter of choice. The surface the plane cuts is one more place the craftsman leaves behind his signature and another element of the design. A noticeable surface texture that enhances the robust design and oak grain of an Arts and Crafts chest of drawers would be inappropriate for a Federal mahogany side table or some other high-style piece, where surfaces just shy of perfectly smooth are more suitable. There are also practical mechanical reasons for shaping the iron. In bench planes with a thin iron, shaping the iron will make it cut a smaller shaving, reducing the pressure upon it and causing it to chatter less. The strokes will also blend together more easily with the outer edges of the iron out of contact with the wood.

Since a smoothing plane should be adjusted to take a very fine shaving, only a very slight rounding of the iron is really necessary. When I want to leave a surface with a subtle but noticeable planing pattern, I shape the iron ever so slightly convex by working it over the grinder in a slight arc, grinding more heavily on the outer edges (see p. 67). After grinding the iron, I hone it to a final consistent shape. I check the profile by holding the iron against a straight block of wood held up to the light. The arc doesn't have to be perfect.

Shape the iron profile gently convex or relieve the corners on a benchstone after grinding the iron. Start with a coarse stone and use light pressure to prevent gouging the stone.

Because my preference is for a barely noticeable planing pattern, I usually shape my smoothing plane irons with only slightly relieved corners (see the photo on the facing page). Using my benchstones, I work these edges more heavily each time I sharpen, making sure they are as sharp as the rest of the iron so they don't leave dull streaks. Relieving the corners still lets me overlap the planing strokes and not leave a distinct edge that would mar the smooth finish. While planing, I check the width of the shaving as it curls in the throat to judge whether I need to alter the iron shape when I resharpen, by concentrating a little more on the middle of the iron or on the outer edges. A shaving nearly the full width of the throat is ideal to smooth most efficiently.

Smoothing Technique

To illustrate basic smoothing technique, I'll use the example of finish-planing a cherry dining table top. By the time I get to this step, the top has been cut to finish dimension and any joinery such as breadboard ends or underside bevels has been completed. If it was important that the top be very flat, I would have flattened it first with a longer bench plane, a #5 or #6, which would likely have left a surface with many planing marks. There could be some grain tearout where there is some figure in the boards. For the final planing I start in with my #4 smooth bench plane. This particular plane has a thick replacement iron with the corners only very slightly relieved and a modest throat, since I also use this plane for other bench work. Holding the plane skewed to the surface—60° or so—and taking a light cut, I stroke down and across the top, and, as best as I can guess, with the grain.

To smooth a large tabletop, the author skews his smoother slightly (here, a #604½ Bed Rock) and planes parallel strokes down the length of the top. He keeps a tin of paste wax handy to lubricate the plane's sole.

Figuring out grain direction is not truly a guess. Any milling or planing I have done up to this point has given me clues and shown me possible trouble spots. To make the final planing easier, when I glue up the boards I take care to orient the grain as consistently as I can and mark it on them (see p. 107). Holding the plane on the skew and working across the grain rather than directly down it gives me some advantage around any trouble spots and helps level out any variation along the glue joints (unless the table has been previously flattened with a longer plane). Where the grain is contrary, I try planing it from a different direction. I work until the surface is leveled and fairly smooth and any tearouts are very shallow. I think of this step as "presurfacing," before a final smoothing with a #604½ Bed Rock.

A #604½ is an excellent smoothing plane for better behaved woods such as cherry. I have this plane tuned as a smoother only: The iron is sharpened ever so slightly convex, and the throat is tight. This plane has two further advantages—a well-machined frog and impressive heft. If this was a figured-maple tabletop or some other ornery wood, the #604½ might not plane it without some tearout. It would be worth a try, but I might have to resort to another plane for my final smoothing pass (such as my high-angle Chinese smoother or one of the Norrises) or expect to use a scraper on the areas where there are small tearouts.

Smoothing with two planes has some advantages. The #4 does the bulk of the work, leveling out the surface as it exposes fresh wood on a top that could have picked up some dirt during construction. The #604½ that follows is set very fine with an iron tuned to leave a smooth surface with a minimum of planing texture. Each plane is tuned for the work it needs to do; using them together I work more efficiently and need to resharpen fewer times. Moreover, the #604½ stays sharper longer, since it is doing only a minimum of work, and cuts a smoother surface as a result.

With the tabletop clamped on my bench, I plane long parallel strokes down it with the #604½ following the direction of the grain (see the photo on p. 163). The technique is similar to the stroke with other bench planes, but there are some subtle differences. For one, the strokes should be as continuous as possible from edge to edge. An incomplete stroke leaves a spot where the iron stopped cutting that can be seen and felt and will need to be planed over again or scraped out later for the smoothest surface. If I want to avoid a spot of irregular grain or for some reason not complete a stroke, gliding the plane off the surface like a plane taking off from a runway usually works. Unfortunately, lowering the plane into the cut somewhere out in the surface is more difficult to do without leaving a few little chatter marks (because the plane and iron don't firmly engage with the cut right away). On really long work this sometimes cannot be avoided, but it is always better to start at an edge and skew the plane to work into the surface or any areas of difficult grain.

Getting started smoothly in the cut is the hardest part of smoothing technique to master. Smoothing planes are small with a minimal amount of sole in front of the iron to balance and guide the plane into the cut. A distorted sole compounds the problem by having no flat reference to start from. I balance the plane on the edge of the workpiece with

the iron just ready to make contact, concentrate my hands and thoughts, and forcibly start in. A slight skew helps a lot in getting started. For long surfaces I walk right along as I plane; otherwise, I lean forward to keep the plane engaged with the surface.

The small size of smoothing planes is an advantage in maneuvering across the surface, changing the skew as necessary, or planing around difficult grain. Holding the plane with your hands quite close together, the natural pressure is as much downward as controlling direction, which helps keep the plane on the surface and engaged with the cut. Wood-bodied smoothers have an advantage over bench planes in hugging the surface. It's natural to hold them low down on the body, since there are usually no totes or

knobs. Holding the plane in this way lowers its center of gravity and improves its stability and performance. Smoothing planes such as Norrises tend to hug the surface due to their heavy weight alone.

Each smoothing cut creates long shavings that need to be cleared from the throat to avoid clogging and preventing the iron from cutting smoothly and evenly. Equally important, clearing the plane after each stroke will help prevent a piece of shaving getting caught on the back of the throat, which will mar the surface as it gets dragged along. Lightly waxing the sole helps, and it also makes each stroke easier by reducing friction. I usually have a tin of soft paste wax and a square of flannel near at hand on my bench just for this purpose and use them often.

Smoothing a table with breadboard (or batten) ends poses a challenge. Plane up to the end, increasing the skew in the direction of the grain of the batten as you approach it. Just past the joint line, swivel the plane and finish the stroke along the batten.

It pays to stop and sharpen the iron regularly. How often depends a lot on the kind of wood you are smoothing and how perfect you want the surface to be. Hard, figured maple will dull the sharpest of irons far faster than mahogany, which means you'll need to resharpen maybe twice as often or more. Even with soft woods like white pine that plane easily, the iron should still be very sharp to shear the soft fibers cleanly rather than beating them down and smoothing them over. As the iron loses its sharpness it takes more effort to push the plane (a warning sign to notice), the surface will not have quite the polished smoothness (another sign), and there is a greater chance that the iron will drive under and tear out the grain rather than cutting the fibers cleanly. Whenever I push to finish smoothing a surface and avoid one last sharpening, inevitably I get a bad grain tearout just as I am nearly done. I have to resharpen and replane, and waste more time than if I had just resharpened the iron sooner in the first place.

Smoothing work has a meditative feeling: one thoughtful stroke after another, clearing the plane of shavings, drawing my hand over and feeling the surface. With light cuts, there is the freedom to keep working until the surface has a satisfying polished smoothness—besides, there is too much pleasure to hurry the work. When I am done planing, there may still be places where the grain refuses to plane to a consistent smoothness, but a scraper can handily finish the work. For this modest tabletop it might have taken only a half hour to plane the top and bottom to a polished smoothness, including sharpening. After a little bit of scraping, if it's needed, the top is ready for a coat of finish. Even without it, the clarity of the surfaces shines.

SMOOTHING CROSS-GRAIN SURFACES

If this tabletop had breadboard or batten ends (see the photo on the facing page), smoothing it would be more challenging and take more time. Strokes can no longer be started straight into the surface, because of the cross-grain breadboard secured against the long grain of the top, nor can a stroke be ended as easily. The same situation happens in smoothing transitions between stiles and rails for drawers and doors (see the drawing below) and in many other places on furniture. By way of example, I will explain how I go about smoothing the stiles and rails for a frame-and-panel door and smoothing the joints between them after assembly.

Only after the joints are cut and fit and the door is ready for assembly will I smooth the individual parts. This technique is no different than with the tabletop; I use the same two planes, #4 and #604½ bench planes, and continuous strokes. Using a smoothing plane with a wide iron (the #604½ has an iron 2⅜ in. wide vs. the #4's 2-in. iron) is a real advantage in this kind of work, because I can smooth stiles or rails nearly the width of the iron in one pass. To do this, the iron should be sharpened mostly square with slightly relieved corners. After smoothing each part, I mark the grain direction on it at each joint with a tiny pencil arrow so that when I later smooth the transition at the joint I will be planing with the grain as much as possible.

Smoothing a Joint

Skew the plane up to the joint and then change direction, always trying to plane with the grain on both parts.

Small pencil arrows marked on the pieces before assembly indicate grain direction.

Stile

Rail

To smooth the joint after assembly, I use either a block plane if the variation is slight or a larger smoothing plane such as the #604½ when more wood needs to be removed. The #604½ is tuned for normal smoothing; the block plane has an adjustable throat set very fine and an iron honed with slightly relieved corners. My hands are a little large to use the smaller bench planes comfortably, but a #2 or #3 similarly tuned would also be a good choice. The only real trick to the technique is to plane the joint at a skew and work in the direction of the grain for both parts as much as possible. Sometimes this is as easy as a couple of skewed passes taking off the high spots.

Where the surfaces of the rail and stile at the joint don't align as well, I plane the higher surface closer to level first before trying to smooth the joint. I lower the higher part by taking smoothing cuts straight along the grain, starting either from an edge or at the joint. The final passes to smooth the joint are at a skew, either with the same smooth plane or more often with a block plane with the iron set for a very fine cut. Sometimes it is still necessary to smooth small variations at the joint with a sharp scraper, which is explained further in Chapter 9.

SMOOTHING CURVED SURFACES

Smoothing curved surfaces with a flat-soled plane might not seem possible at first, but it can be done. Gentle convex curves such as the apron of a demilune table can be smoothed with a block plane, where its small sole is easier to balance and control than a larger smoothing plane. Very gentle curves can be smoothed with a #4. For curves both concave and convex that have a consistent radius, a compass plane tuned as a smoothing plane is the right tool (see the photo at left on p. 208). While it's harder to smooth curved surfaces than flat ones and get as good results, at times I have no choice. I always try to smooth the surfaces of parts first, before steaming or laminating them into curves, to minimize the need for any later smoothing. But inevitably there are small dings, stains, glue smears, or irregularities that will need to be planed out of the finished curved surface.

Smoothing the surface of a convex curve with a block plane takes a sensitivity to the way the plane is cutting—quite different from the force involved with pushing a smoother across a flat surface. The iron must be set for a very fine cut, since the amount of the sole contacting the curve is small and the convex surface actually pushes into the throat somewhat. The throat should be very tight. The trick is to balance the plane on the portion of the sole right ahead of the iron, while guiding the cut tangentially to the surface. I start at an edge whenever possible, although this is less critical than with flat work, and rock the plane as I guide it over the curved surface (see the photo at left). Rocking the plane toward the heel or toe either disengages the iron from the cut entirely or lifts the iron enough that it takes a lighter cut. This technique is useful to begin or end the cut where only a small area needs smoothing, for instance, where there is a ding in the surface. It takes balance and control to keep cutting a continuous shaving without chattering, all the time conforming to either a constant or changing curve. No matter how carefully I try to plane the surface smooth, I almost always still need to scrape out small irregularities or fair the curve slightly with a hand-held scraper.

A block plane works well for smoothing convex surfaces. The trick is to rock the plane, keeping it tangential to the surface and firmly engaged so that it cuts continuously without chattering.

Smoothing with a compass plane is similar to using a #4, but more challenging. I find a compass plane harder to use for smoothing to a final finish than a block plane, except where I want to finish with a truly consistent curve. Where two curved parts need to mate exactly would be such a case, or where I need to cut a consistent curve on the inside and outside of a part. A very slightly convex iron and a fine cut improve its performance. Compass planes are discussed further in Chapter 10.

The Ultimate Smoothing Plane

If you were to seek out one tool for the widest range of smoothing tasks, it would have to be a heavy British smoother like a Norris. British smoothers represent the highest evolution of smoothing planes and some of the most beautiful tools ever produced. The combination of a very thick iron ($^3/_{16}$ in.) and chip breaker, bedded against a high and solid frog, a super-fine throat, and a massive plane body adds up to a smoothing plane that cuts smoothly and consistently no matter how contrary the grain. It's not that the surface it cuts is more perfect than that of other good smoothing planes, but it will smooth woods to a polish few other planes can. Add to this the allure of brass, steel, and rosewood in a finely made tool and it is easy to understand why these smoothing planes have always been sought after by craftsmen doing first-class work in hard and figured woods.

Although Thomas Norris is the best known maker of these heavy smoothing planes, he was really only one of a handful of such plane makers working in Britain from the middle of the 19th century up until World War II. Stewart Spiers of Ayr,

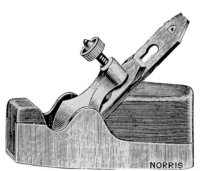

Dovetailed.
Improved Steel Smoothing Plane.
Round Sides.
Fitted with rosewood and gunmetal lever.

			I $\frac{3}{4}$	I $\frac{7}{8}$	2	2$\frac{1}{8}$	2$\frac{1}{4}$″ cutters
No. 4	...	...	18/6	19/-	19/-	19/6 each
No. A4	...	...	21/-	21/6	21/6	22/- ,,
(Patent Adjustable)						
Extra Cutters to fit above	1/6		1/6	1/8	1/10 ,,

Dovetailed.
Improved Steel Smoothing Plane.
Round Sides and Closed Handle.
Fitted with rosewood and gunmetal lever.

			2	2$\frac{1}{8}$	2$\frac{1}{4}$	2$\frac{3}{8}$″ cutters
No. 5	...	...	23/-	23/-	23/6	24/- each
No. A5	...	...	24/-	24/-	24/6	25/- ,,
(Patent Adjustable)						
Extra Cutters to fit above	1/6	1/8	1/10	2/- ,,

No. 6, with parallel sides, same price as **No. 5.**
No. A6 ,, ,, ,, **No. A5.**
(Patent Adjustable)

3

Thomas Norris and Sons of London offered over a dozen smoothing planes, with different shapes, styles of tote, and material (steel, gunmetal, or malleable iron) and, after 1914, with or without their patented adjuster.

Early miter planes, such as this one by Spiers of Ayr, Scotland, inspired the design of heavy British smoothing planes with dovetailed-together steel plates and rosewood infill.

Scotland, was building similar planes to a superior level of craftsmanship some 20 years before Thomas Norris and Sons of London got started (around 1860), as were smaller makers such as Slater of Clerkenwell and Mathieson of Glasgow. For the most part, these were small family-run businesses producing a limited number of styles and planes, mostly by hand.

Just as common as the planes by these makers are the individually made planes of similar design and construction made by the craftsman who used them. Some were made from bought castings, others were cast in the foundries then common in many industries in Britain (probably during lunch hour and using a borrowed smoothing plane as a pattern). Irons, cap irons, Norris patented adjusters, and even screw caps marked "Norris London" could be bought to complete the plane.

The evolution of the heavy smoothing plane was a departure from the wood-bodied planes in common use. The new smoothing planes had steel soles, to hold up to hard wear and last longer, and, because of their construction, far greater mass. The design was derived both from Roman planes with steel soles and sides and most directly from earlier miter planes (see the photo above). The new design evolved to three patterns: a rounded coffin shape similar to traditional wood smoothers, a parallel-sided pattern, and a square-toed body with tapering sides to the heel. Some planes had open totes like Bailey-pattern bench planes developed later, some had closed totes, and some resembled the

shape of simple wood smoothers with no tote at all.

The design of these planes came about in response to the need for a tool that could handle imported tropical woods such as rosewood and ebony that were increasingly popular with a rich middle class. Easily worked native woods were also in short supply. Even though a new heavy smoothing plane cost a craftsman between two and three weeks' pay, the planes were eagerly sought after by the rising numbers of craftsman filling the demand for the best work. For those who couldn't afford one, less expensive wooden planes were still an option.

By the turn of the 20th century, the market for the highest-quality tools was in decline. Industrialization was so pervasive that it was able to satisfy everyone's demand for furniture, and

what demand there was for hand tools, too. Hand craftsmanship was no longer affordable, except by the wealthy. Stanley, meanwhile, was still growing and capturing a larger and larger share of the world tool market with its line of less expensive woodworking tools.

Norris was in a special position at the turn of the century. It was still producing high-end planes in a wide variety of styles—shoulder, rabbet, panel, jointer, and miter planes—whereas the other family businesses (such as Spiers) had lost interest or died. Only Norris was left making the best planes. As the competition with cheaper Bailey bench planes increased, Norris responded by producing a line of lower-quality smoothing planes with annealed iron bodies, stained beech in place of rosewood, and a less precise adjuster. Although these planes hardly compare to those of a few decades earlier, Norris is still the best remembered of the plane makers during Britain's Golden Age of tools—not because the company made the best planes (Spiers' are every bit as good), but in part because Norris was the last maker of these beautiful planes.

The name Norris has become synonymous with British smoothers for another reason: In 1913 Norris patented an adjuster that controlled the depth of cut and lateral alignment. Before then, the iron was set in the same manner as other wooden planes, by tapping on the iron, heel, or toe of the plane body. Norris's adjuster is a single shaft with a knurled knob that engages with the iron by capturing the head of the bolt securing the cap iron to the iron (see the photo below). Rotating the adjuster shaft side to side adjusts lateral alignment, and screwing the shaft in and out on a fine thread adjusts the depth of cut.

The adjuster was a definite improvement over the nonadjusting planes of other makers. It made the plane easier to use, even though it doesn't adjust the iron as smoothly as you might expect for such a fine tool. Its shortcomings are slight; the adjuster is a little sloppy and will not adjust smoothly if the lever cap is tight. Yet, Norris planes sell at a premium in large part because of the adjuster, where similar fine planes without one can sell for half as much.

Apart from the fine work these smoothing planes are capable of, there is at least one more reason to own one— they are a good investment. In this modern age of planned obsolescence, how many tools can you buy, use in your work throughout your lifetime, and every year have them grow in value? As some of the premier antique woodworking tools, Norris smoothing planes and those of similar makers are among the best such investments, but they are not easy to find and are costly when they are. Early planes with a maker's mark are the most valuable, especially ones with the least amount of wear and original irons. Users can often find planes passed over by collectors that have or might need minor or cosmetic repairs or a replacement iron. There is also a wide variety of craftsman-made unmarked planes, mostly without adjusters, that will give a lifetime of service. Chapter 13 has more to say about investing in antique planes.

I am fortunate to own two Norris smoothing planes and similar planes made by the Scottish makers Spiers and Mathieson. It's easy to appreciate the beauty of these planes and their ability to smooth the most ornery of woods. But my feelings are deeper than that. More than with any other tools I own, I feel a connection with the craftsman who carefully hand-built each plane as much as 100 years ago and with the kindred souls who have used these planes in their craft for the many years before me.

Boldly stamped into the wooden parts are their names: S. Simon, G. Harrison, L. Roberts. I don't feel any need to add mine.

Taken together, these planes inspire a reverence I rarely feel for the mass-produced factory tools of today. They represent the evolution of a tool that is as functional today as when it was first made; any further improvements would be slight at best. Some of the tools Stanley Rule and Level produced early in this century, such as Bed Rock bench planes or the #45 combination plane, are the same sorts of tools—they simply work well for what they were designed for. Even though most of these tools are no longer being made, we are fortunate that there still are at least a few dedicated makers of modern Norris-type planes, trying to add their own improvements to the originals. Whether it is a classic old tool or a modern Norris, for serious smoothing work there are very few tools that are as pleasurable to use, or that work nearly as well. You'll never regret having one.

The Norris adjuster mechanism consists of a single shaft with a knurled knob that engages with the iron by capturing the head of the bolt that secures the cap iron to the iron.

9
SCRAPERS

One of the most useful of hand-tools is the steel cabinet-scraper.... Properly sharpened and held correctly the scraper should be capable of taking long shavings of tissue thinness from even the most refractory of timbers, and it is therefore invaluable for the last fine finishing.

—Ernest Joyce, *The Encyclopedia of Furniture Making*, 1978

Scrapers and smoothing planes are like a pair of workhorses; alone, each is capable of a wide variety of work, together, they can do much more. Some woods are either just too wildly figured or have a grain structure (such as roey grain) that makes them difficult to plane smoothly. A scraper can handle these woods easily and leave a smooth surface. Other woods, such as softwoods, are difficult if not impossible to scrape, but they can often be planed quite easily. For smoothing any surface, there are no better tools than a team of scraper and plane.

Scrapers are planes, so what's so different about them that they can curl up shavings and leave a smooth surface that other planes tear out? The biggest difference is in the cutting edge of the scraper—how it's sharpened and shaped to cut a fine shaving when held at a high angle to the surface. The unique cutting edge has a tiny hook, or "burr," worked onto it, quite different from the beveled and honed knife-like cutting edge of a plane iron. It's created with a burnisher or other piece of hard steel by rubbing along the honed edge and deforming the metal.

While it might be simple enough to describe, creating an edge that cuts well is probably the hardest thing to learn about scrapers. It can be very frustrating to feel you are doing all of the sharpening correctly but still end up with a scraper that works poorly. It's too bad that this prevents many craftsmen from either using scrapers altogether or not to their fullest potential. Yes, there are some tricks to sharpening and rolling the burr, but once you learn the technique and finally use a sharp scraper, you'll find it a tool impossible to get along without.

Scrapers as simple as they are useful: a European toothing plane (at rear) and a craftsman-made spokeshave-type scraper with ivory wear plate ahead of the iron. Two miniature planes, one ivory the other beech, sit atop the spokeshave-type scraper.

Simple hand-held scrapers come in a variety of sizes and qualities and can be filed to any shape. Storing them in a slotted block of wood (or individual sheaths) protects the fine cutting edges.

Holders make a scraper less tiring to use and give better control. From the top, a Stanley #12 with two large handles for heavy work; a simple Stanley #80 cabinet scraper readily available new or used; a nickeled Stanley #81 with rosewood sole; and a craftsman-made scraping spokeshave of ebony with brass throat piece.

Types of Scrapers

At first, you might not think of scrapers as planes at all. There is no question about some—those scrapers fixed in a plane body that look and are used just like smoothing planes. Another form looks more like a heavy spokeshave; although held differently than many planes, these scrapers still have the plane characteristics of soles, handles, and a way to fix the blade. (I think of scraper cutters as "blades" rather than irons since they are usually thinner and of a softer temper.)

Also included in this group are scratch molders, profiled scraper blades held in a stock (often wood) that helps guide the cut. (Making and using scratch tools is explained in Chapter 10.) But what about the most basic and most useful of the scraper tools, a piece of flat thin steel held in your hands alone? In this case, the heel of your hands and your fingers both guide the cut and support the scraper just like the sole and frog of a plane. Except for the blade, your hands are the plane.

HAND SCRAPERS

Scrapers are ancient tools. The simplest scraper is nothing more than a shard of window glass or a piece of steel cut from an old saw. Handsaw steel is perfect, being just flexible enough and of the right temper to be able to roll up a good burr edge and stay sharp. Some flexibility is desirable, so you can bend the scraper to concentrate the cutting force in a smaller area, say to scrape out a scratch or imperfection. Today, modern scrapers of this type, no longer cut from handsaws, can be bought from any woodworking catalog in a variety of sizes, shapes, and qualities (such as hardness). Most common and useful for flat surfaces are square-edged scrapers measuring about 3 in. by 6 in. Shaped scrapers such as "gooseneck," concave, and convex scrapers or ones filed to a specific profile are useful for scraping moldings, curved parts, or bowls.

For versatility and quick scraping jobs, nothing beats a simple hand scraper. I use ones of different thicknesses and flexibilities for everything from scraping glue or removing an old finish to smoothing small imperfections or areas of irregular grain on tabletops after smooth planing. Hand scrapers have only one unpleasant drawback; aggressive scraping can create enough heat from the friction to cause you to really take notice! The steel is so thin that it can heat up quickly, right at the point where your thumbs are making firm contact.

CABINET SCRAPERS

The same type blade, or one slightly thicker, can be used more easily when held in a holder of some kind. Different holders give different advantages, but they all help to keep the blade oriented to the cut, avoid the burning thumbs problem, give an added measure of control, and are less tiring. Holders with a flat sole help to scrape a level plane, just as a flat sole does on a bench plane. Any holder helps you scrape more aggressively.

A holder can be a simple handle with a scraper blade clamped at one end, a tool similar to a spokeshave for light scraping of curved surfaces, or a heavier cast-iron holder with two handles in line with the blade for scraping large surfaces (see the bottom photo on the facing page). All these designs are known as cabinet scrapers. Not included in this group, but as a separate scraper type, are holders that look and work like bench planes. Some of the simpler holders are made of wood or have wooden soles added to a cast-iron body for the same reasons some craftsmen prefer wooden

A chair devil will scrape complex shapes, such as the continuous back rail on this Windsor chair, a task nearly impossible with other planes. The tool on the bench is a flat-soled scraper.

planes—smooth operation. The variety in these tools is tremendous, from the craftsman-made scraper for a specific job to common cast-iron cabinet scrapers by Stanley and others. Interestingly, the first design that Leonard Bailey patented (in 1855), and one of the earliest metal planes, was a variable-pitched heavy cabinet scraper of this type, with large rosewood handles. Stanley eventually produced this scraper (the #12) for nearly the next 100 years.

Of this second type of scraper I most often use a Stanley #80 cabinet scraper for leveling modest surfaces that are difficult to plane smoothly; the flat sole and side handles give a controlled cut with less effort than with a hand-held scraper. The flat sole helps me scrape out a ding or tearout without dishing the surface. The blade is beveled rather than

square like a hand scraper, so it is easier to roll up a larger burr and scrape more aggressively. It's particularly useful for veneered surfaces, where there's just too much risk of tearing out the thin veneer with a smoothing plane. Although the #80 works well on open surfaces, the handles get in the way when working in tight places or up against a vertical edge. I also use a few specialty scrapers of this type, such as a "chair devil" similar to a spokeshave (see the photo above), for working curved surfaces or small areas more easily scraped than planed.

SCRAPER PLANES

A third type of scraper is the most plane-like; in fact, these tools all look like planes. Some have the same front knob, rear handle, flat sole, and general shape

Similar to the bench planes they resemble, scraper planes have flat soles and strong handles. Shown here are three rare Stanley designs: from the top, a #87, a #85 with tilting handles, and a #212 that is used one-handed.

Oriental scraping planes have thick irons wedged into low hardwood bodies. The two smaller planes are used to flatten the soles of longer bench planes.

of a cast-iron smoothing plane. Others have similar characteristics and a rabbet mouth and handles that tilt to one side or the other for working in close to a vertical surface (see the photo at left above). Three of the rarest Stanley tools are scraping planes: the #12¼, #85, and #212. Recently, Veritas introduced a scraper-plane insert that fits into a cast-iron bench plane such as a #4 or #5 to convert it to a scraping plane.

Wooden scraper planes look exactly like bench planes with thick irons and wedges and differ only in that the scraper blade is set at a much higher pitch—sometimes nearly vertical (see the photo at right above). Toothing planes are one such type, with a finely serrated blade like saw teeth that can scrape a surface aggressively to create a good glue surface when veneering or to level a highly figured board. (For more on toothing planes, see the sidebar on p. 181.)

All of the scraper planes are used like planes, for the final leveling and smoothing of surfaces. They are the most comfortable to use for long periods of scraping, and their large soles flatten a surface accurately, just as a long bench plane does. They use thick beveled irons, sometimes serrated like a toothing plane, that are better able to resist the heavy cutting pressure and not chatter. Since scraper planes cut slowly but carefully, I use them to smooth large surfaces after first doing as much as I can with a smoothing plane. No matter what tools I start with, I finish with a simple hand scraper on the particularly difficult areas.

Cutting Dynamics

Whether a scraper is held in your hands, in a cabinet scraper, or in a plane-like body, the way it cuts is much the same. Scrapers have two distinct cutting advantages that give them versatility and the ability to work woods that other planes can't. One is that the cutting action of a scraper is like that of a high-angle plane iron, with all of the same dynamic advantages. The other is that the hook rolled onto the cutting edge controls both the depth of the cut and the size of the shaving. At best, scrapers cut like a finely set and well-tuned plane, curling up transparent shavings. They can just as easily be tuned to scrape paint and do other rough work. Even though sharpening and shaping the edge takes learning a specific technique, a sharpened scraper is a tool that nearly anyone can use with good results over a wide range of conditions.

Using a scraper at a high angle or pitch curls the shavings so abruptly that tearout and splitting are less likely, especially if the cut is light. Scrapers cut over a range of pitches, depending upon the size and shape of the burr, but generally the pitch is about 60° or more (see the drawing below). A normal bench plane iron is closer to 45°, and even though 15° might not seem like a big difference, it actually is. The extreme case is a scraper used without any burr formed into the edge at all but just sharpened and honed perfectly square (like the traditional piece of glass). In this case, the tool can be used almost vertically for the finest shavings, very light cuts, and utmost control.

The unique shape of the hooked edge has just as much effect on how a scraper cuts as does its pitch. The burr is rolled onto the edge with a burnisher held against it at anywhere from square to the edge to about 15°. Burnishing different angles creates different burr shapes. The heavier the pressure with the burnisher, the more the steel is deformed and the larger the burr. Whereas a plane uses the depth of the iron and the width of the throat to control the size of the shavings, the size of the burr and the pressure upon the cutting edge do the same for scrapers.

All of the advantages that make scrapers well suited for working hardwoods make them generally less useful for softwoods. Softwood fibers are usually more smoothly cut with an iron at a lower pitch, because they offer less resistance. High angles tend to lift the soft fibers rather than cut them. While it's not impossible to scrape pine or

basswood, for example, only a scraper carefully sharpened with a very fine burr will work, and even then the surface isn't as smoothly cut as with a plane. Part of the problem is that usual scraper technique is to flex the blade slightly and concentrate the cutting force along a small area of the edge, making it even more likely that the soft fibers will be pressed down and deformed rather than cut. Fortunately where scrapers are needed most—for smoothing difficult hardwoods—they also work the best.

Tuning Scrapers

Sharpening a scraper blade is the most difficult part of learning to use scrapers, but it's really not all that different from sharpening a plane iron. Understanding what the edge should look like and how a scraper cuts helps a lot in learning to sharpen. As with a plane iron, there are

many possible ways to create the cutting edge, each yielding different results. An edge suitable for smoothing inlaid veneers is very different from one that's best for leveling a tabletop. Ultimately, the most satisfying results come from trying some of the variations to create slightly different edges and see how they work for you.

All scraper blades are sharpened in essentially the same way. Thin blades have edges that are most often square with the sides and a burr rolled to either side; thicker blades as are common in cabinet scrapers or scraper planes are beveled at 45° or less with a single burr rolled toward the back. A very fine cutting edge can be produced with no burr at all, but most scrapers do have a burr of some kind. Toothing planes need none because the serrated iron cuts well without it. To simplify the explanation of tuning technique, I'll focus on the

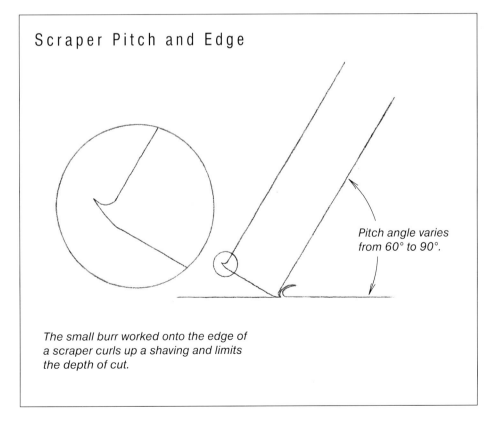

Scraper Pitch and Edge

Pitch angle varies from 60° to 90°.

The small burr worked onto the edge of a scraper curls up a shaving and limits the depth of cut.

process of tuning a scraper with square edges. Tuning a scraper with a beveled edge is in essence the same, with only a few small variations in honing and in rolling up the bevel (see pp. 180-181).

JOINTING THE EDGE

Before you roll on a burr, the cutting edge needs to be carefully honed and prepared. You can roll up an edge on a scraper blade without any preparation and it will still cut, but it will not be truly sharp, it will be finely serrated and

leave scratches on the surface, and it will dull quickly, too. Take the same blade and hone the sides and edge as perfectly as a plane iron bevel and back, and then roll up a fine burr and the scraper will cut extremely fine shavings, leave a polished surface, and have a much longer lasting edge. It lasts longer because more of the edge is working (rather than just the tips of the serrations that break away). The smoothly prepared edge has one more advantage: The edge can be quickly burnished down and rolled

up again and be nearly as sharp as it was originally.

I start preparing the edge by filing it square and straight. To do this I clamp the blade lightly in a machinist's vise (between wooden blocks is best), with the edge I'm filing just above the jaws. You could use a woodworking bench side or end vise, but I prefer to keep metal filings well away from anywhere I'm using planes. For a file I use a very fine 10-in.-long jeweler's file. It leaves a smooth cut, but jointing with a fine mill bastard file and stoning the edge just slightly more will give the same results. I file with the length of the file along the edge, at a slight skew, and use the top of the jaws as a reference to file straight and very square with the sides (see the photo at left).

I find that it's easiest and fastest to work freehand, but you can joint the edge with any of a number of jigs. I have an old commercial cast-iron saw jointer that holds a file at right angles to a fence that rides along the side of the scraper (see the top left photo on the facing page). New versions are available, too. A simple jointing jig (see the top right photo on the facing page) is nothing more than a wide kerf cut in the side of a hardwood block to fit a file snugly (adding a screw or two in from the top will lock it in place). Holding the side of the block along the scraper's side and working up and down the edge files it square and true. Whatever method you use, the important thing is to get a nice square edge. I like to file a straight edge, because it can be more quickly honed, but a slight camber works fine, too. Ideally, it's nice to keep the tiny serrations left by the file parallel with the edge for the smoothest final edge, but with careful honing this is less important.

Working at a slight skew, file the edge of a scraper square in a machinist's vise fitted with wooden jaw protectors. Use the blocks of wood like a shooting board to file square to the sides and straight along the edge.

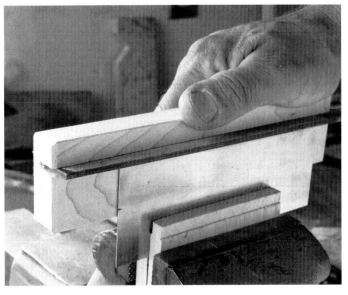

An old cast-iron handsaw jointer fitted with a short, fine file works well for jointing a scraper blade.

A simple jointing tool can be made by cutting a slot in a block of hardwood to hold a file snugly.

HONING THE EDGE

Honing technique is similar to jointing, except that the edge of the scraper is refined with a benchstone instead of a file. Similar sorts of jigs and techniques work, too. Keep one thing in mind, though; scrapers are thin and hard enough that they can easily wear a groove in a soft stone (such as a waterstone). This isn't good for your stone, nor will it hone a square edge. If the scraper does work into a groove, it will tend to round the edge and negate all your efforts.

My preferred honing method is quick and easy. Holding the scraper upright, I work it back and forth down the length of the stone and slowly from one side to the other (see the photo at right). It's something like a sawing stroke using all of the stone. The only trick is to keep the blade square with the stone. Nearly as easy is to run the edge of the scraper against the side of the stone while supporting it flat on a block of wood alongside. Varying the thickness of the block will ensure working different areas of the side of the stone. I hone until the

To hone the edge of a scraper, hold it upright and "saw" on the face of the stone, working back and forth and slowly side to side to avoid scoring the stone.

edge appears polished and feels very sharp. Just as important is honing the flat sides, because, as with a plane iron, they form half of the cutting edge. I hone the sides flat on the face of the stone, working one side and then the other,

shifting my fingers and the pressure often. I finish with a few strokes with the blade on edge to remove any wire edge.

At this point, try out your honed scraper on a block of maple or cherry to see what difference rolling up a burr in

Burnishers for working the burr on the cutting edge of a scraper need to be hard and smooth. The two shown here are made from old files carefully ground and polished; the triangular burnisher is best for straight edges, the oval for curves.

Work-harden and draw the steel along the edge before turning the burr. Lubricate the burnisher with a drop or two of oil, and work it flat along the side near the edge back and forth a few times.

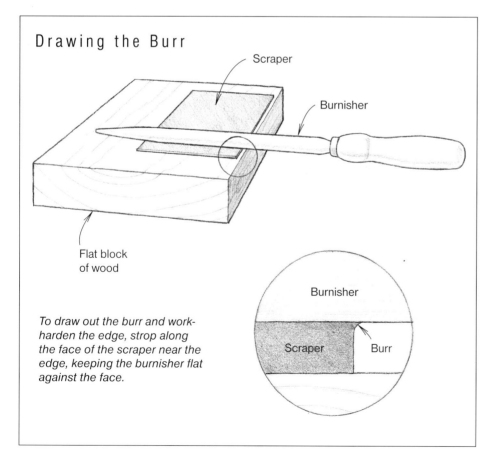

Drawing the Burr

Scraper

Burnisher

Flat block
of wood

To draw out the burr and work-harden the edge, strop along the face of the scraper near the edge, keeping the burnisher flat against the face.

Burnisher

Scraper

Burr

the next step makes. As is, the edge should turn up a nice fine shaving, but it will cut much less aggressively and dull more quickly than a scraper with a burr, and you'll need to hold the tool at a high pitch for it to cut. (If the scraper works up a fine dust, it's not sharp and requires further honing.) I sometimes use a scraper without a burr with very light pressure for careful smoothing around inlays or at joints where the grain meets at right angles.

ROLLING UP THE BURR

So far this sharpening technique is straightforward and should pose no problems to anyone familiar with sharpening planes. What is a little tricky though, is rolling up the burr. This is where most of the confusion about scrapers lies. I suspect that some of the poor results with scrapers are due to not preparing the edge well to begin with and then having to use a lot of pressure to roll up a burr. Such a burr won't last long or cut as well as it could. Another fault is rolling up a burr at too acute an angle to the sides, or in other words farther off square from the edge. This sort of burr might actually curl so much that the scraper practically needs to be horizontal to cut well. By then you're dragging your knuckles, too.

A third common fault is to roll up the burr with the wrong tool or with excessive pressure. The metal deforms and tears, forming a hook useful only for rough work. The best burr is rolled up with light pressure at a consistent angle with a smoothly polished burnisher. A fine burr will cut wonderfully, it will last just as long as a larger burr, and it can be worked down and rolled up again without going through the entire resharpening process.

A burnisher is a useful woodworking tool for a lot of tasks, but it's essential for getting the best results with a scraper. I have two that I made from old files by carefully grinding off the teeth, smoothing the edges, and polishing the surfaces. One is softly triangular, the other oval (see the photo at left on the facing page). The handles are simple hardwood turnings. The alternative is to use the back of a chisel, gouge, or awl, but I prefer the predictability of using a burnisher. There are a number of burnishers and burnishing tools available through some of the better woodworking catalogs meant just for rolling the burr onto scrapers.

A burnisher works well for two reasons: It's harder than the scraper steel and can deform it, and it's the right shape. Scrapers do come in a range of hardnesses. The harder the steel, the longer the edge lasts, but also the harder the tool needed to roll a burr edge on it. The burnisher's shape spreads out the pressure against the edge, gently

To turn the burr along the edge of a hand scraper, start with the burnisher square with the edge, take a stroke, lower it a degree or two, stroke again, and stroke a third time, finishing somewhere between 75° and 85°.

deforming it, but hopefully not so much that the burr is rough and broken. With light pressure this is less likely to happen. I use the triangular burnisher for straight edges and the oval one for turning the edge on curved scrapers, because it more easily follows their shape.

To begin rolling the burr, support the scraper on a flat block of wood, lubricate it with a drop or two of oil, and strop the sides with the burnisher (see the photo at right on the facing page). The idea here is to keep the burnisher flat against the side and work back and forth a few times on each side close to the cutting edge. This ever so slightly "draws" the metal that will be the burr and work-hardens the edge slightly so that the hook lasts longer. If there is an old burr already there, this method will roll it down in preparation for reshaping it. Any wire edges left over from honing and filing are also smoothed out.

Holding the scraper in your hand, roll up the burr by wiping the burnisher against the edge three or four times (see the photo above). The first stroke should be nearly 90° to the edge, and each successive stroke should be at a slightly

more acute angle (as shown in the drawing on p. 180). The pressure should be moderate. Slightly more pressure is needed with the oval burnisher than with the point of the triangular one, only because the pressure of the triangular one is more concentrated. The idea is to deform the edge into the burr, but slowly enough that the steel doesn't have microscopic tears. Until you get a feel for rolling up the edge an oval burnisher will give the best results, because its roundness shapes the metal smoothly. Changing the angle of the strokes and building up the burr slowly helps, too. I repeat this process on the three remaining sides of the scraper.

The burr on the edge should be quite noticeable, and it should feel sharp. The size of the burr is a function of the pressure used and the angle the burnisher makes with the edge. A final angle of about 85° leaves a fine, sharp burr. Don't use an angle any lower than about 75°, because it will create a cutting edge that has to be tilted well forward to cut. Tilt the scraper to feel the angle at which your edge cuts best.

Rolling Up the Burr

SQUARE-EDGED SCRAPER

1
2
3

75° to 85°

Using light, consistent pressure, wipe the burnisher along the edge at 90° (1) and then at progressively lower angles (2, 3).

The greater the angle of the last stroke, the higher the pitch when using the scraper.

BEVEL-EDGED SCRAPER

Using modest and consistent pressure, wipe the burnisher along the bevel (1) and then move it toward the horizontal (2, 3).

10° to 15°

3

30° to 45°

2

1

To turn the burr on a bevel-edged scraper, work from the beveled side, stroking repeatedly with modest pressure. Stop with the burnisher between 10° and 15° from square with the edge.

BEVEL-EDGED SCRAPERS

Part of the beauty of hand-held scrapers is that the angle of attack, or pitch, can be changed quickly and easily. The heavier bevel-edged blades common in cabinet scrapers and scraper planes are adjustable over a much smaller range of pitches, or in some cases aren't adjustable at all. So while they are sharpened in a similar way to the lighter scrapers, to get the best results means a little trial and error to get a hooked edge that fits the tool's pitch. What this really means is paying attention to the angle the burnisher makes with the cutting edge.

The preparation is very similar to the method I have already described for square-edged scrapers, except that the blade is filed and honed at a bevel. Any of these blades can be sharpened square, with the advantage of having an extra edge on both sides. The reason they are beveled is so that an aggressive burr can be rolled on more easily, in that just the metal of the bevel needs to be deformed. The bevel also creates an ample relief angle. A bevel angle between 30° and 45° works fine. Sharpen the bevel the same way as for a plane iron and relieve the corners so there is no chance of digging them into the finished surface.

To create the cutting edge, first work-harden the back with a few light strokes as for a hand scraper. Use a drop or two of oil. Then, with the burnisher resting on the bevel, stroke along the edge. Work lightly a few more times back and forth, each time with the burnisher more square with the edge (see the photo at left). Finish with the burnisher at an angle of between 10° and 15° for a burr of the right shape and angle. Since these blades are used for more aggressive leveling of surfaces, I always work on a noticeably larger burr, with an extra stroke or two or with slightly more pressure than on a hand scraper.

Curved scrapers are sharpened in a similar manner. I have a large variety of different-radius scrapers made from old sawblades, some with beveled edges and some without. The challenge is to hone a sharp edge and then work the burnisher along it at somewhat of a consistent angle. I usually end up just sharpening the area I happen to need, say to fit within a cove molding. Round files and small slipstones help to shape and hone both inside and outside curves. I work the burr edge on with a round burnisher using light pressure.

RESHARPENING

Depending on what I am doing and how sharp I need my scraper to be, I can often roll down the burr and reshape it at least once. It's never as sharp the second or third time, but it does save going through filing and honing the edge again. Thicker bevel-edged blades never resharpen as successfully, because the burr is usually larger and deforming the metal to roll it down and back up again tends to dull the edge considerably.

To resharpen I roll the burr down with the burnisher, in exactly the same way I work-harden and draw the edge originally—by stroking close to the edge with the burnisher flat against the side. The burr edge is then rolled up. The lighter the burr, the more easily it can be rolled down and back up a third time. After that it's back to filing and repeating the preparation, which only gets easier as the sides hone to a smooth polish.

FINAL TUNING

Once you have a feel for rolling on the unique burr edge, the rest of tuning scraper tools is a snap. With a hand-held scraper, sharpening the blade is the complete tuning. The soles of cabinet scrapers and scraper planes should be lapped if they are hollow or warped, which is not a big job considering their size. The throat needs no attention, since the quality of the shaving does not depend on its size as it most definitely does in,

TOOTHING PLANES

Toothing planes are a special type of scraper plane, with a heavy, serrated iron (much thicker than common scraper blades) bedded at nearly a vertical pitch (see the photo on p. 170). The serrations cut like the tiny teeth of a fine handsaw scraped across the surface. Irons vary in coarseness, with 20 to more than 30 teeth per inch. Thinner toothing blades were once available for cabinet scrapers and scraper planes and can sometimes be found on the used tool market.

Originally toothing planes had two uses: to level particularly ornery surfaces and to "tooth" veneers and the grounds they are glued to. The idea was that a rough surface gave a better glue bond. With modern glues little if any toothing of veneers is done.

I don't use a toothing plane much, but sometimes it's the only tool for the job. I think of it as the scrub plane of the scraper family, used to level a surface quickly no matter how difficult the wood. It leaves a rough surface, but one easily smoothed with other tools. Since the depth of the cut is not dependent on the size of the burr—there is none—the iron can be set quite aggressively. Sharpen and hone the bevel like any plane iron (there's no need to flatten the back). It cuts unique shavings—something between coarse sawdust and tiny shavings.

Toothing blades, finely serrated like saw teeth, have traditionally been used in scrapers for roughing the surfaces of the veneer and ground for a better glue bond, but they are also useful for leveling highly figured and ornery woods.

say, a smoothing plane. Any handles should be tight and comfortably shaped.

As for the bed that supports the blade, it's much less important that it be flat in a scraping tool than in a bench plane. This isn't to say that a scraper won't chatter; in fact, it will do so quite easily. But to cut the best surface, the cut should be light, so there is less pressure upon the blade than there is with a plane. There is another reason that the bed is less important: On some scraper holders there is a screw behind the blade to flex it into a curve away from the bed. Flexing the blade serves two purposes. It directs the cutting force into a narrower arc of the blade, and changes the depth of the cut. The arc stiffens the blade somewhat, too.

Using Scrapers

There are no great differences between how each of the three types of scraper tools are used or for what types of surfaces. Naturally, a cabinet scraper or a scraper plane with a flat sole and stout handles is easier to use for smoothing a large surface, where the tool holds and guides the blade. Although a hand-held scraper leaves just as polished a surface, it takes longer and might leave you with hot thumbs.

I hold a hand scraper between fingers and thumb at both ends and flex the blade to concentrate the cut. This puts the pressure right where it's needed, but unfortunately also gives my thumbs good contact with the steel right at the point where the most heat is generated by friction. Some craftsmen prefer using a cabinet scraper or scraper plane just to avoid this problem. Light pressure with a hand scraper and pausing occasionally works for me, or if I plan on doing a lot

To use a hand scraper, hold it between your fingers and thumbs and flex the blade forward into a slight arc. Tip the blade in the direction of the cut, and push with even strokes that glide into and out of the cut.

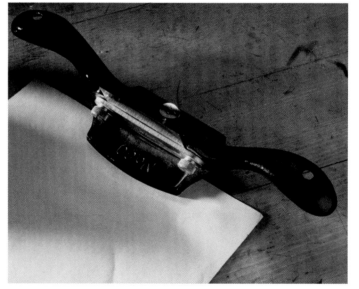

To set the cutting depth of a cabinet scraper, rest the tool on a piece of paper just ahead of the throat, slide the blade in, and secure it. Turn the thumbscrew to tension the blade and to increase the depth of cut.

of scraping I wear the leather "thumbs" cut from an old pair of workgloves.

I use a hand scraper with long push (and sometimes pull) strokes that glide into and out of the cut. My palms guide the cut, and my locked wrists keep the pitch consistent. The beauty of scrapers

is that they can be worked in any direction, but they will leave the most polished surface cutting with the grain. Avoid pressing too hard at the start of the cut, which can leave the surface with tiny dents. If chatter is a problem—and it almost never is with a hand scraper—

work the area from different angles and try pitching the blade differently. Using the tool upright is usually more aggressive than tipping it forward. Try to use the entire length of the edge before resharpening. For working into a corner I hold the scraper in one hand and pull it toward me with my palm still acting as a sole. Rarely do I sharpen the two short edges of the scraper, so that if need be I can use either edge to guide the cut without cutting with it, too. Breaking these edges with a file makes the scraper more comfortable to hold.

On cabinet scrapers and scraper planes the blade depth, and on some tools the pitch, needs to be set before using them. Adjustments are made the same way in both tools. Initially, I set the depth by slipping the blade into its holder with the cabinet scraper or plane lying sole down on the bench (as if it were being used), with a piece of note paper under the sole ahead of the blade (see the bottom photo on the facing page). The paper is just thick enough that once the blade is secured by the hold-down screw, it projects below the sole about the thickness of the paper and parallel with the sole. This might seem like too little, but it's actually about right. If the blade is not parallel with the sole, adjust it by tapping it with a wooden mallet just as if adjusting the iron of a wooden plane. On the Stanley #80 the depth is further adjusted by turning the thumbscrew behind the blade. Turning it in presses the blade into an arc and increases the depth of cut. If you find you need to keep increasing the depth of the cut and the scraper is chattering and cutting poorly, the blade probably just needs resharpening.

Changing the blade's pitch in a scraper plane (such as the Stanley #112 shown here) also adjusts the depth of the cut. Tightening one nut while releasing the other tips the blade forward (for a deeper cut) or backward (for a lighter cut).

The pitch of the blade holder is adjusted with a threaded rod through a post behind it and two locking nuts (see the photo above). Since few of these tools also have a thumbscrew for tensioning the blade, changing the pitch is a way to adjust the cutting depth. First set the pitch high (60° to 80°) and fix the blade in the holder with a piece of paper under the front of the sole. Refine the pitch by loosening one nut and tightening the other to tip the blade forward or backward. Tipping the blade forward deepens the cut; tipping it back lightens the cut.

Scraper planes or cabinet scrapers are used in the same way as hand scrapers, with long strokes and mostly with the grain. Sometimes it's more comfortable to pull the scraper. The blade is held at a consistent pitch and the sole guides the cut, so all you need to do is supply the power and direct the tool. While scraper planes and cabinet scrapers are capable of leveling large surfaces fairly quickly (though more slowly than a plane), they are finishing tools best for smoothing not hogging. A small amount of hand scraping is usually all it takes to bring the surface to a final polish.

At least one or two members of the scraper family should be within an arm's reach of any bench. Whether you use one for scraping glue or for smoothing wild-burled veneers to a polish, no tools have quite the range and flexibility of scrapers. If you get frustrated trying to get the sharpening right, burnish lightly and keep trying. It will be worth it when you realize how versatile and useful scrapers are.

10
PLANES FOR SHAPING

A carpenter stands in need of a great variety of tools, such as saws, planes,

chisels, hammers, awls, gimlets, &c. Common workmen are obliged to find

their own tools, a set of which is worth from ten to twenty pounds, or even

more. But for different kinds of moldings, for beads, and fancy work, the

master carpenter supplies his men with the necessary implements.

—The Book of Trades, or Library of the Useful Arts, 1807

Of the many hundreds of different types of planes, more shape the surface in some way than leave it a flat plane. Whereas a few bench planes sufficed the 18th- and 19th-century joiner, it took dozens of planes to cut the moldings to complete the interior and exterior trim for a house. Planes shaped everything from round-head windows, to the moldings run on their casings, to wide roof cornices. The tools fit the work and changed along with the tastes and styles that demanded them.

When molding machines came along, and later combination planes like the Stanley #55 (see the photo on the facing page), molding planes could have become obsolete. Certainly demand fell off, and eventually all the surviving makers closed shop. Still, molding planes are in many shops today; I use a variety in the course of a year. Why use them, in a modern shop equipped with shapers and routers, or when stock moldings can be bought at any lumberyard? The same question could be asked about any of the other shaping planes—panel raisers,

chamfer planes, spokeshaves, and compass planes.

With the exception of spokeshaves, I don't use any of these shaping planes as much as bench or joinery planes. But even in this age of "time is money," there are times when they are the best and most efficient tools for the work. With the right jigs and cutters a router or shaper can do a lot, but making those jigs takes time. I can take out a beading plane and run it along the edge of three casing boards in less time than it takes to chuck up a router, set up a router table, make a

The Stanley #55, known as "a planing mill within itself," was the most complete combination plane ever sold. It could cut moldings, rabbets, dadoes, tongue and grooves, beads, chamfers, and much more. Almost 100 irons of different profiles were available.

trial pass or two, and sand the router beads smooth. I can cut the same bead as easily well away from the edge—something a router cannot do. Moreover, the plane-cut quirk (the small groove between the bead and the flat) is finer and sharper, the bead as smooth as if polished. Of course, it takes a tuned plane to get such results, but once it is tuned, I can cut many hundred feet of moldings before at most the iron needs a light honing.

There are also aesthetic reasons for using planes. Machine-cut details look like what they are—uniform and exact. Details cut with a plane, guided by hand and eye, have individuality. Shapes have the slightest variation that can be seen and felt. To me, they are more beautiful because they aren't machine-perfect. I want to see the work of a craftsman's hands and sharp hand tools in my furniture, not the product of machines.

Shaping planes offer nearly unlimited design possibilities. In the case of molding planes, I think of the basic shapes as words that can be used to write sonnets, haiku, or exclamations. These moldings can be bolder and more shapely than the machine-cut alternatives, worked by cutters designed around the limitations of grinding carbide. The design possibilities and the ease of using shaping planes might encourage you to work in new ways, to shape a table edge, or to add a curve where you might not have. Such details are functional and beautiful. If this isn't reason enough to use these planes, there is one more—they are some of the most beautiful tools of the plane maker's art.

Hollows and rounds came in matched pairs, as many as 24 different sizes. They are still the most useful planes for shaping a wide variety of molding profiles, used either alone or in combination with other molding planes.

Molding Planes

Molding planes are the first planes to come to mind when you think about shaping wood. Hollows, rounds, ogees, reverse ogees, astragals, beads—there is almost an endless number of shapes. A carpenter of a hundred years ago would have had dozens of different profiles, and bought new ones as moldings changed to suit the fashion of the day. Each is beautiful, with a shapely wedge, a golden beech body, and decorative chamfers run on the edges.

Most molding planes (or molding tools, as they were first known) have a

Most molding planes have a single iron, a simple wooden wedge, a rectangular body, and a side escapement throat. Both the planes shown here cut the same complex shape (a Grecian ogee).

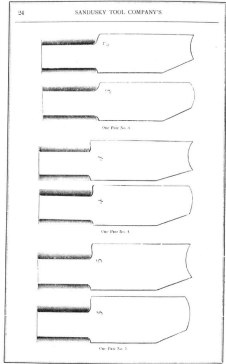

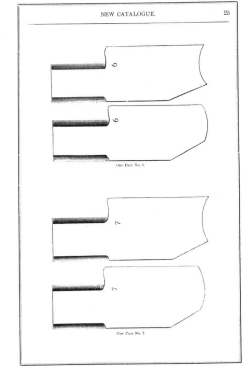

single iron, bedded at a slightly higher pitch than a bench plane. They were designed for working straight-grained softwoods; cabinetmaker's planes for working hardwood need a higher pitch still. Usually the iron is not skewed, although this feature is more common on English planes. Some specialty molding planes have double irons. Most have simple rectangular bodies, a handhold rabbeted out of the body, and a tapered throat cut into the side where the shavings are ejected. Wider molding planes, such as cornice planes, pump planes, and other specialty planes, often have a bench mouth similar to a jack or try plane.

Hollows and rounds are the most basic molding planes, and in many ways they are still the most useful. As the names suggest, hollows have soles that are hollow or concave across their width; rounds have convex soles. Once you could buy them individually or in sets with as many as 24 numbered pairs. Each cuts a specific radius and an arc of about 60°. Every manufacturer had his own numbering system, which was not consistent throughout the trade but was nevertheless useful as a rough way to compare sizes. Those who couldn't afford the luxury of all 24 pairs, or didn't have the space to carry them, got by with a set of 9 even- or odd-numbered pairs.

While a craftsman might be able to buy all of the hollows and rounds, there is no such thing as a complete set of molding planes. Beyond the basic shapes there's a nearly endless variety of profiles for specific purposes. Still, looking through makers' catalogs at the height of molding-plane manufacture, there is surprising uniformity in the shapes. Hundreds of sizes and profiles were available, which could then be combined with one another to suit a particular need or cut larger complex moldings.

This unusual whalebone molding plane (a round) was possibly made aboard a whaling ship during the 18th or early 19th century.

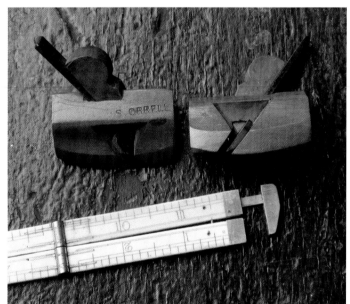

Miniature molding planes such as this pair were craftsman-made for some special work, perhaps for molding the fine mullions of a fanlight window. The planes are mirror images of each other, or "handed," to work with the grain in any direction.

Different trades used different shapes, sizes, and styles of molding planes. The house carpenter and joiner needed the greatest variety for all manner of architectural trim; a furniture maker needed far fewer molding planes. Shipbuilders needed, among others, large hollows known as spar planes for shaping masts and spars. Handle makers used simple hollowing planes called forkstaff planes to shape handles. Large-handled rounds cut pump logs for early water systems. Stairbuilders used wide and often complex handrailing planes and nosing planes for the edge of each step. So it was with coachmaker, casemaker, and sashmaker, all needing different types and profiles of molding planes.

It wasn't until about 1800, when the first broadsides and catalogs appeared, that molding planes evolved to a standard length and style. Except for using yellow birch instead of beech, early American planes closely followed English patterns. With a body as long as 10½ in., boldly chamfered edges, and graceful and rounded wedge finials, the details spoke of a tool made by hand by a craftsman proud of his work. Later planes are not only a standard 9½ in. long, but also show a gradual conformity of details: edges broken by the barest chamfers, rectangular proportions, and wedge finials more elliptical and flatter. Although still made largely by hand (some by prison labor), machines milled out the stock. Details were simplified, as factories emphasized production over quality.

The shortening of molding planes reflects much about the evolution of plane making. One theory is that a joiner could fit more planes into his chest if they were shorter. While this is no doubt the reason that some old planes have been trimmed shorter, a more plausible explanation is that the expansion of plane making gradually improved the tools as they became more consistent. If a slightly shorter plane worked just as well and took less material to make, why make it any longer than the work demanded? And while the decorative wedge finial and chamfers on the plane body are handsome, in a competitive market, why spend the extra time on details unnecessary to the function of the plane?

The peak of the wooden molding plane came between 1870 and 1880. Machinery was replacing hand-cut moldings, both within individual shops and with specialized mills cutting nothing but stock moldings. With more dependable and cheaper transportation, it became economical to ship millwork over a larger area. New combination planes such as the Stanley #45 and later the #55 further cut into the market for molding planes. One patent application for a combination plane touted all the benefits of its design and its "special advantage for carpenters in smaller cities, away from the planing-mills!" Stanley advertised the #55 as a "planing mill within itself," capable of the work of literally dozens of individual molding planes.

No commercial molding-plane makers are working today, unless you include the few craftsmen making a small number of specialty planes (see Chapter 12). Luckily for us, the legacy of all those past plane makers and years of manufacturing is a nearly endless supply of usable and inexpensive old planes. Pick up a few, tune them as I describe later in this section, and try cutting some simple moldings. You'll be surprised how easily the planes work and how enjoyable they can be to use.

CUTTING SIMPLE MOLDINGS

The most useful molding planes are the basic shapes of hollows, rounds, and beads. A variety of sizes of these planes will fill the molding needs of most of us. Add a few specific profiles, such as an ogee, scotia, or ovolo, and you have a far wider range of choices. Each can be used alone to cut a complete profile or in combination with hollows, rounds, and a rabbet plane, to cut a cove and scotia molding, for example. Many molding planes have an integral fence and depth stop cut into the sole to make them easier to use and the work more consistent.

There is a little more to it than just holding the plane against the guiding edge of the work and planing away. Many of these planes have a characteristic known as "spring," or the angle that the plane is held off of vertical in use. Spring angles are different for different sole profiles and not all molding planes need

Some molding profiles are cut at an angle to the sole, or "sprung," for a more consistent throat. Often the spring line is scribed on the toe or heel. In use, the plane is held against the edge with the spring line vertical.

spring, but for two reasons spring is important. If you imagine a shaped molding profile without spring, where the profile is cut deepest into the sole the throat will be quite open (since it tapers wider). Tearout is more likely as a result. Springing the profile places it more horizontal with the sole with a more consistent mouth. Since the plane is held at the spring angle (canted away from the edge), it has a further advantage of making it easier to pressure the plane evenly against the guiding edge of the board.

It's usually easy to determine the spring angle by looking at the heel (or sometimes the toe) of the plane. There you'll see the scribed profile the plane was made to and a long spring line (see the photo on the facing page). Hold the plane with the spring line vertical. Rock the plane slightly side to side and you can feel that the shoulder of the fence also helps hold it at the right angle. Plane away until the profile is complete or the depth stop prevents further cutting.

CUTTING WIDE OR COMPLEX MOLDINGS

An 18th- or 19th-century joiner lucky enough to own a large cornice plane could cut a large and complex molding with one plane. Since such planes were expensive (about as much as six pairs of hollows and rounds) and they are not all that common today, I imagine that most joiners owned few if any wide cornice planes. Those successful enough to own one used it to cut the largest molding of the roof trim or a bold molding at the juncture of wall and ceiling in a formal room.

To cut the hundred or more feet of crown molding needed for a modest house took considerable effort. After cutting just a few feet with such a plane, I can understand why molding machinery was so quickly adopted. For

A cornice plane, with its unusually wide iron and wedge and front handles, can cut a crown molding. The alternative is to use a series of narrower planes.

one, it takes a great amount of force to cut the full width of an iron 5 in. or so wide. This is why some cornice planes have a pair of handles attached to the toe (see the photo above), so that someone (usually an apprentice) could pull, while the master pushed from behind and steered. Planes without handles have a hole for a rope, again to be pulled by someone or possibly to be wound around some sort of waterwheel.

Another reason cornice planes are not easy to use is that sharpening and tuning them is difficult. To cut well the iron of any molding plane must follow the sole exactly. The wider the iron and the more shapely the sole, the harder this is. Seasonal swelling and shrinking of the

plane stock made matters worse. As a result, a cornice plane would have been used for the final few passes to refine a shape roughed out with a plow plane, rounds, hollows, and whatever else fit the profile.

I use essentially this technique to make complex moldings of any width, only without the benefit of cornice planes. I rough out the molding with a router, shaper, or table saw and cut it to a final profile with basic molding planes. For very large profiles, which are most difficult to cut with any method, another solution is to make the molding up in parts. This is exactly what an 18th-century joiner would have done.

Drafting a Crown Molding

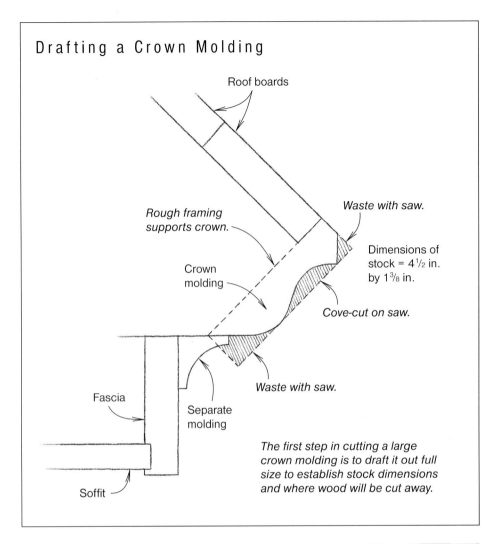

Roof boards

Rough framing supports crown.

Crown molding

Fascia

Separate molding

Soffit

Waste with saw.

Dimensions of stock = 4½ in. by 1⅜ in.

Cove-cut on saw.

Waste with saw.

The first step in cutting a large crown molding is to draft it out full size to establish stock dimensions and where wood will be cut away.

After roughing out the molding profile with a table saw, the author fairs the curves and brings it to final shape with molding planes.

I start by designing the molding to fit the space, its height and horizontal projection, and draft it out full scale. As an example, let's say I am making a 4½-in.-wide cornice molding for the first element in a roof-trim soffit (as shown in the drawing at left). Once I establish the profile, I make a wooden pattern of it out of thin hardwood. This pattern will be used to trace out the profile on each end of the stock, and later the mirror image made from it, to check the molding profile.

One reason stock moldings look so flat is that they are cut into thin stock, obviously to save money. Bolder profiles require thicker stock, usually 6/4 or 8/4, with the added benefit of being a more durable molding. Using my original full-scale profile drawing, I figure the best orientation of the stock to remove the least amount of material. This then establishes the stock width and the bevels on each edge.

The first step in cutting the profile is to mill the stock to dimension and cut the bevels. It's important that the stock be accurately dimensioned, because all future cuts are parallel with one edge or the other. I rough out the profile with a router, shaper, or table saw. An 18th-century craftsman would have plowed grooves to specific depths across the profile, to guide later cuts with hollows and rounds. The same thing can be done with a table saw and dado head to "waste" the entire profile. This works fine for any molding, but it's tedious and takes careful setup. For a 6-ft. length, it might very well be the quickest method. A shaper or router also takes time to set up and often requires special fences or jigs, but these tools have the advantage of roughing out the profile on many feet more completely and consistently.

Combinations of tools sometimes work best. I often start on the table saw cutting the flats that make the transition between curves. Using a large cove cutter and many passes on the shaper might be the next step. A router is best for smaller details. For this particular profile I use a table saw, cutting obliquely across the blade as for cove cutting. This method wastes away the most material quickly. The trick is to cut a small amount at a time—especially for the last pass—and to be very careful to keep all of the pieces oriented in the same way.

With the profile roughed out, I use planes to bring it to final shape. Start with the largest section of the profile, in this case the wide concave curve forming half of the ogee form. Round planes are the tools for this work. Since the radius changes, a few different planes are needed. Rarely will I have a plane that fits the profile exactly, nor is it really important that it does. Start with a round with a slightly tighter radius and plane from end to end, using the machine marks and profile line on the ends of the stock as a guide. Try to plane away the machine marks (or grooves from a dado head or plow plane) consistently, from end to end. For the final pass and the fairest curve, use a round with the widest radius that fits (see the photo on the facing page).

A mirror image of the wooden template comes in handy at this point. By holding it against the profile I can see where I need to keep planing. This is most important where pieces are going to be mitered together, where consistency is necessary. Small variations down the length of a single piece only add to the molding's appeal. The convex part of the profile is faired in the same way, with hollows of various sizes or with a block plane. On other moldings with curves joining into flats, a rabbet plane or side rabbet might be needed. I finish with a shaped scraper and light sanding to fair the molding to a smooth profile.

The completed cornice on the author's shop was made in two pieces and shaped entirely with molding planes.

BEADS, REEDS, AND FLUTES

Beads are among the simplest of molding profiles, yet they are beautiful and incredibly useful. They are one of the few profiles that Shakers, known for their simplicity of design, used throughout their architecture and furniture. Some beading planes cut what is known as a side bead: a bead cut on the edge of a board, flush or slightly below the surface and separated from it by a small square-bottomed groove known as a quirk. A center bead plane cuts a similar bead anywhere in a surface away from an edge. A quirk to either side defines it. Commonly beads are semi-circular, but there are planes that cut

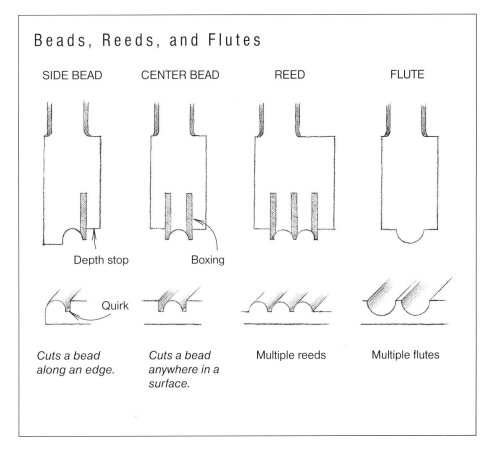

Beads, Reeds, and Flutes

SIDE BEAD   CENTER BEAD   REED   FLUTE

Depth stop   Boxing

Quirk

Cuts a bead along an edge.   *Cuts a bead anywhere in a surface.*   Multiple reeds   Multiple flutes

A complete set of high-quality side bead planes such as this one by E. Preston cuts beads from ⅛ in. to 1 in. wide or larger. The light-colored wood set into the narrow part of the sole that rides in the quirk is tough boxwood capable of holding up to the wear.

pointed gothic beads or elliptical torus beads. The shape of the quirk varies, too, from a sharp groove to a wide bevel.

There is a third type of bead, known as a cockbead, which is proud or above the surface. Although there is a plane (called a "cockbead plane") that will cut the bead and the surface around it, for example, to cockbead the edges of a drawer, it's highly unlikely you'll use such a tool. It's far easier to cut the beads with a side bead plane, separate them from the stock, and let them into a rabbet cut along the edges of the drawer. Any of these beads can also be cut with a scratch stock, as explained later in this chapter.

Reeds are multiple beads. Just as with beads, they can be cut along an edge or away from the edge. Each reed is defined with a distinct quirk. The mirror images of reeds are flutes, rounded grooves cut into the surface. Both reeds and flutes are high-style details found on table legs and ornate columns and pilasters. Beads, on the other hand, show up on the simplest country furniture, as well as on high-style Chippendale designs.

The numbering marked on the heel of a bead plane notes the size of the bead, usually including the quirk. But as with rounds, hollows, and other molding planes, dimensions are not standard. I have a range of side beads, from ⅛ in. to 1¼ in. The smaller beads find the most use, to soften an edge and give it

definition, to create a shadow line, to hide the joint between parts, or even as a convenient way to hide a nail—by driving it into the quirk. I use center bead planes far less often, partly for reasons of taste. What they are useful for is fairing the shape of a side bead or reed for some reason cut against the grain and slightly irregular because of it. Since center bead planes have no fence, they can be used in any direction. To cut a center bead requires clamping or tacking on a temporary fence.

Cutting a bead

A well-tuned side bead plane is easy to use. The plane has a fence and a depth stop cut into the sole, so it's just a matter of keeping pressure on the fence and guiding the plane evenly. I like to finish-plane the guiding edge straight and true first and have the top surface smoothed close to final dimension. It's also easier and neater to bead the stock before cutting any joints. Besides the necessary tuning (see pp. 194-195), three other things help to cut a sharp bead.

One is to increase the depth of the fence by screwing on an extra piece. Most planes have too shallow a fence to begin with, and what's there might be worn. Nothing is more frustrating than having a plane jump out of the cut and plow a new quirk across the finished surface of your work. The simplest of added fences will help steady the plane, and add greatly to your peace of mind.

The second way to improve the cut is to chamfer the edge of the board before cutting the bead. A light bevel is all that is necessary; the side bead plane will cut it away completely as it cuts the bead. As it is, the dynamics of an iron cutting around the two sides of a hemisphere (the bead) is quite challenging. Along these sides the cut is more of a scraping action—nearly as polished a cut, but slower than the cutting action of the rest of the iron. The bevel helps the plane get seated in the cut more easily and removes some of the wood along the side of the bead that's hardest to cut.

The third aid to cutting a sharp bead has to do with technique—a technique useful with any molding plane. I don't always use this method, but it's helpful when I need an accurate profile from end to end. Rather than starting from the front end and planing down the length, start at the finishing end about a plane's length in. Hold the plane against the edge and cut toward the end. Back up a little more and plane to the end again. Keep on backing up and planing forward. The reason this technique helps is that more of the plane is engaged with the cut and guiding the plane. Working in the usual manner, the shortest and likely most worn part of the plane, the toe, is guiding the cut.

As with any woodworking process, when cutting beads it's nice to have an inch or more of extra stock on each end to allow for slight irregularities. This is especially true with any molding profile mitered together or made in parts and meant to appear continuous.

Cutting reeds and flutes

Cutting a reed is quite similar to cutting a side bead. The simplest design is a series of reeds run along an edge. While I suppose it would be possible to cut them with side bead and center bead planes, ingenious reeding planes make it far easier. The sole of the plane has two or more round grooves (flutes) running down the length.

There are different designs, but all have some means to cut one or more reeds by running the plane along an edge or a fence and then moving the plane over. The previously cut reed now guides the plane to cut another parallel reed. The difficulty is working accurately, because slight irregularities in the first reed affect later cuts and can be quite noticeable.

Some fluting planes work on the same principle of the first flute guiding the plane to cut subsequent flutes. Other fluting planes have arms and a fence as a plow does, to guide the plane along an edge as the iron cuts out in the surface. The simplest fluting plane looks like a round plane with depth stops to either side of the iron.

Part of the difficulty of cutting flutes (and sometimes reeds, too) is that they are often stopped shy of the end of the work. To create a place for the plane to cut into, the rounded end of the flute has to be cut out first with a gouge. It's the same idea as a stopped dado or rabbet (see p. 131). I cut the flute either by guiding the plane against a fence or working freehand, following pencil layout lines (see the photo at left). Working freehand is actually quite easy to do. As the plane cuts more deeply it straightens out any wobbles. By tipping the plane right or left I can cut more to one side or the other to center the flute. I continue until the plane stops cutting or until the flute is a consistent width and depth.

To cut a decorative flute, the curved stopped end is first cut out with a gouge and then the flute is cut along pencil layout lines. The fluting plane cuts straighter as it cuts deeper and stops when the depth stop cut into the sole contacts the surface.

New life for two old side bead planes. The bottom one has a new sole, boxing, and fence; the top one new boxing, fence, and a profile shaped with a scratch stock. A frugal woodworker of a century ago would have readily shaped an old plane to fit his needs.

In a well-tuned plane, the iron should exactly parallel the shape of the sole (sighting down from the toe).

TUNING MOLDING PLANES

No molding profile is going to be easy to cut without a well-tuned plane. The tuning is not difficult, but it can be tedious. The sole must be straight and a consistent profile, any boxing (the box-wood strips let into the sole) must be complete, the wedge must be snug enough to hold the iron tightly, and the iron must have the same shape as the sole and be sharp along the entire profile. The results are worth it—a plane set and ready to cut any number of feet of molding and requiring only minimal maintenance from then on.

Little can be done about a plane twisted in some way—except to avoid buying such a tool to begin with. The same is true with a worn sole profile. I have sharpened up the profile with scrapers filed to the shape, but it takes time, and you risk opening the throat if you cut too much. At one time a crafts-man could send back his hardest-working molding planes to get the sole recut or a new iron fitted. Since we can't today, buy planes with good soles if you can.

That said, I have taken a worn plane, cut off the sole completely, added a new one, and shaped it (see the left photo above). It might seem like a drastic measure, but if the body, wedge, and iron are good, recutting the sole is a modest amount of work for a desirable or needed profile. Adding a sole has the further advantage of tightening the throat. Be careful when picking a plane to do this to that it's not a valuable

18th-century tool (the price will be a good indicator) but a common shape produced by the thousands. Shape the new sole with hollows, rounds, other molding profiles, or a scratch stock ground to shape. (For more advice on shaping wooden molding planes, see the feature on Ted Ingraham in Chapter 12.)

Quite often an otherwise good plane will be missing a piece of boxing. Boxing, usually fine-grained Turkish boxwood, was added to planes to reinforce the sole at points of greatest wear. Some boxing with sliding dovetails or tongues is as complicated as any of the most complex joinery and is obviously not easy to repair. Stick to repairing simple strip boxing glued into a groove cut into the sole, the same maintenance a past craftsman would have done. Fine boxing, as along the quirk of bead planes, is strongest set into the groove with the grain oriented at an angle of about 45° to the sole. The wear is then against both end grain and side grain, and the boxing will be less likely to split out. Rosewood or any very hard and tough wood also works well. I cut angled pieces off of a piece of stock as thick as the groove is wide and glue them in place one at a time. For thicker boxing, a simple long-grain strip set into the groove works fine. Shape the new boxing to fit the sole profile with other planes or a scratch stock.

Wedges rarely need much work. Since they are small and often improperly hit against to free the iron, they're likely worn but usable. Make a new wedge if necessary, using the old one as a pattern. The wedge should hold the iron snugly for at least the first third of the iron. Adjust it with a block plane if necessary. It's best if the tip has a smooth bevel to help eject shavings from the throat.

The real work of tuning molding planes is shaping the iron to match the sole and sharpening it. This is far easier with a simple profile like a round than with a complex shape, even though the process is the same. The ideal end result is an iron that, when viewed down the plane from the toe, exactly parallels the sole's shape (see the photo at right on the facing page). If you have bought wisely, this might be as easy as honing the back and maybe the edge slightly.

I use three methods to shape the iron. For irons that are only slightly off, trial and error honing off the high spots works. For irons further out of adjustment, I wedge the iron in place with the lowest point just flush with the sole. Then, with well-oiled slipstones and using the sole as a guide, I hone off all the high spots until the iron's profile exactly matches the sole's. Naturally the iron is now very dull. Working on a grinder with a narrow stone (often using the corners of the stone), I grind the

bevel freehand as much as I can and finish it with slipstones. As with any iron, the back should be polished. The third method works best for really misshapen irons or where I've recut a new sole. In this case I take the temper out of the iron, file it to shape (using the sole as a guide or a line scribed onto the back of the iron), and then reharden and temper it. This takes some skill, a propane torch, and a pail of water.

The tricky part about sharpening the iron once it's shaped is honing along a profiled bevel. Various shaped slipstones make the job easier (see the photo below). When I need to, I custom-shape one against a diamond stone. Pay special attention to any parts of the iron's profile that cut even slightly horizontal, for example, along the two sides of a bead. As I explained previously, the dynamics of these cuts are partly scraping, partly cutting. For a smooth finish, keep these edges sharp and beveled well back.

BUYING MOLDING PLANES

Tuning will be a lot easier if you carefully pick the planes you buy; it's really no different than buying other old tools. Luckily many thousands of molding planes survive. There are enough around that some collectors specialize in specific makers, or planes from a certain area, or even certain types of molding planes such as cornice planes. Eighteenth-century planes with clear maker's marks command the most money, sometimes as much as many thousands of dollars for an individual plane. Leave these to the collectors and historians. For a fraction of what one of these planes costs, you can buy all of the perfectly usable molding planes you'll ever need.

As with other planes, there is a big difference in the quality of the tools available. Some planes are too worn or

Use shaped slip-stones to hone the profile of a molding-plane iron. To work into difficult shapes, reshape a slipstone against a diamond stone (shown at far right).

worm-eaten to use, while others look as fresh as the day they were made. Profiles seldom used or that passed out of fashion can look brand new. The most useful profiles, the ones you want, were made by the thousands and are inexpensive. Skip any by fancy makers (unless you're a collector); you'll pay extra just for the name, and the plane won't be any better than one made by one of the larger manufactures such as Auburn, Ohio, or Sandusky Tool Company. Fine English planes can often be bought quite reasonably from dealers more interested in American makers.

American planes with skewed irons are not common (by contrast, English molders with skewed irons are), probably because of their higher cost new—as much as a third more. They are no harder to tune and they work better, so I always look for them. Check that the body and sole are true, not kinked,

twisted, or badly worn in any way. Only a plane with an unusual profile would be worth trying to straighten, and even then with no guarantee of success. I always sight down the sole looking for irregularities. Check for missing boxing. Some boxing can be easily replaced, some with a lot more difficulty.

Ideally what you are looking for is a plane that a craftsman tuned, used, and stored away idle for all the years since. The iron will be shaped to the sole, maybe even sharp, too. Such a plane tunes quickly and is worth the little more it might cost. Take any plane apart and look at the condition of the iron, bed, and wedge. A little surface rust on the iron is to be expected, just avoid one so rusty it's pitted. An iron can be hard to replace, but a broken or missing wedge isn't.

Chapter 13 delves further into the subject of buying old planes, where to find them, cleaning them to use, and

where a weakness to "buy just one more" for use or pleasure can lead. Collect a sampling of hollows, rounds, and side beads first, and then add other profiles as you find or need them. I store many of mine in a deep drawer, just as they would be in the bottom of a carpenter's chest (see the photo at right on p. 255). Often-used profiles sit on a shelf in my tool cabinet where I can see the shape of each. I don't think it's important to back the wedge off slightly before storing a plane away. Don't drive the wedge too snugly and the plane will be ready to go whenever you need it.

Scratch Stocks

Scratch stocks are an alternative to molding planes and are as versatile and useful molding tools as you could ask for. A scratch stock is a scraper, a piece of steel filed and honed to some profile and

A Stanley #66 Universal beader is a good general-purpose holder for scratch tools. With different-shaped cutters and fences it can cut a wide variety of molding profiles, such as the triple reed shown here.

A #69 hand beader, shown here cutting double reeds, is one of the rarest Stanley tools.

held in a simple wooden guide. These tools have two advantages over molding planes: They are quick to make to suit a specific need, and because they are scrapers, they work figured or hard woods well. Their only disadvantages are that they cut slowly and have a very short sole to guide the cut.

Stanley made two versions of scratch tools, the #66 Universal beader and the #69 single-handed beader—a very rare tool today. The #66 came with eight cutters and two fences, for straight or curved work; the #69 had seven cutters. A new set of cutters can be bought for either. A Windsor beader is another beading or reeding tool.

The advantage of any of these tools is the ease with which a new cutter can be shaped, clamped in place, and put to use. Yet, just as useful is a homemade version. I make the cutters out of pieces of old heavy hacksaw blades or any good steel

about as thick as a handsaw with the same springy temper. The guide is nothing more than an L-shaped or rectangular scrap of hardwood, with a slot sawn in it. The cutter is firmly held by a couple of small bolts that clamp it in the slot, or if it is small enough, by friction alone. The holder is as flexible as the work required. I have made curved ones to bead around a round window and straight ones for cutting along a table edge. If you can imagine the way the cutter should be held against the work, making the holder is easy.

Shaping and sharpening the cutter is not difficult either. If the steel is not too hard, I file it to shape and hone it with slipstones. It's not easy on the file, but it is quick. For harder cutters, I have to grind the profile with a narrow-faced grindstone (shaped with a diamond dresser, if necessary), and then hone it to final shape. For either method, both

faces of the cutter should be stoned to a polish. Sharpen it like a cabinet scraper with a perfectly square edge and no burr.

To use a scratch stock, I tip it in the direction of the cut and use the fence to guide the tool along. Push or pull. It should cut cleanly, curling up fine shavings. I prefer my wooden scratch stocks over the #66 beader because I can rock the cutter to the optimum cutting angle and I like the longer fence. Working the profile on the ends of parts is a little more difficult than with a plane, so leave some extra stock here. I keep cutting until the profile is complete, or until the tool stops cutting because the built-in depth stop in the holder hits on the surface. No matter how careful you are, the profile will need a small amount of fairing with a piece of sandpaper. When you consider what these tools are capable of doing, it's a small price to pay.

Two types of Windsor beaders. The one at rear has a cutter wheel with different cutter profiles filed into the circumference; the one in the front takes individual cutters. Both have adjustable fences.

Homemade scratch stocks for cutting details such as a small bead can be as simple as a shaped piece of hacksaw driven into a saw kerf in a wooden block. An old marking gauge also works well.

An early panel-raising plane with single iron, wedged nicker, and open tote. The iron is heavily skewed to give the best finish on end-grain bevels.

Panel Raisers

With shapers and routers and a wide variety of panel-raising bits, there are few of us today who still use another type of shaping plane, a panel raiser. It's a shame really, because these are beautiful tools and a pleasure to use. An 18th-century joiner would have used one for cutting raised panels for everything from beautifully proportioned wainscoting to doors and the deep jambs of splayed windows.

A raised or fielded panel is a harmony of beauty and function. By cutting a beveled edge all the way around the panel, the center section is left prominent and fielded or raised. By beveling the edges, the panel fits neatly into grooves run on the stiles and rails. For strength, most of the panel is still full thickness. Most important, the panel can shrink or swell with the seasons, yet it's firmly held and it gives rigidity to the overall structure of stiles and rails. Used for doors and paneling, raised panels have a function and beauty that is unsurpassed.

Panel-raising planes look like jack planes with a heavily skewed iron (to work the end-grain edges of the panel more smoothly), a tote, an integral fence and depth stop cut into the sole, and usually a single nicker. English planes are shorter and more massive, with a sliding fence attached to the sole (see the bottom photo at left). This feature allows them to cut bevels of various widths, whereas American planes cut a specific width. Both planes are a variation of the rabbet plane, in that the iron extends to an edge of the sole to cut the shoulder of the panel.

Since panel raisers cut relative to the face of the board, the same plane can be used to field panels on boards of

The stocky English panel-raising plane In the background has a rabbet mouth and a sliding fence to allow for cutting bevels of different widths. The American plane in the foreground looks no different from a jack plane with a skewed iron.

different thicknesses. Those with a pronounced wedge-shaped body cross section cut without spring, others cut perpendicular to the bevel. An interesting feature of both is that they don't cut a square shoulder on the bevel, but a greater angle. Although a slight fillet or angle here is attractive, the main reason is that the same plane can field panels in thin or thick stock and not undercut the shoulder, which would look awkward. The soles on some of these planes are also convex or shaped so that the bevel is cut a more uniform thickness where it slides into the groove. Both features show the ingenuity of the 18th-century cabinetmaker trying to make his tools and efforts more efficient.

Panel-raising planes are tuned like any bench plane, with the addition of a nicker to sharpen. The leading edge of the iron that cuts the shoulder has to be beveled back and sharpened, and set slightly proud of the side, just like a skewed rabbet plane (see p. 127). I relieve this corner of the iron ever so slightly.

To raise a panel, first dimension the stock and smooth-plane the surface. Then with a marking gauge set to the groove width and using the back as a reference surface, scribe around all four edges. This line defines a depth to cut the bevels to. Cut the end-grain bevels first, so that any tearout can be planed out when working the long-grain bevels. Tap the nicker down so that it just scores the fibers, hold the plane tight to the guiding edge, and plane along. Take the last few passes with a very light cut for the smoothest finish. Cut the long-grain bevels the same way, without the nicker. I finish by using a block plane at the corners to fine-tune a sharp miter between bevels.

Chamfer Planes

Chamfers can be a detail hardly noticed or an obvious design feature. Certainly a wide stopped chamfer with decorative lamb's-tongue transitions doesn't go unseen, nor does one inlaid or fluted. But a fine chamfer run on the edge of a table apron blends in with the play of light, shadows, and wood grain. Run your hand or knee against the same edge without a chamfer, and it will be sharp and uncomfortable. Just the slightest chamfer softens and protects the edge.

The simplest chamfer is a small bevel cut into the edge, usually at 45°. When it runs from end to end, a bench plane can cut it as well as any tool. While not strictly a chamfer, a slightly rounded arris cut with a roundover plane is beautiful and just as functional. The most elaborate chamfers are wide, sometimes even with details such as flutes or reeds cut into the surface. Any chamfers

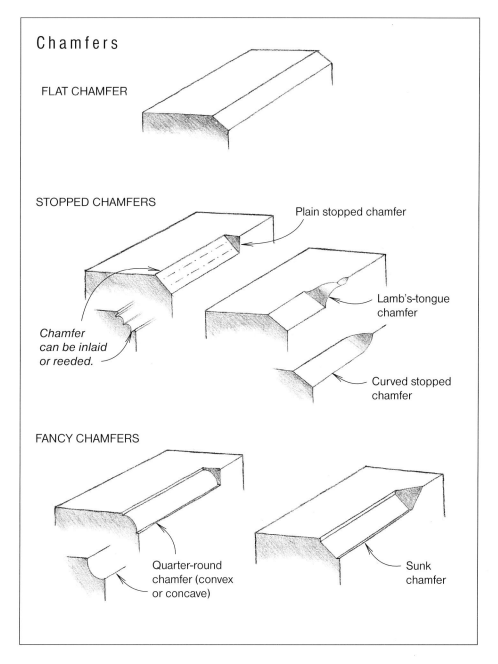

Chamfers

FLAT CHAMFER

STOPPED CHAMFERS

Plain stopped chamfer

Chamfer can be inlaid or reeded.

Lamb's-tongue chamfer

Curved stopped chamfer

FANCY CHAMFERS

Quarter-round chamfer (convex or concave)

Sunk chamfer

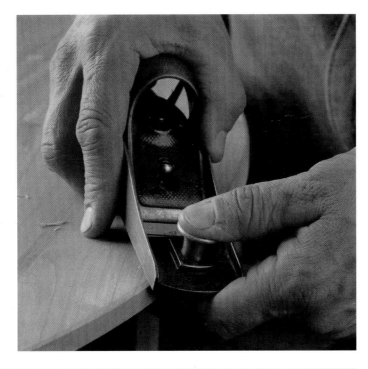

The author's hand becomes a jig to support and orient the plane when cutting a consistent chamfer along a table edge.

can be stopped or ended, with any number of decorative transitions at the ends. A chisel and block plane will cut any of these chamfers, but a chamfer plane makes accurate work easier.

I cut chamfers on many edges of my furniture, even if they are out of view—the inside edge of a rail that a hand will touch when lifting the piece, every edge of a drawer or door. Chamfers blunt the edge, for comfort and to prevent chipping, and to show wear less. I chamfer the edges of panels or tenons to ease fitting the parts together.

The simplest chamfer, a small bevel, requires nothing more than a sharp plane and careful control. If I am relieving the edge of a drawer side, I hold a block plane at a skew at about 45° to the edge and plane from end to end. I use a roundover plane in the same situation. To cut the same chamfer on the edge of a table or around a frame is another story. For this I want a very consistent bevel. I use my hands as a jig to orient the plane to the edge (as shown in the top photo at left), or I use a chamfer plane or chamfer shave.

All chamfer planes have the same unusual feature of a sole in the shape of a deep right-angled "V" to guide the plane along a square edge. The iron is adjustable in different ways to cut a wide or narrow chamfer. In the Stanley #72, the iron is held in a separate front that's movable up or down to adjust the width of the chamfer. In English planes, the whole center section of the plane with iron, wedge, and throat moves up or down. In the case of Japanese chamfer planes and the Stanley #65 chamfer spokeshave, the iron doesn't move, but the V-sole opens or closes to cut chamfers of various widths. The Japanese tool has one further refinement:

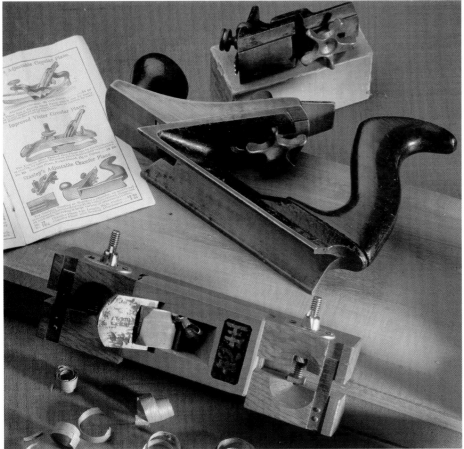

Chamfer planes have a sole in the shape of a deep right-angled "V" to guide the plane along a square edge. In the background is a Stanley #72, behind it a separate front piece that holds scratch cutters for detailing wide chamfers. The Japanese chamfer plane in the foreground has an adjustable-width sole and a sliding carriage for the iron.

The iron is held in a "carriage" that slides across the plane to allow using the full width of the iron before resharpening.

Any of these chamfer planes work best for cutting long consistent chamfers, for example, on the posts of a pencil-post bed. Even if you have never seen or made such a form, imagine cutting four equal chamfers on a tapering square. It's possible with a jack plane—you'll still need to use one to fair the chamfers end to end—but easier with a chamfer plane. Layout is easier, because only the ends need to be marked, and the chamfers are accurately beveled at 45° across the corner.

For the sake of simplicity, let's assume that the chamfers do not stop at the bed rail as they usually would, and save the explanation of stopped chamfers for a moment. I first cut the bulk of the waste with a coarsely set jack plane. Then, with the chamfer plane set to the width of the chamfer at the top of the post, I true up all four chamfers (see the bottom photo at right). If the chamfers weren't tapered, I could complete them with this setting of the plane. Since they are, I reset the plane and cut the last foot of the bigger end to final depth. For long posts I work another section in the middle, and for that matter could keep working sections up the post. It's quicker to complete a few sections and fair the whole chamfer with a long bench plane, using the completed chamfers as a guide.

A stopped chamfer is a little fussier. I lay out the stop and chisel the waste close to the final depth for at least a few inches. This creates a place for the toe of the plane. For the #72 there's a bullnose front just for working tight into the stop. Since I don't have this part (it's very scarce), I use a chisel plane or even a wide chisel. But before cutting the chamfer to

In the stop chamfer plane by Joseph Lee (1883) at left, half the sole slides open or closes to adjust the width of the chamfer. In the E. Preston chamfer plane at right, the whole center section of sole, iron, wedge, and throat moves to cut wide or narrow chamfers.

Shaping wide chamfers on a bed post is relatively easy with a Stanley #72 chamfer plane. The author roughs them out with a bench plane, sets the depth of the #72, and planes each chamfer.

final dimension, I shape the transition at the stop—a lamb's-tongue or a curved stopped chamfer—so that if I happen to cut into the chamfer I can clean it off with a final plane pass. One of the advantages of the chamfering spokeshave is that it's easy to cut a sweeping end to the chamfer, since the sole is short and curved. This is a nice detail for the underside of large floor-joist timbers exposed in the ceiling below.

There is one more nice feature about the #72 chamfer plane; it has a separate front that fits scratch cutters (see the bottom photo on p. 200). This opens up a lot of design possibilities, such as reeds, flutes, or inlay lines cut into the chamfer bevel. The plane is heavy, stable, and far easier to use in this situation than a wooden scratch stock.

Combination Planes

If I were to offer you one plane that could do all the work of the various shaping planes, and cut rabbets, dadoes, and grooves too, wouldn't you be interested? No longer would you have to lug a chest full of wooden molding planes to the job (not that you do now), but a single modest wooden box containing a plane and an array of interchangeable irons. This was one of the appeals of the combination plane, a single plane combining the work of many. In its highest evolution, the Stanley #55 was said to be able to do the work of 93 different planes!

The idea wasn't exactly new. The earliest combination planes, from sometime back in the 16th century, were wooden plows with interchangeable irons for plowing grooves and cutting rabbets. Right through the mid-

19th century some clever minds were still trying to improve the wooden plow, while others were taken by the idea of a cast-metal plane to replace it. It was no different than efforts to develop practical and economical cast-iron bench planes. In 1844, Elihu Dutcher of Pownal, Vermont, came up with the first cast-iron plow, which naturally resembled its wooden relative. Others followed over the next 50 or so years, each with their own improvements and capable of more and more of the work of other planes—plows, fillisters, beading, and matching planes.

"Among the many advantages afforded by making these tools of metal instead of wood are the following: They are much less cumbersome, are more durable, the parts are much more readily and perfectly adjusted, they work better and easier, because they never choke or clog with shavings, and they can be sold for less than one-half the cost of wooden planes of the same variety." Despite this sales pitch in one patent application, some of the early combination planes were cumbersome. Fale's patent plane of 1885 required two soles for every cutter profile, plus all the cutters and main

With a combination plane, one tool could do the work of many. To work as a hollow, round, or nosing tool (for the front edges of stairs and window sills), the Stanley #45 needed special bottoms, which were sold separately.

With an adjustable fence, a Stanley #45 combination plane easily cuts a center bead (or, with multiple passes, reeds). The wooden center bead plane in the background requires setting a guiding fence for each bead or reed.

stock. Even though it weighed almost 20 lb., it was still advertised as requiring "but small space in [a] carpenter's chest." What was appealing was a metal tool not prone to the swelling, shrinking, or warping of wooden molding planes, and taking one plane on the job not dozens.

As would be expected, Stanley developed a number of combination planes. The two most famous are the #45, introduced in 1884 (see the photo above), and the even more sophisticated #55, introduced in 1897 (see the photo on p. 184). Although by no means

simple, the appeal of the #45 is its simplicity and utility compared with the #55. Many are still in use in shops around the world. The #55 is appealing for what it was, for what it could do, more than for what it actually did. It's an amazing tool, easily one of the highest achievements of a plane maker's cleverness, but it's not easy to use. Others must have agreed; few #55s show much wear—it's common to find a box of cutters never touched to a stone. Still, plenty were sold, just like fancy plows and other status tools.

Combination planes appealed to our predecessors in the same way that Shopsmiths do to some of us today. It's the same idea, a basic tool with a whole range of interchangeable cutters and functions. But like any tool that tries to do everything, it ends up doing few things really well. Take, for example, setting up a #45 to cut a side bead. In the few minutes it takes to adjust everything—the fence, the depth of the cutter, the distance between the main stock and sliding section, the alignment of

Three wooden versions of a very useful shaping tool. At top, a shapely beech spokeshave, the square tangs of the iron simply drilled into the body to hold it; middle, a Stanley #85 boxwood razor-edge spokeshave; and, bottom, an owner-made simple spoke-shave showing typical wear ahead of the mouth.

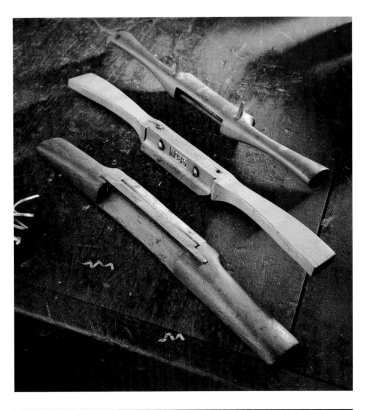

A strongly curved shave, called a travisher by some, is one of the tools used for shaping the concave solid-plank seat of a chair such as a Windsor.

everything, and a trial pass to check the settings—I could run 10 ft. of the same bead with a wooden plane. Moreover, because I work more often with hard-woods than straight-grained pine, the bead produced by a molding plane is more polished and the edges of the quirk are smoother. The entire sole of the wooden plane conforms to the shape of

the bead and guides the cut, while the modest throat helps to cut cleanly. Neither the #45 nor #55 has a throat; only two narrow runners guide the cut.

There are some things the #45 and #55 can do well, such as cutting center beads, flutes, and reeds easily (see the photo on p. 203). Since the iron doesn't have to conform to any sole profile (as

in a molding plane), sharpening it is easier. And for when a special shape is needed, it's simple enough to grind an iron and go right to work. Still, even if we owned one, I doubt many of us would use a combination plane much, considering all of the alternatives.

Spokeshaves

As the name suggests, spokeshaves were once used to shape the spokes of wheels. Whether some still are or not, furniture makers, carpenters, and others have gladly adopted these useful shaping tools. I think of spokeshaves as small planes held by shapely handles in line with the edge of the iron. The handles afford a lot of control of the tool, rocking it to conform to the shape of a curve and regulating the cutting depth.

As would be expected with a tool that found use in many trades, there is wide variety among the styles of spokeshaves, their sizes, and the shapes of the handles and soles. The simplest ones are wood, usually beech, or for better ones boxwood or a hard tropical wood (see the top photo at left). The iron is thin and knife-shaped, similar to a miniature drawknife, from 1½ in. to 5 in. long. The ends of the iron are forged into square tangs and bent at right angles to the cutting edge. The tangs are held in place by friction in holes drilled through the body, and the iron is adjusted by tapping it or the tangs—a simple but workable arrange-ment. Better wooden versions have threaded tangs and thumbscrews for adjustment, and bone or brass wear plates let into the sole ahead of the throat. Most wooden handles are straight and gracefully shaped. Some, called travishers, are almost semicircular, to work the hollowed plank seats of chairs (see the bottom photo at left).

Cast iron opened up a whole range of new designs. Stanley made at least 20 different spokeshaves; other toolmakers made many more. Cast-iron spokeshaves look more like planes, with short flat irons and a cap iron of sorts that clamps the iron against the bed much like one on a block plane. Handles range from straight to gracefully up-curved. The greatest variation is in the shape of the soles: straight, concave, convex, and rounded. Each style works a particular-shaped curve most easily.

Spokeshaves can be found everywhere at flea markets and sales. They're cheap, because so many lack maker's marks that they don't seem to be that collectible. The most common shape has a short flat sole, but there are always other shapes in any miscellaneous box lot of tools. Look for a variety of shapes, even if you don't happen to shape a lot of curves; you'll find a use for them. And even if a shave is a little rusty, tuning it is quick.

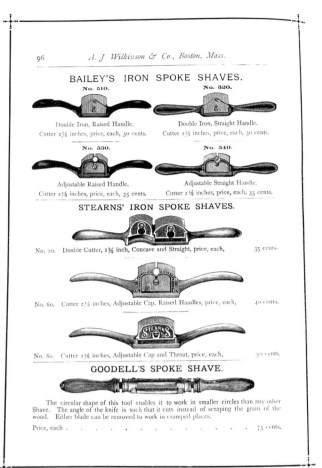

Cast iron allowed many new spoke-shave designs, with gracefully shaped handles and long-wearing soles.

These three spokeshaves are typical of the designs by English maker E. Preston, with ornate castings and comfortable and decorative handles, and made to tight manufacturing tolerances.

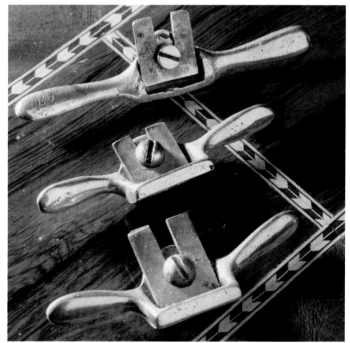

Tiny patternmaker's or modelmaker's spokeshaves cast in brass are useful for fine work. With three different sole shapes—flat, concave, and convex—this set can cut a variety of shapes.

Many curves of different radius can be cut with these three spokeshaves: a Stanley #54 (at work), a cast-iron Millers Falls #1 (left foreground), and a rosewood and brass shave (right foreground). The #54 has the handy feature of an adjustable throat that also changes the iron's cutting depth.

There are only three things to be concerned with in tuning a spokeshave: the iron, the cap iron, and the sole. Sharpen the iron as for a plane, at a bevel of about 25° or slightly less, and polish the back. It can be a little challenging grinding and honing such a small iron. One trick is to make a holder by cutting a saw kerf in the end of a hardwood block; then slip the iron into it, and either clamp or wedge it in place. A wooden clamp alone works well, too. Irons curved across their width for concave or convex shaves (for shaping round handles, for instance) are most difficult to sharpen. I sharpen them with slip-stones as I would a molding-plane iron. Hone the bottom of the cap iron and polish and wax its top surface. As for the sole, lap it on a benchstone or lapping table, or shape it with a fine file. Except for flat-soled spokeshaves, it's less important than with a plane that the sole be perfect. The sole still guides the cut, but so does the way you hold and orient the tool to the work.

Setting the depth of the iron can be tricky. English makers Record and Preston made designs with adjustable irons, through one or two screws behind the iron and engaged with it. Unfortunately, I've never cared for the feel of my adjustable Record shave, so I've had to set my nonadjustable ones by trial and error. I start with the iron barely proud of the sole, tighten the cap screw just snug, and then, with the handle of a chisel, lightly tap the iron to a depth that cuts well. Trying any shave on a scrap is the best way to see how it cuts, but especially ones with shaped soles that are hard to set by feel alone. For spokeshaves tuned for finish cuts, I set the iron parallel with the sole. For rough-cutting shaves, I keep one corner lower so as to have a variety of cutting depths.

I have about eight spokeshaves. Each works well for different shapes. My favorite is a Stanley #54 (shown in the photo at left), with the sole ahead of the iron adjustable by a thumbscrew, to tighten the throat and regulate the depth of cut. If you were to have only one spokeshave, this would be a good choice. Then I have a range of straight, rounded, and concave-soled shaves. All of these are useful for curves of not too tight a radius. If the curve is too tight, the sole can't contact the wood and the spokeshave doesn't cut. For tight curves, say for a decoratively scalloped apron, I have two shaves almost round in cross section, one by Millers Falls and the other by Cincinnati Tool. Look for either of these. The irons are so round that both are a little tricky to sharpen, and they are not the easiest to use, but they will cut a tight radius that no other shave will.

Shaping curved parts can be challenging, because the grain is change-able. Use the spokeshave as you would a plane, as much with the grain as you can and at a slight skew if it feels comfortable and works. Since most of my shaves have a modest throat, a skew usually helps get a smoother finish. Where skewing distorts the cut, I slide the tool to the

Most wooden compass planes have convex soles, though they are not a consistent radius down their length. The plane in the background is one of a set of three ebony compass planes, all with different sole curvatures. The plane in the foreground has an adjustable toe piece for changing the effective radius of the sole.

right or left as I cut, which gives the same sort of slicing cut as skewing. I usually start with a light cut to get a feel for the way the wood responds to the tool. Two things control the cut: the depth of the iron and the way you orient the tool. Since the sole is so short, it's easy to rock the tool forward to cut a little more deeply or backward to lighten the cut. Using a spokeshave isn't difficult, but when you think about rocking the tool while also following a curve, you can see it might take a little time to develop a feel for it.

Compass Planes

Whereas spokeshaves cut a wide variety of shapes, compass planes have their usefulness shaping curved work. Wooden compass planes look like coffin-shaped smoothing planes with a sweeping convex sole (not a consistent arc, though), and they work like bench planes. Some have the clever addition of an adjustable toe piece that has the effect of changing the radius of the sole to cut a wider range of curves. Metal versions show the same ingenuity of a whole range of plane

designs only possible out of this material. The two types Stanley made, the #113 and #20, can cut both convex and concave surfaces. The sole is a band of flexible steel, pushed or pulled into a radius through a large screw (see the photos on p. 208). All of the cutting parts and frog are similar to ones in a bench plane.

Partly because I have found them frustrating to use and partly out of the nature of my designs, I don't use a compass plane much. A wheelwright

Two versions of Stanley's #113 compass plane. By turning the large knob, the flexible steel sole is pushed or pulled into a convex or concave circular radius.

The Stanley #20 works well for fairing the outside curve of a tabletop as long as it's the arc of a circle. Varying curves are better shaped with spokeshaves.

shaping the felloes making up a wheel or a carpenter making curved head windows and doors would find one very useful. Both of these uses point out their main advantages over a spokeshave: They can take heavy cuts and cut to a consistent radius. Since the most consistent radius is an arc of a circle, this is what the Stanley compass planes cut best. Wooden compass planes can fair a concave elliptical curve, but they're frustrating to use, too.

Both planes clog far more quickly than I would like. Part of the reason is the dynamics of cutting a curve. Take the case of cutting a convex shape with the #20, perhaps the edge of a demilune tabletop (see the photo at right above).

Until the sole solidly guides the cut, some of the time the plane is going to be supported at the mouth, taking too big a bite and clogging. As the curve is faired, more of the sole supports the cut and the plane cuts more consistently. The trick is to creep up on the final curve by starting with a tighter sole radius. Keep the cut light and slowly adjust the plane to widen the curvature to the final arc. Fairing a concave shape is similarly tricky. Either technique works best if the curve is the arc of a circle. Compounding the problem with a wooden compass plane is that, in order to cut a tighter radius, the iron must be driven further out, leading to more tearout.

If compass planes can be some of the more frustrating tools to use (even

though they're still the most efficient and accurate tools for some work), most shaping planes are no more difficult to master than bench planes. Each has its specific uses, a shape or detail it cuts best. Depending upon the work you do, you might get by with very few shaping planes. For example, buying only a half-dozen molding planes, along with a rabbet plane you likely already own, you can make a surprising variety of moldings or details that will add immeasurable interest to your woodworking. Even with the simplest of the shaping planes—scratch stocks and spokeshaves—and lots of ingenuity and patience besides, you'll be amazed at the incredible variety of shapes and details you can cut.

I don't remember where I learned the trick, but planes are useful shaping tools on the lathe. Since I'm not as good with a skew chisel as I'd like to be, I use a plane to cut gentle curves, straights, or tapers. I still rough out the shape with a gouge and cut the details with a skew, but keep a block plane handy for any of the longer cuts.

Actually planes have been used on the lathe for some time. About a hundred years ago, when nearly everything was packed in barrels, production shops smoothed the outsides of barrels on huge lathes with planes. To fit the barrel the planes had concave soles and, on some, wide steel rollers at the toe and heel. A movable rod above the lathe hooked into a stout ring at the toe of the plane to help hold it against the rotating barrel (see the engraving below).

My lathe technique is not too different. The cut is similar to one with a skew, but the mouth and toe of the plane give me a much more controlled cut, just as they do when planing a flat surface. Set the iron for a light cut, angle it at about a 45° skew, and plane down the spindle. Keep the cut toward the center of the iron, so as to avoid catching the corner, or relieve the corner of the iron. For shallow curves, rotate the plane to follow the shape as you would planing it off the lathe. Use a greater skew with more of the sole against the wood for the most accurate straight cuts. It's amazing how the curls fly.

Planes were used on a barrel lathe to smooth the outside of barrels. The plane (visible at the right end of the lathe) is attached to the lathe by a movable rod. (Courtesy Roger Smith, *Patented Transitional and Metallic Planes in America, Vol. II.*)

Barrel and Keg Planes

No. 16¾

Combined Barrel Lathe and Sander

11
SPECIALTY PLANES

Here Wratten, cooper, lives and makes / Ox bows, trug-baskets and hay-rakes.

Sells shovels, both for flour and corn, / And shauls, and makes a good box-churn,

Ladles, dishes, spoons and skimmers, / Trenchers, too, for use at dinners.

I make and mend both tub and cask / And hoop 'em strong to make them last...

—Early-19th-century cooper's sign from Hailsham, England

In an age when everything was made by hand, the cooper, carpenter, chairmaker, coachmaker, and others fulfilled all of the needs of the farm, village, and town. With native materials and ancient skills passed from generation to generation, they made objects of beauty and utility. As the sign quoted above amusingly relates, the work was of infinite variety, from cradles to coffins, milk pails to barrels. Craftsmanship was valued; craftsmen were respected members of society.

Craftsmen combine a unique understanding of their materials, methods, and tools. Some of this is taught, some learned, and some just intuitively known from years of thoughtful observation. Chairmakers know that pine makes a stable and easily carved seat; ash, finely shaped and strong spindles; oak, tightly bent bow backs; and maple or birch, strong legs easily shaped on a lathe. They also know what tools to use for every step in making a chair, and the easiest and fastest way to go about it. Their craftsmanship is the purest melding of form, function, materials, and technique. What tools chairmakers need they make, or they refine traditional tools.

Where once many of these tools were simply made of wood and reinforced with iron at points of wear and stress, industrialization spawned a huge array of long-wearing cast-iron designs. Some were old patterns recast in iron, others were new tools that manufacturers like Stanley were only too happy to design, make, and sell. Along with industrialization came the mechanization of most trades, changing them forever. Certainly some trades prospered (patternmaking for one), but for the most part as machines did more of the work, there was less demand for traditional tools and the craftsmen skilled in using them.

Coopering is one of many trades that adapted tools to its special needs, in this case to shape and smooth the sides of curving barrels. The stoup planes at the back of the table smooth the inside; the scraper shave in the foreground, known as a "buzz," shapes the outside.

This chapter is about some of these specialty or unusual planes, often used by a single trade for a specific purpose. Some are unusual because of the way they work, such as cutting useful shavings rather than a surface as most planes do. Some push the limits of what a plane is. Although some of the trades that used them are nearly obsolete, all of these planes once were, and many still are, the best tools for certain work.

Cooper's Planes

Coopering is an ancient trade, well known to the Romans and mentioned in the Bible. Before cardboard and plastic, barrels, firkins, and hogsheads were the universal containers. Beer, whale oil, dry goods, fruits or nails, they were all shipped in barrels easily rolled along wharves or into wagons. The village cooper used the same methods and tools to make sap buckets, milk pails, churns, water tubs, and more. Every village needed a cooper. Although the trade is much diminished today, coopers are still at work fashioning tubs and barrels for aging wine, whiskey, vinegar, and hot tubbers.

To make a barrel takes a keen sense of measuring by eye and knowing your materials—how they will respond to the shaping and steaming needed to bend them into the characteristic bulging shape. Each barrel is made to hold a specific measure, liquid or dry, which requires a certain number of staves of a length, taper, and bevel to fit together tightly. Making and fitting the hoops is a challenge, too. Hardest to make are watertight barrels, strongly bulging and made of stout staves to withstand the pressure of fermenting liquids and the rigors of shipping. Less demanding are coopered barrels for dry goods, or the so-called "white coopering" of pails and

Ron Raiselis, the cooper at Strawbery Banke Museum in Portsmouth, New Hampshire, shapes white-oak barrel staves on a long and heavy cast-iron jointer plane. This is the way coopers have always done it, trusting their hand and eye to get the taper and bevel right.

churns. While some of the necessary tools are familiar to the carpenter or furniture maker—a jointer plane or drawknife, for example—most fit the needs of no other trade.

"Wet" coopers usually work with green wood, preferably straight-grained and split-out white oak. It bends well, is tough, and resists rot. The cooper shapes the staves with a drawknife and ax and puts them aside to dry to reduce any shrinkage that could open up the joints later. By eye, he cuts the tapers and bevels on each stave, pushing them over a long

jointer plane used upside down and with the toe end raised on a small stand (see the photo above). Although the plane looks and works like a carpenter's jointer, its great length (up to 6 ft. and more) and heft make it easier to bring the work to the tool. The taper of each stave defines the eventual shape of the barrel; the greater the taper toward the center, the more pronounced the bulge and the stronger the finished barrel.

The next step is to draw the staves together at one end with temporary hoops and place the barrel atop a blazing

An early German etching of a traditional cooper at work shaping staves.

With a topping plane, which is nothing more than a curved jack plane, the cooper levels the tops of the staves to create a smooth surface to guide the next tools (howel and croze).

The howel cuts a shallow hollow around the inside edge top and bottom; it is followed by the croze (shown in the foreground), which cuts a narrow groove to fit the beveled barrel head. Both tools have large round fences that ride on top of the leveled staves.

kindling fire built in a metal basket called a cresset. The heat and moisture in the wood (plus an extra swabbing of the inside of the barrel) soften and steam the staves. The cooper drives on more temporary wooden hoops to bring the staves together in the shape of the completed barrel. With a drawknife or adz he then bevels a "chime" or chamfer around the inside edges at both ends. The chime helps the barrel take the abuse of shipping without worry of breaking away the short grain where the head joins into a groove cut just below the chime. The cooper then levels the top and bottom of the barrel with a plane resembling a curved jack called a topping plane (see the top photo at right).

Next follow two tools that are unique to coopers, a howel and a croze. The howel is really no different from a compass-soled plane attached to a large curved fence that rides along the top of the staves (see the photo above). The howel cuts a smooth shallow hollow, to give a level place to cut into with the next tool—the croze that cuts a narrow groove for the barrel head. The croze has a similar wide fence that rides on the ends of the staves, but with either a saw-tooth type cutter or two nickers and a single tooth like a router plane. The head that fits into this groove is made up of two or three boards doweled together and smoothed with a large shave called a swift. The cooper cuts the edges to a fine bevel to fit snugly into the groove cut by the croze.

Before setting the barrel head, the cooper smooths the inside surface of some barrels with a stoup plane and an inside shave (or inshave). A stoup plane has a convex sole in both directions to work within the doubly curved staves

(see the photo on p. 210). The cooper smooths the outside with a downright, another large-handled shave, and a similar scraping tool called a buzz. The final step is to fit the head and drive on wooden or steel hoops.

Making the barrel has taken a number of planes similar but different from those of other trades, each perfectly adapted to a cooper's work shaping curved surfaces. And if he has done his work well, the barrel will hold the exact amount of liquid and not leak.

Shaves are used to smooth different parts of the barrel. From the top, a large shave called a swift, with a flat sole for flattening the head; an inshave, used with a stoup plane for smoothing inner surfaces; and a large shave for cutting the bevel on the head.

Violinmaker's Planes

Although it's much more subtle, many stringed instruments have the same bulging shape as a barrel. Violins, cellos, violas, and basses have it—and for the same reasons that a barrel does. The gently curved top and back give the instrument strength with lightness. The parts can be very thin (as thin as a millimeter at the edges of the back in a violin), yet require little internal bracing and still be strong enough to hold up to centuries of being played and handled. Just as important, the thin, bowed shape is flexible to give power to the instrument's sound.

To shape the back and top, violin-makers use the smallest of planes—finger planes. Many are less than 2 in. long, with flat soles or soles curved in two directions like the cooper's stoup plane. They are finely made of gunmetal, with curving sides and beautiful screw caps or wedges. For hollowing against the grain, or for planing a highly figured tiger-maple back, a violinmaker can replace a straight iron with a toothed one.

To shape a back or front, violinmakers cut a blank roughly to shape and refine the outside with a gouge and straight-soled planes. They shape the inside with the same gouge and tiny finger planes. Where the top is a uniform thickness,

Violinmakers use some of the smallest and most beautiful planes to hollow to a gentle curve the inside of the top and back of a violin and larger stringed instruments.

Small planes for shaping chair seats (here, resting on a pine seat for a Windsor chair) have doubly compassed soles to work into the hollow.

These two unusual shaves could be used to hollow a plank seat or just as easily to shape a shovel or scoop.

the back tapers from thicker at the middle toward a thin edge. Consistency of the thickness is important for the tone of the instrument. Small finger planes just fit this work, accurately and carefully hollowing the back and top.

Chairmaker's Planes

Chairmakers hollow plank seats with larger versions of finger planes, with the same doubly compassed soles. Many of these planes are either craftsman-made or modified to work a particularly favored seat shape, from deeply hollowed to one more shallow. Just as useful are large shaves, often called travishers, with strongly radiused irons and handles curving away from the work to keep the user's knuckles out of harm's way (see the bottom photo at right). As with the planes, a chairmaker needs a number of travisher shapes to fit specific seat shapes.

To shape a seat, chairmakers start with a thick plank (usually white pine or basswood) cut roughly to shape. They hollow the center and shape the edges with shaves and planes, leaving a shape that's both comfortable and practical. The hollow is deeper toward the back to give the sitter a slight backward cant, and it's left thickest where strength is needed to joint in legs, spindles, and rails.

Chairmakers have adapted one other plane to their needs: a scraping spokeshave known as a devil (see the photo on p. 173). It's used to shape and smooth spindles and the "bows" for rails and arms. With a short sole shaped to fit the circumference of the part and a bone or brass insert ahead of the blade to counter wear, it's the most practical tool for smoothing curved parts. A devil can follow complex shapes, such as the continuous back rail on some Windsor chairs—a task nearly impossible with other planes.

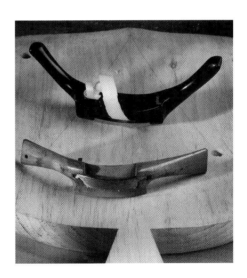

Travishers are shaves used to hollow and shape a seat. They have upward-sweeping handles to keep the chairmaker's knuckles well out of the way.

A large handrail plane (at right) shapes the sides of straight or gently curving sections of handrail. An ogee, hollow, or capping plane (at left) cuts the rounded top profile.

Short-soled molding planes shape the curved sections of the handrail. No matter how many shapes stairmakers owned, for some stairs they had to make special planes.

Stairmaker's Planes

In all of their ornate detail, stairs were once one of the dominant architectural features in a house; some still are. Stairmakers who build such stairs share a similar problem with chairmakers who fair curving chair rails—that of shaping a continuous curved handrailing. Even the simplest handrail has a decoratively molded top and sides. Elegant handrails have even more elaborate profiles and curves that follow the turn and rise of the steps between newel posts, around landings, and between flights. More complicated still are circular staircases with curving handrails, requiring great skill and a number of special tools.

Straight and gently curving sections of handrail are molded with large handrail molding planes (see the photo at left above). A capping plane cuts the rounded top profile, and another (or others) profiles the sides. The trickiest part is shaping more radically curved sections—such as a sweep up to a newel or the scroll that starts the railing at the first step. Planes and spokeshaves are the first tools used, to rough out the shape and molded profiles. The stairmaker refines the profile with shaped scrapers and shaves or uses a number of short-soled molding planes (sometimes custom-made for just that stairs). Miniature finger planes are useful, too, especially where the curve is tight.

Molding planes of all sorts are also needed to build a flight of stairs. Nosing planes (large hollows) cut the semi-circular shape on the edge of each tread. Under each is another fine molding, straight or curved to fit the tread. Newels that aren't turned are often made from a number of applied moldings and small beveled panels. Any good joiner is likely to own many of these planes. Even today with routers and shapers, building a gracefully curving stairs and handrail takes a variety of special shaping planes.

Coachmaker's Planes

Many trades were involved in building carriages and coaches, from the wheelwright fashioning wheels to the upholsterer fitting the seat cushions and the blacksmith forging the iron axles and fittings. The coachmaker built the wooden coach body, curved in every direction as much for elegance as practicality—for strength and to maximize the interior space suspended between the wheels. Working with few straight lines, coachmakers required a number of short-soled and specialty planes for cutting curved rabbets, grooves, and moldings. Such tools were useful in many other trades as well, such as for a joiner fitting the interior of a ship, a furniture maker cutting curved moldings, or a sashmaker molding shaped windows.

Just as each set of stairs is different and poses specific challenges, so it was in building coaches, carriages, sleighs, or any one of the many designs of horse-drawn vehicles. Building large coaches required the most skill. They had to be strong to withstand the abuse of rough roads, yet light enough to be able to be moved easily by a team of horses. To the strong frame the coachmaker fitted panels, doors, and windows, often curved in one or more directions.

A coachmaker's planes had to have short soles to work curves; there was less need for the long, straight work that a longer-soled plane could do. Many are either very short, or the heel is cut away into a beautiful and functional curved "pistol grip" (see the top photo at right). To cut moldings, rabbets, or grooves around curves, the sole is often compassed. To work into tight places, some rabbet planes have a sole wider than the rest of the body, known as a T-rabbet (see the bottom photo at right). This unusual design allows the plane to be used on its side, much like a side rabbet plane, to adjust a curved groove.

Coachmakers showed real invention in their plows and routers for cutting grooves along tight or changing curves. The simplest tools are routers with large handles and very short soles and fences. Most have two irons, on opposite sides of a fence, to work right-handed or left-handed with the grain. With shaped irons, the same tools could mold along a curving edge. Plow planes such as the

A coachmaker needed short-soled planes to work curved parts. The shape of the plane body evolved to an elegant and functional pistol grip, allowing one-handed control.

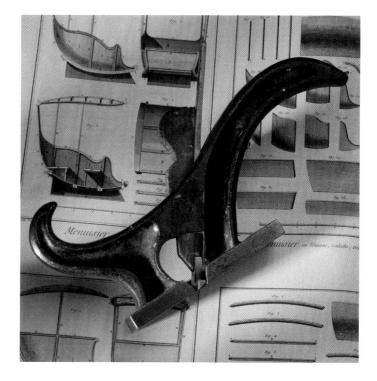

One of the few coachmaker's tools made of cast iron rather than wood, this T-rabbet plane has a sole wider than the body for working in tight places or for use on its side to adjust a groove.

To plow grooves for panels in curved frames, a coach-maker's plow plane had to have a very short skate and fence. The top plow has an adjustable fence; the simpler one below it has a fixed wooden fence. In the foreground is a small molding plane.

one in the rear of the top photo at left have a very short skate and fence to allow the plane to follow any curve. Stanley used the same design idea in the #196 curved rabbet plane (see the top photo on p. 125). A rare tool today, this plane would have been useful to the few coachmakers still working by the early 20th century. Coachmaking has not disappeared quite yet. The tools and skills survive with the few makers left restoring and making coaches and the wooden parts for some fine horseless carriages.

Patternmaker's Planes

Patternmakers use some of the same curved-soled planes as the coachmaker. They were once some of the most highly skilled craftsmen in every foundry, producing the wooden patterns from which each casting was made. Although patternmaking is a disappearing art, patternmakers are not yet all gone. For example, there's a full-time patternmaker at Lie-Nielsen Toolworks, designing and making patterns of every plane and part they cast (see pp. 237-238).

Patternmakers have to understand their materials, both the wood for the patterns and cast iron, bronze, aluminum, or whatever the eventual casting will be made of. Every metal shrinks differently as it cools, which means that the pattern has to be made slightly larger to compensate. It's also the patternmaker's job to design the pattern so that it can be cast accurately and so that it has all of the necessary details and tolerances for later machining.

Patternmakers make their patterns from a stable fine-grained wood such as mahogany or cherry. To release the pattern from the sand mold easily, they shape every surface with a slight taper known as draft. Where surfaces join at

To save space in a tool chest, patternmaker's planes often had interchangeable wooden soles and irons to work the different radii common in their work.

right angles, they often fit small leather or wood fillet strips to strengthen this joint in the finished casting. Curved sections they shape with spokeshaves, planes with shaped soles, or finger planes when necessary. To take up less space in their tool chests, patternmakers use a variation on the combination plane. The plane has a cast-iron body and thin interchangeable soles and irons, each with a different curvature (see the bottom photo on the facing page).

The most unusual patternmaker's plane is a corebox plane (see the photo above). While the name and appearance of the tool might be familiar to some, what it makes and how it does it are far less obvious. Whether owner-made of wood or either of the two versions Stanley made of cast iron, corebox planes have two wings that meet at a right angle where the V-shaped iron projects.

To see such a plane you'd have no idea that it is capable of cutting an exact semicircular hollow of any diameter

(depending on the width of the wings). It works on the principle that only a right angle—the sole of the plane—can be inscribed in a semicircle. Patternmakers first plow two grooves with a plow the exact diameter of the desired half-circle and either parallel to each other or diverging so as to cut a tapered hollow. They waste what wood they can with hollows or other planes and finish it to a consistent shape with the corebox plane, one pass after another across the whole curve. The Bayley corebox plane (shown

The Bayley corebox plane cuts a semicircular hollow. The plane rides along the top of the stock, and the cutter rotates a few degrees with each pass.

Rounder planes work on the same principle as a lathe, shaving a piece of wood round as it is fed up through the middle. The large rounder in the foreground cuts only one diameter; the more complex "witchet" at rear is adjustable and will cut tapers and tenons.

in the photo at left above) works on a similar principle, except that the plane stays in the same position and the cutter rotates a few degrees after each pass.

Why make such an accurate semicircular hollow? By making a section twice as long as needed, cutting it in half, and joining the parts, the patternmaker has an exact cylinder that is a mold for a core (made from sand and a binder to give it strength). Some castings, such as a large sheave meant to slide onto a shaft, are better cast with a hollow for the shaft rather than solid. Casting it solid would mean drilling a hole for the shaft afterwards—not easy to do if it's a large diameter. The solution is to make a pattern of the sheave as mounted on a short shaft, make a sand mold, remove the pattern, and slip in a sand core the size of the shaft. The core fits neatly into the sand-mold impressions left by the short wooden shaft. It's a simple and elegant solution involving an unusual hollowing plane.

Rounder Planes

Whereas the patternmaker's corebox plane cuts a perfect semicircular hollow, a rounder cuts a cylinder, such as for ladder rungs, handles, or dowels. Not to be confused with a round plane (the mate to a hollow), rounders shave around the outside of a bolt of wood like a simple pencil sharpener. Dynamically, it's a difficult cut, so they don't leave a perfectly smooth surface.

The photo at right above shows two versions of rounders. The simpler one is nothing more than a tapered hole drilled into a burly hunk of hardwood, with two handles and an iron mounted tangentially to the hole. It might have been used to taper the ends of large pump logs, joined together to form the earliest water systems. Smaller versions cut long handles or stails far more easily than on a lathe. The idea is simple enough that any craftsman can make his own rounder, for such needs as cutting dowels of any diameter on or off a lathe.

The rounder at rear in the photo, known as a witchet, has more bells and whistles. It's adjustable to cut different diameters, the "sole" is plated to resist wear, and it has two irons. The shorter iron cuts into the end grain, the other shaves the diameter. It's possible to cut tapers by turning the handscrews and changing the cutting diameter while working down the length of the stock; it's also possible to round the end into a tenon.

Price, each, ... 62 cents.

STEARNS' PATENT SPOKE POINTERS.
Nos. 1 and 2.
WITH GRADUATED ADJUSTABLE SHANK.

Spoke pointers cut a round taper on the end of a spoke, ladder rung, or round tenon.

Spoke Pointers

Spoke pointers work on the same pencil-sharpener principle as rounders, but they are more acutely tapered and the stock does not pass through the tool. The name suggests their association with wheelwrights and pointing the ends of spokes. I find them useful for tapering the end of any round part—dowels, round tenons, or the small pins I drive in to lock a mortise and tenon.

I have a number of sizes. The smallest is an inexpensive pencil sharpener with two sizes of holes. It will round pins or dowels as small as ⅛ in. diameter. Since the iron is set at a very low angle and the cut is a slight skew, it cuts fairly cleanly. I also have two larger-diameter spoke pointers with square drill shanks meant to be used in a brace. These are handy for pointing many parts consistently (by counting the revolutions, for instance), but it also means clamping up the parts to have both hands free to run the brace. It's quicker to hold the wood and screw the spoke pointer around the top a few times by hand. I set the irons in all of them for a light cut and fine-tune by trial and error.

Price, No. 1, each, ... $ .75
" " 2, " 1.25

Used in a bit brace, this adjustable hollow auger by E. C. Stearns cuts various sizes of round tenons to fit any mortise exactly. The cutting end looks and works like a small plane. In the foreground is a small spoke pointer.

Hollow Augers

Another variation of the rounder is a hollow auger, a bit-brace-driven plane. The cutting end looks like a miniature plane with a sole, an iron, and a cap that clamps it in place. It cuts round tenons on the end of round or square parts, for such things as chair stretchers, ladder rungs, and wheel spokes. As the hollow auger cuts around the shoulder of the tenon, the tenon feeds into the throat and helps support and guide the tool. There are many variations. Some cut one size tenon only; others are adjustable over a range of sizes. They can have two irons or one.

I have an adjustable model made by E. C. Stearns sometime in the last quarter of the 19th century (see the photo above). It's most useful whenever I'm cutting many identical round tenons, or when it's easier to bring the brace and hollow auger to the work, rather than turn the tenons on the

One of the more unusual planes, a shoe-peg plane cuts uniform square-tapered points on an end-grain block, which is later split apart into hundreds of tiny shoe pegs.

peg planes or if it's a recut bench plane. The sole has 15 sharp V-grooves running down its length, similar to a reeding plane (though a reeding plane would have 3 or 4 at most). The iron is toothed like a saw but cuts only over about half of the grooved sole.

A shoe-peg maker used this plane on the end grain of a very straight grained chunk of maple or birch, so that the finished pegs could be split off easily and consistently. First he ran the plane a few times in one direction across the block, using the fence or a temporary wooden strip as a guide. By setting the plane over and using the cut grooves as a guide (just as with a reeding plane and explaining why only part of the iron cuts), he cut progressively over the whole width. He then planed at right angles to the first grooves in the same way, to leave the block covered with evenly spaced square-tapered points. He split the pegs off in strips with a chisel, and then into individual pegs—each only about $1/12$ in. square with nicely pointed ends—ready for driving into a heel.

Sashmaker's Planes

One of the few other planes designed specifically for shaping end grain is a sash coping plane. A sashmaker used one to cope or profile the ends of each rail and sash bar (or muntin) in a window, to neatly fit the mirror-image profile cut on the stiles. Coping is not possible with every molding profile, but it's the fastest and neatest way to join the molded edges of stile and rail. To minimize tearout, either the work is put into a special saddle template with an end shaped like the coping cut, or a number of rails and muntins are clamped side by side and coped together. There are a number of different versions (and profiles that like most planes conformed to prevailing

lathe—for long pieces, for example. This model will cut tenons from $1/4$ in. to $1\frac{3}{8}$ in. diameter to fit any mortise exactly, but not always easily. The iron is tricky to set—it must project just enough to the side, as in a rabbet plane. On this tool, the tenon feeds through two V-shaped jaws that open and close to accommodate different diameters. If the iron projects too much, the tenon is slightly undersized and it wobbles in the guides; if it doesn't project enough, it's too tight. It's typical of the shortcomings of any tool meant to do everything.

Shoe-Peg Planes

Another unusual plane that cuts a specific shape in end grain is a shoe-peg plane, used for cutting small, square-tapered pegs. There was a time when these small hardwood pegs were used to attach heels and soles to shoes and boots. Burlington, Vermont, was once the shoe-peg capital of the nation, where the single largest factory cut as many as four hundred bushels of shoe pegs daily!

The shoe-peg plane by A. Gillet shown in the photo above looks like a jack plane with a removable fence. It's such an unusual design that it would be hard to say if it is typical of other shoe-

tastes), but all cut along the end grain in the same way.

Sashmaking takes skill and a number of other special molding planes. While they don't look or cut any differently from other wooden planes, the profiles are specific to sashmaking. What they better represent is how sashmakers combined cutting functions to make the most efficient planes possible. Take, for example, cutting muntins, the thin bars that divide the panes of glass. An old method was to cut the putty rabbets to hold the glass and putty, then mold one side of the face and then the other—four cutting operations with two planes. Eventually someone had the idea of joining together a rabbet and molding plane, a so-called stick-and-rabbet or sash plane, to cut the molding and rabbet at the same time (see the photo at right). Cutting muntins this way takes one plane and two cuts, and it's a lot more accurate.

There are more reasons why sash planes are efficient. Some versions have a single body and two irons (easier to sharpen and tune than a single wide iron). Others are split, so that with shims between the plane bodies or separated by adjustable screws of some kind, the same plane will work thicker stock. Only the flat between molding and rabbet is wider; the molding profile is the same (so the same coping plane still works). And since the plane references against the outer edge of the molded profile, any slight variation in the stock thickness shows up as a wider putty rabbet, which is easily planed down after the window is assembled. This saves time in that the stock doesn't need to be thicknessed carefully or planed smoothly to start. A minute saved here, or a tool that worked more accurately, added up to considerable time savings when fashioning all the many windows for a house.

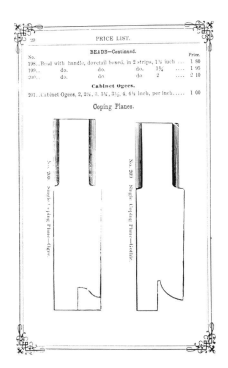

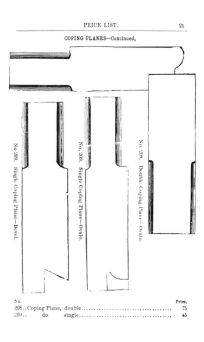

Sash coping planes shape the end grain of rails and muntins to neatly fit the mirror-image profile cut on the stiles. Since these planes cut lying on their sides, some ingenious plane makers added another plane body at right angles to the working plane, for a handhold.

Rather than use separate molding and rabbet planes, a sashmaker's stick-and-rabbet or sash plane combines the work of both. It efficiently and accurately cuts the molded profile and putty rabbet at the same time.

Planes whose purpose is to cut shavings rather than a surface are particularly unusual. A spill plane cuts tightly twisted shavings, just right for lighting a pipe or candle from the fire in the hearth.

Spill Planes

Taking a break from his work (since he is working so efficiently), a sashmaker might run a piece of scrap pine across his spill plane. The long, tightly twisted shavings called spills were just the thing to light his pipe from the embers in the fireplace. Such planes are not rare, but they are very unusual in the plane world. They're one of the few planes where the shaving is the object, not the surface the plane cuts.

Spill planes are all different. A few commercial plane makers offered them for sale, but most are simple enough to be easily made by the owner. All that is necessary is a sharply skewed iron and a fence either to guide the scrap against or to guide the plane. A common design looks like a molding plane with a wedged iron and side escapement throat (see the photo above). Another I've seen has a small, round exit hole for the shaving, to help curl it all that more tightly.

Making a tight spill is trickier than it might seem. Set properly, the skewed iron does all the work, but it still takes a slow and steady stroke. Cut too quickly and you'll make a nice shaving, but it will not be twisted much and will burn up too quickly. Take too coarse a cut and the shaving won't curl well either. Once you have it, the spills are uniform and tight. With matches so common today, we forget how spills were once one way our ancestors moved fire from hearth to candle, lantern, or pipe.

Spelk Planes

There is another plane whose purpose is to make shavings—a spelk plane. There are many variations, some of which have different names, but they all work basically the same. A spelk plane makes shavings of a certain width or thickness, for weaving baskets, bending into small boxes, or if they are wide enough, for bending into traditional round cheese boxes. Shakers in Canterbury, New Hampshire, used a spelk plane of sorts to make the fine poplar strips the sisters wove into the poplarware boxes they were known for. Another variation is a Japanese plane that shaves long, wide shavings used for wrapping paper. The super-surfacer planer evolved from this spelk plane (see the sidebar on p. 154).

Some spelk planes resemble old-fashioned cabbage graters, with a spokeshave-type iron mounted across the heavy stock. The low angle of the iron works well with the grain, cutting and splitting the spelks (which are left somewhat rough). The thickness of the shaving is regulated by exposing more of the iron and opening the throat. Driving the plane over the stock or the stock over the plane takes such force that most planes have a number of handles for additional hands. Cutting stock slightly green is easiest.

Basketweavers and hatmakers use a type of spelk plane for cutting flat strips or for sizing them to a consistent thickness. To produce uniform strips, the stock is first scored with a knife or a series of knives ganged together and then passed through the spelk plane. Shaker sisters used this method to make fine poplar strips as narrow as $\frac{1}{8}$ in.

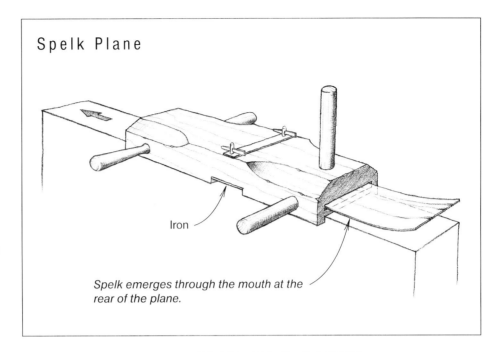

Spelk Plane

Iron

Spelk emerges through the mouth at the rear of the plane.

Stanley's #96 blind-nailing plane (or chisel gauge) is as scarce as it is unique. It guides a narrow chisel or gouge to cut a shaving that's perfect for hiding a nail when the shaving is glued back in place.

Blind Nailers

Falling somewhere between these unusual shaving-making planes and ordinary planes that leave smooth or shaped surfaces is a blind-nailing plane. Its name clearly identifies what it does—cutting a shaving from the surface to hide a nail. It's how it does it that's quite different from the way most other planes work.

For one thing, a blind nailer is unusual in that it's small, only $2\frac{1}{4}$ in. long. For another, the plane's function is to guide a small chisel (or a gouge) in place of the small iron you might expect. This is where it gets its other name: a chisel gauge. Clamped on the end of a chisel, it guides the cut to curl up a shaving. The idea is then to back the tool out and leave the shaving attached, drive a nail under it, and glue it invisibly back

This butt mortise plane by C. M. Rumbold Co. has an unusually wide throat, so the user can see how the plane is cutting as it levels the bottom of hinge mortises or similar recesses.

Another plane could make the same cut, but here's where the unusually large throat helps—you can see where you're cutting. A router has an open throat for the same reason and could be used with care, but the sole is not the best shape to work on the edge of a door easily. The lack of a sole just ahead of the iron of a butt mortise plane is unimportant, since a perfectly smooth surface is not the main object.

Interestingly, this was one of the few useful plane designs that Stanley *never* made. Although wooden versions had been around a long time, it wasn't until the 1950s that C. M. Rumbold Co. started making this design in cast iron, not too many years after Stanley was starting to cease production of some of its specialty planes.

Table-Leaf Planes

As the name suggests, table-leaf planes are used to cut the joint for a drop-leaf table. While no different from other molding planes in appearance or function, table-leaf planes are one of a number of unusual planes meant to be used in pairs to cut a special joint. The same sorts of planes were used by many trades, such as the casement-sash maker for the meeting joint of sashes, a case maker cutting dustproof joints between doors, or doors and frame, or a plane maker cutting complex joints for inlaying boxing.

Table-leaf planes are actually quite simple, just a pair of fenced hollow and round. At first glance, the joint they cut doesn't seem all that complicated either, but actually making a properly fitting table-leaf joint is quite subtle. You can use a matching pair of hollow and round or scratch stocks, but it's easiest by far with a well-tuned pair of table-leaf planes. With large fences, it's easy to hold

into place. Simple enough, but it still takes a feel for the tool to get it right. Too deep a cut and the shaving is brittle; too shallow and it's hard to get the thin edges glued back down. I prefer using a shallow gouge, for a fine chip that's strong and flexible. Blind nailers might seem like funny little tools, but they're perfect for what they do.

Butt Mortise Planes

A larger relative to the blind nailer, a butt mortise plane works on the same principle of a simple plane body supporting a chisel iron. What's unusual about a butt mortise plane is

that its throat is wider than the length of the blind nailer—nearly 3 in. wide! No other planes but routers have such wide throats.

The main use of a butt mortise plane is to true the bottoms of mortises for locks, hinges, an inlay recess, or perhaps the background of a carving. The easiest way to use it is first to score and chisel the recess, remove most of the waste, and then use the tool for a final smoothing and leveling. In cutting a mortise for a hinge, this eliminates the additional step of marking out its depth. I set the depth of the iron to the thickness of the leaf held against the sole next to the iron. With the same setting, all of the hinge mortises are identical.

Table-leaf planes are no different from a matched pair of hollow and round, with the simple yet very important addition of fences to guide the planes for greater accuracy.

the planes against the leaf and table to cut a consistent and tight-fitting joint. Tuning the irons to one another is then the only tricky part.

What these and many other planes like them represent to me is the way that craftsmen adapt their tools to work more accurately or more easily. Perhaps it's adding a special fence and curving the

plane's sole as with a cooper's croze, shortening a plane to work the complex shapes and curves of a handrail, or combining the functions of two tools into one as with the sashmaker's sash plane. The special demands of each trade require unique tools. Some of these tools are unusual because they are unfamiliar, from a trade long diminished from a

century ago. While none of us is likely to use a shoe-peg or spelk plane, the usefulness of their basic concept might never be obsolete. As for the rest of the planes in this chapter, many are still useful today—maybe not every day, but for those situations where no other tool works quite as simply or as well.

12

CONTEMPORARY
PLANE MAKERS

Of course the really good plane becomes an instrument, it becomes

something that you want to make music with.

—James Krenov, 1996

Craftsmen have been making their own planes for a very long time. In earlier days, plane making was an extension of the woodworking profession, and fashioning a kit of tools was a natural rite of passage from apprentice to journeyman. As commercial plane making expanded to supply every type of wooden plane imaginable and later manufacturers like Stanley began to produce an incredible variety of metal planes for a modest cost, there was less incentive for a craftsman to make all but the most specialized tools. He simply bought the planes he needed.

During the many years that Stanley dominated the hand-tool market, many competitors came out with their own plane designs. Some of the tools were excellent, every bit as good as what Stanley was making. Yet every one of these companies has since stopped making planes, not because their products were poor (Stanley's were quite mediocre for many years after World War II), but rather because, up until quite recently, there has been a declining market for all hand tools. It was the same way in England, as some of the finest toolmakers—Norris, Spiers,

Preston, and others—closed up shop. Woodworking machinery captured imaginations; hand tools represented hard and sweaty work.

Some of the romance of working with one's hands for pleasure or income has returned. I am certainly among those craftsmen who have chosen to make a living designing and building furniture rather than, say, pursuing engineering or law. Every one of us needs all types of quality tools for our work. Up until recently this has meant hunting for old tools at flea markets, auctions, and tool dealers. Simultaneously, collectors and

While greatly diminished from almost a century ago, plane making goes on. A number of small businesses like Lie-Nielsen Toolworks of Warren, Maine, are making beautiful planes based on classic designs (here, the Bed Rock #604).

historians are just as interested in hand tools and the technology they represent. The result is pressure on the market for the classic tools of Stanley, Norris, and others. The rare tools get ever more expensive and beyond the reach of most of us. Luckily, some of those same craftsmen have turned their energies to redesigning and remaking some of these classic tools.

This chapter tells the stories of five of those plane makers. All of them have been captivated by the romantic vision of making beautiful hand tools as good as or better than the originals. They got started for different reasons. One maker was frustrated trying to work with the best tools he could find. Others just relished the challenge. Some had to work hard to establish their businesses, but all found a market for their tools. There will always be a demand for good tools.

At the very least, these stories will offer insight into how metal and wooden planes are made. While the subtleties of the design, materials, or machinery might be different, plane making has changed very little over the years. I hope that these stories might also inspire you to make a plane or two for yourself. It will give you a different perspective and understanding of your tools. Cabinet-maker and plane maker James Krenov shares this thought when he says that his "first little attempt with [making] a plane that succeeded might have been the turning point in my life, because it opened up the fact that tools can be better, that tools can be personal and more intimate. Had I failed, I might have just fallen back into the general pattern, which doesn't mean I wouldn't have been a cabinetmaker, but it might mean that I would never be able to make music."

Plane-making techniques vary, but almost none of them are beyond the reach of anyone with curiosity and modest skills. Anyone can make a wooden plane. While casting bronze planes would be difficult if not impossible in a home shop, making the pattern is not. Then it's just a question of finding a foundry to do the casting and taking it from there.

Ted Ingraham: Wooden Molding Planes

For a long time, wooden planes were literally made by the millions. During the years of peak production (1870–1880), catalogs such as Ohio Tool Company's offered a dazzling array of nearly a thousand different planes, from bench planes to complex cornice planes to simple hollows and rounds. Meanwhile cast-iron planes, with their positive adjusters and soles that stayed true over a lifetime of work, were becoming more competitive in terms of quality and price. When cast-iron bench planes finally came to dominate the market, new combination planes (such as the Stanley #55 and #45) further eroded the market for wooden molding planes.

At one time a finish carpenter needed a huge set of different molding planes—as many as 60 different pairs—for cutting specific moldings for everything from window and door trim, to ornate crown moldings, to small base moldings completing the baseboards. As molding machines and mill-cut moldings became readily available, fewer moldings were cut by hand with planes. Most houses

In the tradition of past plane makers, Ted Ingraham stamps the toe of his wooden molding planes with a stamp he cut and filed. This plane cuts a large cornice or crown molding.

built today have generic millyard moldings, if any, certainly none cut with planes. But the need for molding planes has not disappeared altogether. For authentic moldings for restoration work or building period houses, or as a way to create any molding profile, wooden molding planes are still the best tools.

Ted Ingraham started making molding planes out of curiosity. Always interested in the tools and methods of the 18th-century woodworker and restoring old houses at the time, it was only natural that he would try his hand at making planes. The success of the first ones encouraged him to keep going. Since then he has made dozens, including many to cut specific moldings for his period Georgian house. When I met him he was taking careful measurements of a very early square-armed plow plane, to add to his growing log of planes to reproduce someday. In his shop a few months later he made a molding plane and explained the process.

MAKING A WOODEN MOLDING PLANE

The stock for the plane is a piece of straight-grained, quartersawn yellow birch. Birch was the choice of early American plane makers, distinguishing their work from English beech planes. By the time plane making became a commercial trade and the first catalogs appeared, American makers had switched to beech. Both woods are hard-wearing and stable and, as long as the stock is well seasoned, make good planes. Ted often starts with a hunk of firewood cut into rough blanks and seasoned upstairs in his shop. Earlier makers first steamed the wood to speed the seasoning (and enhance the color) and then set the blanks aside for three years or more.

In some descriptions of plane making great importance is put on cutting the

After dimensioning and squaring the stock, Ted cuts the handhold with a fillister plane.

blank so that the sole is cut from the wood closest to the bark. Years of experience showed that this wood is better able to hold up to wear and thus is somewhat "harder." Just as important is orienting the blank so that the grain slopes toward the heel of the plane. In use, the fibers will be smoothed down and are less likely to catch and tear out, damaging the sole or marring the work. Few pieces of wood are perfect, and it's here that Ted's experience is important in knowing his material and the defects that can be safely ignored.

Ted dimensions the blank (into the plane stock) slightly longer than 10 in. by 3¼ in. and slightly thicker than the molding profile, in this case 1½ in. wide. A first and important step is to accurately square the stock—the long-grain edges and the ends. Accurate layout, upon which all the cuts depend, will then be much easier. The next step is to cut the handhold, 1½ in. deep and one-third the width of the plane body. Ted uses a fenced rabbet (a fillister) to

sink this wide rabbet accurately and quickly (see the photo above).

Molding planes vary in width, but they are cut to a uniform length and height. Blanks can be made ahead of time to speed large production runs, but standardization also makes it easier when cutting only one plane, because the same jigs can be used to mark out all the cuts for the throat, mouth, and wedge mortise. Ted uses a pitchboard (see the top photo on p. 233) laid alongside the stock to lay out the throat at a bedding angle of 50°, which is standard for many molding planes. Carrying the lines across the top of the plane he lays out the wedge mortise in the center and one-third the thickness of the handhold. Depending upon the type of molding plane he is making, he might also mark out the sole for a fence cut into it. Even though this plane will eventually cut a reverse ogee, so far nothing distinguishes it from another similarly sized plane meant to cut an entirely different molding profile.

The molding profile is scribed on the toe and heel from a wooden template. For some profiles, the molding is "sprung" or angled for a more consistent throat, as can be seen on the old molding plane on the left.

The various wooden templates shown in the foreground speed layout, while the metal scrapers at rear are used to fine-tune the sole profile after it has been shaped with other molding planes.

Ted shapes the sole profile to the layout lines with hollows and rounds.

Commercial plane makers shape the sole with a "mother" or backing plane with a mirror-image sole profile.

To lay out the profile for cutting the sole, Ted uses a wooden template against the toe and heel (see the top left photo on the facing page). Interestingly, the layout lines are not square with the sole, but at an angle to it (known as the spring angle). Springing the profile places it more horizontal with the sole and gives a more uniform throat opening, which reduces the risk of tearout. (For more on spring, see pp. 188-189.)

Commercial plane makers cut the throat and wedge mortise next, and the sole profile after that. Ted prefers to profile the sole first, to make sure he gets it right before any further cutting. He cuts the sole profile with molding planes, specifically hollows and rounds (see the bottom left photo on the facing page). Deep profiles are roughed out with a plow plane by plowing one or more grooves to a specific depth to guide later cuts. The sole is finished with a scraper ground to the molding profile. Ted clamps the stock in a special jig that holds it either upright or on its side for the different cutting operations.

Plane makers doing production runs of specific profiles use "mother" or backing planes to cut the sole (see the bottom right photo on the facing page). They look like the same molding plane, except that they have a mirror-image sole profile. The new profile is shaped by merely planing it on with the backing plane. The same backing plane can be used to create more complex molding profiles by using it along with special molding planes that add such details as beads.

Once the sole is shaped, the mouth, throat, and wedge mortise are cut next (see the top photo at right). Using a fine backsaw, Ted saws along the lines defining the mouth and throat, stopping just shy of the fence and base of the handhold. With a fine chisel he chops

The mouth and throat of the plane are cut with a fine backsaw and then chopped out with a chisel. The pitchboard in the background is for laying out the throat opening.

After defining the wedge mortise and then boring through to the throat, Ted uses floats and chisels to enlarge the mortise and true the bed.

out the waste and deepens and refines the throat. The wedge mortise is first defined by chopping it about ½ in. deep and then boring through to the throat with a small-diameter bit. To refine the mortise Ted uses a narrow chisel and floats (see the bottom photo on p. 233).

Floats are special plane maker's tools that are a cross between a rasp and a chisel (see the top photo below). It's most important that the bed line is true right into the throat. Ted uses a pattern wedge to check the dimensions and then to cut a wedge for this plane.

For the iron, Ted cuts up a section of an old heavy circular saw (sawmill sized). He forges the blank into the distinctive molding-plane iron shape, tapering thinner away from the cutting edge and with a long narrow tang (see the bottom photo at left). He fits the iron to the plane and checks that the wedge secures it well close to the cutting edge. If necessary, Ted improves the fit by twisting the iron slightly or hollowing the bed. The next step is to shape the soft iron to the sole profile with a file. After hardening and tempering it in the forge, Ted hones and refines the iron to the exact profile.

The plane is now finished, except for chamfering the edges to soften the hand-hold and refine the plane's appearance and rubbing on a coat of oil to protect it. Each plane maker's style is distinctive in the way he cuts the chamfers and details the finial on the wedge. Where once molding planes made by hand had pronounced details, over time some of these disappeared as planes became more uniform and plane making turned into an industry. Ted Ingraham's plane shows those handmade details. With only an occasional honing of the iron, it will last for years and years.

Floats are plane maker's tools, a cross between a rasp and a chisel, that cut smoothly and quickly. Many floats are made from old files.

The wedge for the plane is cut from a pattern in a shape distinctive for each plane maker. The iron is forged from a blank cut from an old circular saw and filed to the sole's profile.

Leon Robbins: Specialty Wooden Planes

Leon Robbins, of Bath, Maine, came to making planes after a career selling antique tools and restoring furniture. "I took the challenge to make one," he explained, "but it wasn't easy." Traditional methods frustrated him: "I burned every other plane." A deeply religious man, he prayed about it and one day had a vision about a different technique. Today, almost 20 years later, he is making a living turning out a steady run of traditional wooden planes: compass hollows and travishers for chairmakers, panel-raising planes, dovetail planes, coachmaker's planes, miniature planes, and bench planes.

Although he loved the challenge of making the planes, selling them was hard. He had some contacts from his years dealing tools to craftsmen and collectors. He tried ads and a tool distributor. A colorful old-timer in an unusual business, it was just a matter of time before *Yankee Magazine* and others found him. Today he sells mostly through Garrett Wade, Woodcraft Supply, and by word of mouth.

To see his shop you would never expect it to be a plane "factory." Compact, with machinery, tools, and jigs packed in everywhere, it feels more like a shop on one of the ships built nearby at the Bath Iron Works. He has two low benches opposite each other for shaping and fine-tuning planes, and an old swiveling office chair he rolls between them. As we talked, he pulled out planes, tools, and jigs to explain his method.

Most of his planes have a bench throat, the kind of throat cut into the center of the plane and quite different from the side escapement throat on most molding planes. This type of throat requires a different construction technique. Leon's frustration early on was in finding a way to cut a consistent throat in a solid-hardwood plane body. Today he laminates the body out of two thin sides and two center pieces—one the bed and rear of the plane, the other the toe and throat. Working this way lets him control the width of the throat more exactly; since the sides are most visible, he uses eye-catching curly or bird's-eye maple for them.

Leon Robbins makes traditional wooden planes. Shown here (clockwise from top left) are a miniature bench plane, a panel-raising plane, an unusual molding plane, a compass hollowing plane, a rabbet plane, and a coachmaker's plane.

The center pieces and sides are cut out on the bandsaw with jigs and then trial assembled. On large planes, gluing the parts together in perfect alignment is the challenge, because clamping pressure inevitably makes one or more parts lubricated with glue shift. To prevent this shifting he drills and pins the parts together dry with very small dowels, using a wedge in the throat to keep things aligned. The pins are cut off later when the body is trimmed to size and the sole is trued. Lately, he's been making a lot of compass hollowing planes for shaping chair seats, a design worked out with the help of chairmaker Michael Dunbar. Leon shapes the complex soles of these planes on a sanding jig chucked in the drill press. He cuts and shapes the irons for many of his planes from hardened tool stock that he buys from a specialty supplier.

What started as a challenge has turned into a business that's growing every year. When I was visiting him he was filling an order for 125 planes—far more than he can comfortably make alone. He tries and fine-tunes each plane until he's satisfied. Only then does it leave his shop. I left with a sense that even greater than the financial security the business has brought him was the satisfaction of making good tools that others appreciate.

Lie-Nielsen Toolworks: Re-engineering Metal Planes

Although their makers live fewer than 50 miles apart, there is a world of difference between Leon Robbins' hand-made wooden planes and Tom Lie-Nielsen's elegant metal tools. While they are both making traditional tools, Lie-Nielsen Toolworks is re-engineering and remaking some of the best of Stanley's classic designs. Tom Lie-Nielsen is clearly interested in redefining our perceptions of just how good a new tool can be.

Tom Lie-Nielsen's whole life prepared him for making planes. Still, he never expected to end up as the driving force behind a small Maine company making the best modern production planes. Full of the energy of someone obviously in love with his work (he never takes stairs at any less than two or three steps at a time), Tom gave me a tour of his modest factory while explaining the steps involved from idea to finished plane and how he ended up a plane maker.

He grew up among the wooden boats and old-timers of his father's boat shop in Rockland, a town or two away from Warren where he lives now. It was there that he learned woodworking skills and, in the shop's small machine shop, how to machine and fabricate boat hardware. Tom learned casting by pouring a huge lead keel in the beach sand behind the shop. When he finally left and headed to New York, he took with him the most important skills that would later serve him as a plane maker—the ability to design and make things with his hands.

His time in New York taught him more—what woodworkers wanted in the way of tools. He ended up at Garrett Wade, selling tools and dealing with customers. They would lament that

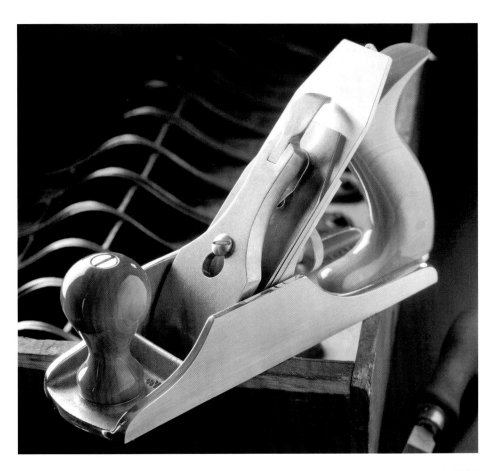

Lie-Nielsen Toolworks is redesigning classic Stanley planes. This version of the Bed Rock #604 has a heavy body cast from manganese bronze for beauty, durability, and good performance and a heavy iron and precision-made parts throughout.

"they just don't make it like they used to," to which Tom responded that "we have the technology, they just don't care." Stanley, who long dominated the industry with innovative and well-made woodworking hand tools, had basically written off the market. Although the company was regularly turning out 30,000 planes a week, producing a few thousand specialty ones a year didn't interest Stanley. Tom saw that the interest in working with one's hands and woodworking in particular was growing.

There was another key to the woodworking hand-tool market that Tom quickly realized. Used tools were plentiful, but for all but the most basic planes (#4s, for example), the market seemed specialized and mysterious to the uninitiated. If they were to buy an older tool, what was a fair price, would the quality be okay, and would it be usable? To buy new tools felt safer.

By the time Tom left Garrett Wade, he understood the woodworking tool market well enough to believe there was a demand for quality tools. It also brought him into contact with Ken Wizner, the maker of a bronze version of the Stanley #95 edge plane. Ken wasn't that interested in plane making and was never quite able to keep up with demand, so he gladly sold the business to Tom. When Tom brought out the skew block plane the following year, he was still a long way from where he is today, but he was making planes.

Designing and making the skew block plane was trial by fire. Manganese bronze (an alloy of mostly copper and zinc with trace amounts of manganese and other elements) was used for the casting. It still is for all of Lie-Nielsen's bronze planes, because it is strong (it won't crack if dropped as cast iron will), it holds up to wear well, it is heavy and doesn't rust, and, maybe most important, it has a beauty and warmth that are hard to resist. After it was cast, machining the skew block plane involved the challenges of milling compound angles and holding odd shapes. The first year he made only a couple hundred planes and sold them all through Garrett Wade. Gradually new designs were added, as well as more machinery and some employees.

A low-angle block plane and a jack plane followed. All were specialty designs, long since dropped by Stanley. The Stanley #1 was the next step, because, as Tom tells it, "I wanted to experience what goes into making bench planes." The #1 involved learning how to make a large number of identical parts, chip breakers, and handles, all nearly miniature in size. From there the Bed Rock bench planes #602, #604, and #605 followed.

The dozen or so designs in production today are all based on classic Stanley patterns. A question that comes to mind is what about the patents that Stanley had on most of their tools and even specific parts of some, such as adjusters and lever caps? What Lie-Nielsen is doing is no different than what other manufacturers did a century ago. As patents expired (they last only 14 years), others readily borrowed the successful designs. And while Lie-Nielsen's planes are based on the same designs, the new patterns are refined and re-engineered beyond anything Stanley ever did. To work better and more easily, plane bodies are heavier, adjusters are designed into

planes that never had them, much thicker irons are designed into every plane, and all parts are machined and polished to very high standards.

MAKING BRONZE PLANES

To make cast-metal planes takes a surprisingly modest amount of tooling and technology. It shouldn't be surprising, given that cast-metal planes have been made for over 150 years, well before Bridgeport vertical mills or computer-driven machine tools were invented. The steps involve casting the body and body parts; machining the throat, sole, sides of the body, and all of the areas that mate with other parts; machining and polishing the parts; and assembling them all together. Although it might not be high tech, making the 34 parts in a smooth plane, machining them accurately, and assembling them in a high-quality tool is challenging. To be efficient at it and be able to produce

affordable tools makes it more challenging still.

At Lie-Nielsen Toolworks, raw materials literally come in the back door, move through the various departments as they are cast, machined, and finished, and move out the front door as completed planes. What I didn't expect is how raw the materials actually are—ingots of bronze, brass and steel rods, flat bar stock for the irons, and cherry planks for the knobs and handles (see the photo below). Of all the parts on the #604 bench plane, for instance, only two small Phillips-head screws aren't made right on the premises.

Well before the casting or milling comes the careful designing of each tool. This involves the skills of a patternmaker, who makes a wooden pattern and mold of the tool. The pattern is essentially a wooden version of the plane; each part requires a separate pattern. It's more complicated than that, though, because the hot metal shrinks as it cools. Some

To control quality, almost every part of every plane is made in Lie-Nielsen's small factory from raw materials— ingots of bronze, brass, and steel rods, flat bar stock for the irons, and cherry planks for the knobs and handles.

metals shrink more than others—cast iron less than 1% and bronze about 4%. The wooden pattern has to account for this shrinkage. Then there is something called "draft," which is the taper built into the parts so that the plastic pattern made from the original can be more easily removed from the sand when making the sand mold for casting. Beyond this, the patternmaker also has to design the pattern so that it can be cast well and not leave thin sections incomplete.

Plastic versions of the plane are cast from the mold of the wooden pattern. Depending upon their size, a number of plastic planes are attached to what is known as a matchboard, a 16-in.-square wooden board. This is the pattern the actual casting is made from. It's also the patternmaker's job to lay out the path that the molten metal takes. It enters through a funnel-shaped sprue, flows along the runner filling the cavity of individual planes, and proceeds into gates connecting the parts. Each casting also has a riser, usually behind the thickest part, that is a reservoir of molten metal to help compensate for shrinkage.

Making the sand molds and casting the metal is ancient technology. The sand is a very special natural sand that looks and feels like fine black loam. It has to be fluffy to dissipate the air displaced by the molten metal and moist enough to hold its shape. The matchboard is dusted with talc (to help release it from the sand mold) and captured between two halves of a mold that is filled with sand and tightly tamped. Separating the molds releases the matchboard and leaves a void with exactly its shape, complete with runners, gates, and risers. The sprue is cut in, and the mold is ready to be poured.

Depending upon the size of the plane, only between a dozen and two dozen planes are cast in one pour, in about six molds. For smaller parts such as frogs and lever caps, far more can be cast at a time. The pour is a drama of intense white heat and flowing molten metal. The entire vessel holding the golden liquid bronze glows a bright orange when it's pulled from the furnace. There are no flying sparks, only the quiet concentration of two men pouring the metal as consistently as possible. Just a short while later the molds are knocked apart and the process is started again.

From the time the individual planes are cut apart until the plane is boxed and shipped, every pair of eyes is checking for quality. A slight pit in the casting, an asymmetric shape, a surface not perfectly milled—almost anything can send a plane back to the foundry. The acceptable castings are stress-relieved in an oven, for

Plane bodies and other parts are cast in small batches in traditional sand molds. The heavy bars atop the molds prevent the sand from buckling as the molten metal fills the mold.

As each rough casting passes through the machine shop getting its body milled to size, its sole ground flat, and its throat opened, operators constantly check tolerances and quality.

just the same reasons that wood is seasoned before it can be reliably milled and worked.

From the foundry the planes pass through the machine room. Using old Bridgeport milling machines and a handful of computer-controlled lathes and vertical mills, all of the important surfaces of the casting are machined. The throat is opened, the bedding surface of the frog is milled, the sole and sides are surface-ground flat, and holes are drilled for such things as frog screws and rods to secure handles. A steady stream of lever caps, adjuster yokes, frogs, and many small parts is also moving through.

Plane irons are among the parts in motion. Lie-Nielsen irons start out as bar stock, which is cut to length, shaped, and beveled. Their irons are good not because they use the best steel (there are more expensive alloys available), but because they take great care with the next step—tempering. The irons are hardened in small batches in a salt bath, a vat of molten salt about 1,500°F, and quenched in a 55-gal. barrel of water. It's the same process as hardening steel red hot with a fire, except that it's far more predictable. From there the irons go into an oven to draw the temper. The hardening warps the irons slightly. They are surface-ground flat, the edges are trued, and the bevel is ground and, finally, honed by hand.

All the while in the woodshop a crew is turning knobs, shaping and sanding handles, and stuffing the few planes that require it. Another crew is grinding, polishing, and hand-filing the completed metal parts. In the machine shop, parts such as lever caps are assembled. The last step is bringing all the parts together and assembling the finished plane.

By the time a Lie-Nielsen plane is shipped, many eyes have looked at it through the dozens of separate operations that went into making the

parts. If one thing above all distinguishes these planes, it's their high quality. Everything about the way they are made contributes to the quality—small batches, manufacturing nearly every part on every plane, and trying new techniques to constantly improve the finished product. Very few of the best tools wear out, except under the hardest conditions and constant use. These are some of the best tools, destined to last many generations and give pleasure and satisfaction to all who use them. To those disappointed with the mediocre quality of new tools, Lie-Nielsen planes prove just how good a tool can be.

Jeff Warshafsky: Modern Norris Planes

Jeff Warshafsky started making planes out of frustration with both new and old planes. While working with Ian Kirby making furniture, he was introduced to a Norris smoothing plane. It worked better than any of his Record planes, but as he told me, "I liked the plane, but not the

adjuster." Still, he went to buy one, they were expensive, and "they all needed work." So he set out to build his own and improve on the original. Being mechanically minded and an optimist didn't hurt.

Luckily his brother, a manufacturing engineer, guided him through the difficult parts. Jeff made a mahogany pattern and sent it off to have one iron plane cast at a foundry. He milled all the important surfaces on a small Bridgeport machine while he thought about how to redesign the adjuster. For the iron he used a special alloy, cryogenically treated to hold a keen edge (see the sidebar on p. 240). Anyone familiar with Norris planes, quite possibly the highest evolution of the plane, will understand something of the high standards Jeff expected. Whether he succeeded or not is a matter of opinion, but by then he had the urge to keep making planes. "If I'm interested," he thought, "then maybe someone else is."

An ad in *Fine Woodworking* magazine generated some sales. Jeff tried to sell the idea to the larger tool catalogs with no

Reed Plane Company made four sizes of bench planes. Shown here are its heavy bronze smoother patterned after similar Norris designs and a low-angle block plane.

If I told you that freezing your plane irons is going to make them take and hold an edge a lot better, you might not believe me. I'm not exaggerating the results, but there's a little more to it than popping your tools in the freezer. That is unless yours happens to be set for -310°F.

Cryogenic tempering has been done commercially since the early 1980s. I first heard about it from a woodworker friend who supercooled his chisels with good results. When I tried out the super-cooled iron in a Reed Plane Company's smoother, I was convinced there was something to it.

Cryogenics seems as much magic as science. How else can you explain a process that gives musical instruments a clearer tone or makes panty hose last 6 months? Each company has its own technique, only adding to the mystery. Essentially, for less than $2, you can have one of your plane irons slowly cooled to -310°F in liquid nitrogen. It's held there for a day and then warmed to +310°F. What you get back is an iron free of stress, and while it's no harder, it is permanently more resistant to wear. Quite simply, the edge lasts longer. Microscopically, the austenite component of the steel is converted to harder martensite. Easier to understand is to think of it as an extension of the heat-tempering process, where beneficial changes happen from a deeper "quenching."

To end up with a finished plane free of casting defects, Jeff started with oversized castings made from a wooden pattern. After many hours of milling and hand filing, the plane body (shown in the foreground) was ready for its wooden infill.

the handwork making and fitting the wood infill and adjuster, opening the throat, and polishing everything. In the end, he made a little over 100 planes before Mahogany Masterpieces went out of business. Jeff's life and interests changed, too. He realized there was too little profit to continue, but by then he had the satisfaction of knowing he had made many beautiful planes.

Jamestown Tool Company: Planes as Art

Jay Gaynor and Joseph Hutchins had a similar romantic idea about making English planes. Like Jeff Warshafsky, they had little experience. Joseph had built some furniture and knew about wooden planes and hand tools. Jay's interest in tools was more as a historian, as a curator of a tool collection. Not long after they met they took over Jay's basement, and, working evenings and weekends with tools that were not

luck. It wasn't until he met Robert Major of Mahogany Masterpieces that Reed Plane Company really got going. Jeff chose the name, by the way, because it sounded quite fitting to a company making English planes. Robert Major wanted to sell Jeff's planes. He suggested casting them from bronze, making different sizes, and marketing them in individually fitted mahogany boxes along with shavings the plane had cut.

While it was exciting to be making planes, it was demanding work. The planes had to be perfect. Not so romantic were the hours it took milling oversized castings beyond possible casting defects,

particularly sophisticated, they built planes as beautiful as any ever made. As Joseph explained, "We attempted to make tools as art in much the same way that Spiers, Norris, and Mathieson did, with shaped yokes and curving plane sides beyond the functional." Over the next three years they made about 50 planes in four patterns: a miter, thumb, shoulder, and chariot plane.

Each described the adventure as "diving into new things, learning patternmaking and all of the steps to making a plane." There were a lot of new techniques to learn. The first step was to make a wooden pattern, based on planes that they borrowed, and then urethane castings of it (with glass beads to give the body rigidity). A local foundry cast them in bronze. They milled the inside surfaces, sole, and sides, soldered on a steel sole, and then began hours of hand filing, fitting, and finishing. They had help from some friends making guns who advised them on finishing techniques and how to inlay the wood infill common on all of their planes.

What distinguishes Jamestown planes is the care with which they were finished. Finishing took as long as all of the rest of the manufacturing. It's easy to understand why. Every edge was shaped with a file and sanding sticks and then polished. Each tiny pit in the casting was chiseled out, a small piece cut from scrap from the same casting (each saved and numbered in a box) was fit to it, and the surface was peened over to make an invisible repair. Screw slots were always aligned parallel with the sole or with each other (as seen on the chariot plane in the bottom photo at right). This meant using special fillister-head screws and turning them in tight, marking the screw slot, backing the screw out, milling

Jamestown Tool Company set out to make planes as art, as beautiful as the traditional British tools that served as patterns. They made four different planes, including the low-angle miter plane shown here. (Photo courtesy of Jamestown Tool Company.)

it flat, filing a new screw slot, and finally tightening it once again. Every detail was important.

The final test for each plane was to take an end-grain shaving from an oak plank. The final test for Jamestown Tool Company was that it was economically unsuccessful. I doubt that Jay and Joseph ever really expected it to be. Far more captivating was the romantic idea of making planes patterned after some of the most elegant tools ever made. Their planes are a testimony to that vision.

Meeting these plane makers has convinced me that making planes does not have to be a dream. While there might be a place for more small companies like Lie-Nielsen Toolworks making 10,000 or so planes a year, the rewards can be just as satisfying making a few planes for yourself. And who knows where it might lead?

The careful alignment of the slots in the screws that secure the adjustable throat in this chariot plane is typical of Jamestown Tool Company's attention to every detail. (Photo courtesy of Jamestown Tool Company.)

13

BUYING PLANES

If a tool appeals to me I keep it. After all, it can always be sold tomorrow—

or the day after!

—A collector commenting on the "squirrel syndrome"

When I think about buying planes, my first thought is always of old tools. Old tools appeal to many, but for different reasons. Some, like myself, are users. I like the feel of a tool worn by some past craftsman—a tool rich with history from an earlier age when hand tools were deeply valued and each was built with quality and care. Today, few of the hundreds of different planes once available are still being made, and sadly most are not that good. Yet there is a nearly endless variety of old planes to discover, to tune for use, or to search for—just for the pure fun.

Others love and collect old tools out of curiosity. Some are attracted by the beauty and variety of the tools alone. Others feel a connection through the tools to their trade and the working methods once used. Tool historians and others study tools to understand specific trades, their traditions, and how tools changed the work, and the work the tools. As little as 30 years ago there were few books about old tools, their makers, and how they were used. Today, with more collectors and more interest, our knowledge has grown of how and why many of these tools evolved.

Buying old tools to use is deeply satisfying. One of the most astonishing stories told to me recently by someone selling new tools was how often he heard people express fear about buying old tools. Perhaps they imagine a fraternity of dealers trying to get top dollar for worn-out and less than usable tools. This isn't entirely untrue; some of the most expensive tools are a little worn out, mostly because they've had long, hard lives. But these aren't the tools you'll want to collect to use anyway. Usable and useful tools are to be found everywhere, for prices often lower than new tools.

Old tools have a beauty and appeal that new tools lack. While it would be hard to build a boat with these tools as the inside lid of one of these boys' tool chests suggests, the tools reflect the simple beauty of wooden hand tools.

Every large flea market has someone selling tools, or, in this case, the entire flea market is tools. So many planes were made over the past 200 years that you never know what might turn up.

Bargaining is part of the fun at flea markets.

This chapter is a guide to where to look for good tools, what to look for and to avoid, and where it can lead if you love old tools a little too much.

Buying Planes to Use

When I first started collecting planes over 25 years ago I asked Vern Ward, one of the oldest and most respected dealers, for some advice. By then I had acquired the usual Stanley bench planes and wanted to buy some of the more specialized planes for my furniture work. The market was still a little bit mysterious to me; I wondered if I would pay too much or get tools hard to tune and actually use. His advice was to "(1) Buy the best planes available. (2) Buy the tools you love. (3) Look everywhere—from dealers, auctions, flea markets, barn sales, wherever." It has turned out to be sage advice.

Old planes are everywhere. Go to any barn sale, flea market, or country auction and you are bound to find at least a few worn-out molding planes, or quite likely a whole lot more. Most common are the planes that many trades used: cast-iron bench and block planes, and wooden planes like smoothers and simple plows. Literally millions were made through the 19th and mid-20th centuries. Less common are planes for specific tasks or trades, such as coachmaker's, furniture maker's, or cooper's planes. The most rare (and expensive) are early planes, both wood and metal, with early attempts at patented or unpatented improvements, or ones that were never made in large numbers because they were very specialized, proved unpopular, or were expensive (the Stanley #9 block plane, for example). The best planes of this last category always fetch the highest prices.

Competing for all of these tools are users, dealers, and collectors. Rarely is

Dealers are a good source of all tools, from the common to the unusual, but expect to pay the market price. This dealer specializes in molding planes.

At any tool auction there's just as much of the action in the parking lot. Dealers and "tailgaters" sell tools from tables or right out of the back of their cars.

there a pure distinction between them. Dealers can be users and collectors, too. Collectors become dealers when selling off excess planes from their collection. And a user can easily become a collector, and then a dealer selling some of the surplus. What hat any of them wears on a particular day depends on the tool, how much money they have in their pocket, and how much discipline they happen to have.

Where to look for planes depends upon how much time, energy, and money you happen to have. Common and inexpensive planes can be found at flea markets, yard and barn sales, country auctions, and sometimes antique shops selling things other than tools. If you are looking for a #4 bench plane, any of these sources will turn one up at a reasonable price, but it will take

some energy and time. By just keeping an eye out over the years I've found a number of interesting planes where I least expected. And while it's still possible to find a rare tool for a bargain, books and price guides have educated more and more people to the value of old tools.

For the less common and rare tools, dealers and specialty auctions are the best sources. This is the easiest and most direct way to find the tools you're after, but there are fewer bargains. Expect to pay a price consistent with the market. Buying from a dealer you get the benefit of his advice and of establishing a relationship that can mean other desirable tools coming your way. Most dealers will bargain or swap and keep an eye out for tools you are looking for. Some have tool lists they send out a number of times a year for a fee.

Some tool auctions include shows that attract a wide array of dealers showing some of their best tools and hottest recent finds. This is the best place to see and feel some of those planes you have only seen in books and to talk with other interested tool people. It's why I jokingly refer to auctions as my "continuing education" about tools. In the parking lot there are often a huge number of "tailgaters," either selling out of the back of their car or from small tables. The prices are competitive and there are literally tons of planes to look over. But it's at the auction that the real excitement happens.

One of the first auctioneers to specialize in tools, Richard Crane attracts buyers and sellers from as far away as England. He has an annual spring and fall show and sale and six country tool auctions in his cow barn in Hillsboro, New Hampshire.

BUYING AT AUCTION

At most, something like $3 million worth of tools pass hands every year at auctions, through dealers, at flea markets, and at similar venues. This is a tiny part of the antiques market, barely equal to the price of one Impressionist oil painting. To understand all of the players and forces coming together at a tool auction, I talked with auctioneer Richard Crane. Since the early 1970s he has been a major player in the tool market, selling everything from box lots of parts to the most expensive and rare tools. Today he has an annual spring and fall show and sale, and another half-dozen country auctions at his cow barn in Hillsboro, New Hampshire. Dealers, collectors, and users come from throughout the United States and from as far away as England to swap, sell, and share stories.

Richard started selling tools almost by accident. Some tools were in among the lots at one of his country auctions, and as it turned out he sold them for a high price. Knowing a good thing when he saw it, Richard found more tools to auction, including some of his own. When Lee Murray became a partner, they auctioned off Lee's tool collection (which filled a three-story barn) to avoid any conflict of interest. It took buyers a while to find them so far off the beaten track, but they did. At auctions they sold everything, or as Richard tells it, "If we couldn't sell 'em, we gave 'em away." That got people's attention. It wasn't long before he specialized in tools and gained a reputation for satisfied sellers and buyers alike.

Tools come from all over. Lee Murray travels to see collections the owner (or, sadly, often the widow) would like to sell. Rarely will dealers buy a large collection, because of the large up-front expense and the long time it might take

to sell it all. More tools come from collectors trying to focus their collection or to part with tools that no longer interest them. The commission is a set 20%. Dealers with rare or special tools put them up for auction in the hopes of getting the best price, or use it as a place to unload surplus tools anonymously. And at any auction you'll find the tools that are someone else's problem—maybe just a bad buy, a tool with improper parts, or a hardly noticeable repair; whatever the reason, an auction is a sure way to sell a tool quickly. Not knowing what you are likely to find is part of the fun of auctions, but it's also why the advice "buyer beware" is often repeated.

Buying tools at an auction doesn't need to be any riskier than buying from a flea market or tool dealer, and it's far more exciting. The only way to "know a bargain when you see one," as Richard describes it, is to educate yourself. He

suggests picking up a few books and learning about the tools, and talking with other collectors and dealers. At the very least, before the sale carefully inspect each tool you intend to bid on. The more you know, the more likely you'll get what you expect.

I was nervous and somewhat timid at my first few auctions—most people are. As with many things, there are certain procedures, and each auctioneer has his own style. Before every auction the tools are arranged in numbered lots on long tables. Most people look more than they touch, so naturally at first I was reluctant even to pick up many of the tools, for fear of dropping something or damaging it. One day I got up the courage to take a plane apart to check its condition, to check the frog, and to check for repairs or cracks where they might be hidden. Now I freely pick up and take apart whatever tools interest me, even ones I don't bid on.

When it comes to bidding, it's a matter of style and discipline. The surest way to walk away satisfied (and not kicking yourself for buying something you don't really need for more than you had hoped for) is to set limits at the beginning. When I'm examining the tools before the auction I write down the most I'm willing to pay for each one that interests me. Then I stick to it.

You're bidding against collectors, users, dealers, even museums, each with their own ideas about what a tool is worth. A lot of things can affect what the tools are worth on a given day. In Richard's experience, "If the stock market was up yesterday, I'll have a better sale today (higher prices)." Collectors always seem to have the most money to spend. Two who want the same tool can push the price to levels that will amaze you. At auctions that attract dealers from different regions, their bids reflect what tools sell for back home, or what a collector they represent is willing to pay. Usually, watching the dealers will give you a sense for the market price. They expect to make a profit by buying low and marking it up one-third to one-half. Don't worry about scratching your nose and buying a $1,000 ivory-tipped center-wheel plow, get into the excitement and bid on something.

There are two other ways to buy planes at auctions: through a dealer who will bid for you on specific items (whether you are there or not), and from special auctions conducted by mail and phone bid only. Dealers bidding for you charge a small commission and will even ship the tools to you afterwards. The risk is buying tools sight unseen. For a mail/phone auction there is a catalog with descriptions and photos of all of the lots. Then through an ingenious system (obviously thought up by a tool dealer), you can call in up until the last day to check on your bids and raise them as you like.

THE INFORMED BUYER

The key to success in buying old planes (or any tools for that matter) is to educate yourself. It's easy to read the short descriptions in a new tool catalog and get a fair idea of what you are getting. You know the plane will be complete and in working order, or at least you can send it back if it's not. While some dealers and auctioneers will take back unsatisfactory tools, more than likely once you buy a tool, it's yours. Quite possibly it's this fear that deters some from the old tool market. It's understandable; after all, who wants to spend $100 on a plane and find out that it's missing important parts or is unusable for some reason?

When plane hunting I always carry a reprint of the classic Stanley catalog #34, originally printed in 1915. Every tool is described, along with exploded drawings, descriptions of variations between model numbers, finishes, and dimensions, and often an explanation of how the tool is used. Carpenters and others would have had this catalog tucked into their toolboxes to read during lunch—and daydream about new tools. There are many other such reprints and texts about tools, some of which can be bought from dealers who sell books along with tools. The bibliography on pp. 258-259 lists some of these, any of which are well worth the investment.

Experience also helps. For a long time before I bought any expensive planes, I asked a lot of questions and looked a lot. I still can't tell a Bed Rock #608 type 3 from a type 6, nor do I really care, but I can recognize if a plane is complete and if the parts are roughly the same vintage. The more valuable the plane, the more you need to know. Planes obviously vary widely in quality and styles, but even the same models changed over time. Usually the price will reflect seemingly small differences, such as an added $\frac{1}{4}$ in. in length, a certain style adjuster knob, or a frog factory-painted orange. Most of these subtleties mean more to collectors than to users.

To further illustrate my point, imagine that I've put two planes in front of you that look identical. Both are basic, inexpensive homeowner bench planes,

The key to success in buying old tools is education and experience. Ask questions, read books, or bring along a copy of a reprinted Stanley catalog, so that when looking through a box of tools you'll know what to look for and what to avoid.

with simple modern lines and painted gray-blue. One is a Defiance #3 and the other a late-series Victor #1103. If you saw them at a flea market, you would expect to pay no more than $20 for either. That's what the Defiance is worth; the Victor is worth more than $1,000. There would be no way of knowing how valuable it is without experience and knowledge.

Dealers are another source of information and help. While they are ultimately trying to make a living (or support their own tool collecting), it's to their benefit to help you learn about the tools. They want you to come back and buy more someday. Don't expect a lot of help on tuning and using planes; most know more about their history, subtleties, and scarcity.

Patience is another key to plane-buying satisfaction. For the most part, these planes are manufactured items (some of them by the millions), and another is bound to turn up somewhere. Even the rare tools show up regularly at the bigger shows and sales. Part of the thrill of collecting old tools is searching for them and waiting for the right one to come along—one that appeals to you, is in good condition, and is at an afford-able price.

WHAT TO LOOK FOR AND AVOID

As a user starting out you'll likely be looking for the basic planes—common, functional bench planes. There are so many that you'll be able to choose just what you want, risk less than what a new tool would cost, and get a premium plane. The next step is buying less common and more expensive specialty planes, such as shoulder rabbet planes, dado planes, scraper planes, and compass planes. The third step, should you take it, is collecting some of the rare and

In your search for planes, you're apt to find everything from the common to the unusual, from standard cast-iron bench planes to these wooden cornice planes.

costly planes such as a Stanley #9 block plane, a #52 shoot board and plane, or a Norris A5 smoothing plane. By then you're verging on being a collector. If you know how to buy a good #4 bench plane, then the next steps just take more experience, knowledge, and patience.

The first test is to pick up the plane and just feel it in your hands. Not only will this give you a sense of its balance, but also of how the tote and knob feel. Are they smooth and polished, or do they feel loose, rough or chipped, cracked or repaired? Part of the beauty of older planes is the beautifully shaped and polished rosewood handles. While loose handles are no problem (see pp. 52-53), I wouldn't buy a plane with cracked, chipped, or repaired handles if I had a choice. Such planes will be less expensive, but making or buying a new tote or knob will take time and add to the cost. And when it comes time to

resell, a repaired or replaced handle devalues the plane.

Look the whole plane over. Does it look complete? Bench planes are fairly simple to evaluate, but when buying a rabbet plane, for instance, empty threaded holes will clue you to a missing depth stop or fence. Do the parts look natural together? Look for cracks and chips, especially around the throat. Grime coating a plane can conceal cracks. Hearing a hollow ring when you rap the body with your knuckle might indicate a hidden crack. Chips devalue the plane but, except for ones along the throat, don't affect the performance. However, chips along the sides that your hands will rub against while using the plane are uncomfortable.

Inspect the sole for wear and bad scratches. Most used planes (and new ones, too) are going to need some lapping to polish and true the sole, so expect this.

The planes listed here are useful in nearly any woodshop for a wide range of work. The Stanley numbers refer to specific planes commonly available or can be used to compare sizes with planes by other manufacturers. Many of these planes are available new. All of them can be found in the used tool market with a little luck and patience.

The list is very flexible and should be used as a guide only. What planes are useful to you ultimately depends on the kinds of work you do. Every craftsman should have at least one of the first six types; the rest can be bought as you need them.

- Block plane, a #60½, #9½, or Lie-Nielsen low angle
- Smooth planes, #4 size for rough smoothing and a heavy, finely made plane such as a Norris-type Bed Rock #604 or #604½ or a Lie-Nielsen #604 for finish smoothing
- Jack plane, #5 size
- Jointer, #7 or #8 size
- Rabbet plane, a basic bench rabbet #78 or a heavier #289 with a skewed iron
- Hand-held scrapers, square and "gooseneck"; and #80 cabinet scraper (or similar handled scraper)
- Router plane, #71 or #271
- Two spokeshaves (straight and round soled)
- Shoulder rabbet plane, #93 or #92 (either also functions as a small chisel plane)
- Bullnose rabbet plane, #75, #90, or a beautiful British example by Preston or others
- Bench rabbet plane, #10 or #10½ (smaller version of #10 and more scarce)
- Narrow dado plane, #39¼ or #39⅜ or a wooden version
- Chisel plane; the small Lie-Nielsen version of the #97 is a wonderful tool

- Medium-diameter spoke pointer and a simple pencil sharpener
- Side rabbet plane, #79, or #98 and #99
- Miter plane or low-angle heavy plane for shoot-board work
- Scrub plane, or retuned smooth or jack
- Various sizes of side bead planes (³⁄₁₆ in., ¼ in., ⅜ in., and ½ in.), or #45 combination plane
- Range of wooden molding planes, hollows and rounds (three or four sizes of each)
- Beading tool, #66 with cutters
- Compass plane, #20 or #113
- Chamfer plane or shave, any pattern

Although I don't own one myself, many craftsmen rave about the Lie-Nielsen low-angle jack plane. They recommend putting it near the top of the list.

Planes best for children

- For the youngest kids, a finger plane #201, #101, or #100
- Block plane, #102 or Lie-Nielsen low-angle (basically the same plane)
- Spokeshave or set of inexpensive small bronze spokeshaves (three)
- Bench plane, #2 or #3 size

Bad scratches can be lapped out, but they are rarely too deep to cause problems. I try to carry a straightedge with me to check the sole for flatness, nevertheless. Often the seller will have a square handy. Hold the plane up to the light and sight under the straightedge as

described in Chapter 4. The truer the sole, the less work it will take to tune the plane.

With the plane still assembled, move the adjusters (if there are any) to see if they work smoothly. Rotate the depth adjuster through a wide range to feel for

any looseness or roughness from damaged threads. It's rare that the cast yoke capturing the brass adjuster wheel is broken, but check it all the same. If the plane looks good so far, take it apart.

First look at the frog and the setscrews that secure it to the sole and, on planes that have it, the screw that adjusts the frog's position. It helps to have a medium-sized flat-head screwdriver handy. Rust covering the frog or screws indicates the plane has been sitting in a cellar or unheated garage long enough that the screws might be frozen. Try turning the frog adjustment screw first to see if it's free. If you want to be very thorough, check that the frog setscrews are not frozen or stripped. If you get this far, you might as well remove the frog and inspect it. It will need a thorough cleaning, but is it complete and unchipped? Check that the screw that holds the iron and lever cap in place is free, not bent, and that the head is not damaged.

What do the lever cap, cap iron, and iron look like? Irons are replaceable and often were. If there is less than about an inch of iron left before the slot, it will need to be replaced again before too long if the plane is used a lot. The steel is sometimes soft close to the slot, too. Most irons will be discolored with a slight amount of rust, but definitely avoid an iron with a rusty back or one that's noticeably pitted. Such an iron will take hours of lapping and even then not sharpen well. Neither the cap iron nor the lever cap should be too rusty, chipped, or deformed, but, like the iron, these parts can be replaced if need be (though not always easily or inexpensively). The locking lever on the lever cap should work smoothly. Check that the screw that secures the cap iron to the iron is not stripped and that the slot in the head is not too badly worn. I wouldn't worry about the cap iron fitting the iron, since few craftsmen either knew about or took the time for this important tuning step.

Before you buy, inspect the plane carefully for cracks and mismatched or missing parts.

There are other subtle things to check for that increase the plane's value. Is the plane complete with original parts? This is sometimes impossible to tell without a lot of experience, because even at the factory older parts were sometimes fitted to the newest model. My Stanley catalog helps here, but I also look for consistent patinas and matching patent dates (if any) on the iron and plane. Look at the japanning, the black "paint" covering the unmilled areas of the casting. Japanning in fine condition adds to the plane's value, although it in no way affects its use. The finer the overall condition of the plane, the higher its value now and in the future.

Inspecting potential planes will take some time, but it will further your experience and help you end up with some satisfying tools. While most problems are repairable, you'll have to weigh your skills, the amount of time you want to invest in making the plane right, and the difference in price between it and a perfect tool. The least expensive tools can sometimes become the most expensive.

If you like a tool, buy it. Among my many regrets are the tools I for some reason passed up. I can remember many of them, including a mint-condition Bed Rock #607 that was sold when I returned from a brief walk to "think it over." This isn't to say you should buy everything you like; few of us have those kinds of resources. But it's not always true that a better tool will come along for a better price. Except for the more common Stanley planes, most tools are different enough that some have more appeal than others. Meanwhile you have missed out on all of that time using and enjoying the one you passed up.

REPAIRS AND CLEANING

There's an ongoing debate among collectors about cleaning and repairing tools. One side feels that tools should be left as found, with only the slightest cleaning where really necessary. The other side believes that tools should be restored and cleaned to an as-used condition, typical of a craftsman who cared for his tools. One thing both sides do agree on is that overcleaning ruins a tool's historic, aesthetic, and monetary value.

Since I am buying tools to use, I naturally favor cleaning and repairing to the point the tool is functional. As users, we are less likely to buy rare or historically significant tools (such as early molding planes), both because they are usually vastly more expensive and because they are not always the best tools for the work. For rare tools such as these, I favor only the most necessary cleaning. A complete cleaning runs the risk of removing tool marks showing how the plane was made and the beautiful patina that only comes from years of handling and use. Stick to working by hand, with mild solvents and fine abrasives, and you'll run little risk of overcleaning.

Cleaning a plane is part of its hidden cost. I usually start by taking everything apart. I clean wooden parts with very fine steel wool (0000) and turpentine, or kerosene for really thick grime. Usually a thorough rubbing will clean off the dirt and leave the patina, but sometimes I have to lightly scrape a paint splotch or dried-on glue. For a finish coating I use a mixture of boiled linseed oil and beeswax melted together (to the consistency of warm butter), which I rub on and buff off. Wooden planes finished with linseed oil alone and stored in a damp place run the risk of molding badly, since the oil actually feeds the growth. A polish of

Repairing cast iron takes experience and great skill to do well and can be quite costly as a result. These three repairs are of varying quality.

shellac is fine, but generally you shouldn't use varnish.

I clean and finish metal parts that are not too badly rusted the same way. A slightly coarser steel wool removes more serious rust. On parts such as the lever cap and cap iron, I sand the working edges with fine sandpaper such as 220 or higher. Fine wet-and-dry paper and kerosene as a lubricant work well for a final polish. Avoid overcleaning any brass or gunmetal parts because it's easy to leave the patina splotchy and remove any protective varnish. A wipe of the linseed oil and beeswax finish brightens any japanning.

Repairing the boxing on a molding plane or making other wood repairs can be challenging, but it is rewarding, especially if the tool is a bargain. Yet metal repairs can quickly become beyond the skills of the average craftsman. I would avoid most tools that need such repairs in the first place, but occasionally you'll find a rare tool that's quite

reasonable and worth repairing. It's very tricky to weld cast iron, especially where the material is old and thin. There are a few specialists who do it; ask some of the bigger dealers and collectors for recommendations. When you figure in that even the most basic repair can be $100 or more, perhaps the plane isn't such a bargain after all. And, remember, even the most skillful repair is going to devalue the plane somewhat and make it harder to sell to someone other than another user or impetuous collector. Another downside is that it might not work as well as it could. The alternative is to keep looking and find a "parts" plane to replace the damaged part.

Investing in Tools

When you spend hundreds of dollars on individual planes, you can't help but wonder about their value, say 10 or 20 years down the road. If you heed Vern Ward's advice to "buy the best," you have little to worry about. While some would disagree about the value of buying tools purely as an investment, historically the high end of the market has grown consistently. As users, we have another distinct advantage to buying fine old tools. What other things can you enjoy, make a living with, and then sell for considerably more than you paid?

When pressed about investing in tools, auctioneer Richard Crane opines that the value of tools has risen about 20% a year. Others think that this is far too optimistic for all but the very best and rarest items. Driving the market is the underlying fact that there is a finite number of old tools. For some of the rarest of these, maybe only one or two survive. As for the most common tools, a Stanley #5, for example, there might be millions still around. Prices are always going to reflect the basic law of supply and demand.

Richard likes to think of the tool market as a stock market, with each type of tool—levels, saws, planes, edge tools, rules—as individual stocks. Some years planes are hot, other years it could be levels or saws. "Buy some of each," he advises, "hedge your bet." The same advice applies to any collection, especially one where the investment potential is even being considered. A collection that's too narrowly focused, say, one of shipbuilder's spar planes, might be valuable to you (and costly to acquire) but be worth far less auctioned off all at once.

Prices reflect only what someone is willing to pay. Auctions most specifically establish values that day and sometimes indicate where the market is headed. Lots of factors drive the market and establish prices, such as the number of new and old collectors, their disposable incomes, the quality of the tool—even such factors as a tool's size. Larger tools

are not always so appealing because they are hard to move and display. Subtle things like an original box or a clear maker's mark can increase the value of a plane two times or more.

The reality is that for most of us tools are not the best investment. It's hard to make much money when the non-dealer collector or user has to buy at retail and sell at wholesale. The price has to appreciate quite a bit just to break even. The market is just too small and specialized. But then there are the stories—nearly every dealer has one—of a flea market find that turns out to be worth thousands. Richard Crane told me of the "clunker" of a molding plane he bought from a woman at a flea market for $50. It turned out to be a signed cornice plane worth $3,800. I've heard about yard-sale Stanley #1s bought for

$15 and early plow planes worth many thousands bought for $300. Certainly these kinds of tools can make you some money, but it's more often due to someone's knowledge of the tools and labor in bringing it to market, not a true "investment."

I still feel that tools are a worthwhile investment for some. They might or might not be growing in value as fast as a CD, but the ones I own and use in my work give me a different kind of pleasure than money in the bank. It's the same feeling expressed to me by another friend and collector: "I often think that if my addiction had been horse racing instead of tools, I might easily have had as good a time, but would have a whole lot less to show for it. In that sense I suppose you could argue that tools are a good investment."

An original box greatly increases the value of any plane. To find the original box for a rare plane, such as many of the ones shown here, is even more valuable.

A few of Scotty Carter's miniature planes are bench planes, similar in every detail to ones like the brass-soled smoother in the rear. The larger of these might be a salesman's sample.

Collecting Planes

Whether or not you call it an investment, it's still easy to buy a few planes, and then a few more, and before you know it you're collecting. Perhaps you're the user who buys some planes to build that Queen Anne highboy you've always planned on making "someday." The process can be so subtle that, before long, planes fill every vacant space in your shop. Some of us take Vern's advice to "buy the tools you love" too far.

Every collector has his own stories about how he got started, the first plane he bought, or the rare ones he found in unlikely places. Yet one of the funnier quirks I discovered among collectors is how many carefully follow every movement of tools they would like to own someday. More than one collector discouraged me from photographing a rare tool, saying it would only revive interest and generate more phone calls. Still, for the rarest of the rare tools, you

can bet that a number of people know where they are and the chances of getting them. Some wait years. Collecting takes patience.

Collecting also takes judgment and discipline. Few of us have the resources to buy every plane we like, nor would such a collection be very interesting. Some of the finest collections I've seen are modest, but they showed consistency and judgment. The collection is an extension of the collector's interest not only in the tools but also in their history and the society that created them. Most never imagined where collecting a few planes would lead.

SCOTTY CARTER, COLLECTOR

It's fairly obvious at any tool show or auction that nearly all the buyers and sellers are men. Tools from the trades have always appealed more to the masculine half of the population, probably because of man's long history of designing, making, and working these

tools. In England there are a few woman tool dealers, but here the few women you'll notice are wives helping to run the business and peddle the tools their husbands are busily out buying and swapping for. Scotty Carter stands out in this crowd—as a dealer in high-end English (and some American) tools, as a long-term collector of miniature planes, and as the white-haired grandmother she is.

It was in her and her husband's shop in Portsmouth, New Hampshire, that I saw my first Norris plane many years ago, long before I appreciated what they were or could even afford one. I would go down into her tool cellar and buy a few English molding planes or carving tools. She always stocked an incredible variety; they were good tools and inexpensive. She is still in the same shop, a restored brick and granite grain-storage warehouse overlooking the waterfront. Since her husband, an avid and early collector of New Hampshire tools, died in 1983 she has run the business alone. She still travels to England a couple of times a year to buy tools—finding a few Norris smoothers or shoulder planes among the more usual planes, chisels, and saws.

With all of the beautiful tools passing through her hands over the years, the only ones she has been tempted to collect are miniatures, planes no longer than an inch or two, made from beautiful materials and complete in every way. Since she bought her first one in 1965 for $12, a tiny whale-shaped horn plane lying on a blanket at the Amsterdam Flea Market, she has collected perhaps two dozen. "They're no different than other antiques that appeal to you graphically or for their form," she explains. And as more than one collector has admitted, "You don't know you are collecting until one day you realize that you are."

STORING AND DISPLAYING PLANES

Part of the joy of owning and collecting fine tools is showing them to others. Even the most simple or basic tool can incite curiosity and interest. Many of the people who visit my shop comment on how seldom they see a craftsman at work, let alone the variety and beauty of the tools involved. And I have just a small and specialized collection. While glass cabinets might be nice, the most simple shelves or even drawers can show off your tools handsomely.

As a user, I want the tools I need accessible. I store large planes on the wall right next to my bench; a few are on shelves, but most are arranged in a bank of drawers just for planes. The smallest are housed in shallow drawers with dividers. Medium-sized planes and ones not needed that often fill the center drawers. The large bottom drawer is filled with molding planes on end just as they would have been in the bottom of a carpenter's tool chest. Everything stays dust-free and organized.

Dampness can ruin a good plane. In a heated shop such as mine, rust is never a problem. Other tools are not so lucky. It's common to find planes with pitted soles and irons, or at least covered with a layer of surface rust. Wooden parts or whole planes can mold or be ruined by damp storage. Even a dry place exposed to big swings in temperature, can be damaging. Metal cooled by a chill night will condense a fine layer of moisture on it as the day heats up, causing rusting. The best place to store any tools is in a heated building or one massive enough to change temperature slowly.

Simple shelves organize a collection of planes, keep them accessible, and show them off, too.

Drawers are an alternative for dust-free and efficient storage. They need to be designed to take a lot of weight and to fit planes of various dimensions.

Her complete collection is spread on a piece of black velvet laid out in the bottom of a low carton that once held four six packs of some soft drink. The display might not be elegant, but it's obvious that she gets a great deal of pleasure from each tool as she picks them up to show to me. "They don't show up anymore," she laments. She remembers where she got each one or the different dealers who gave her certain special ones. With her warm charm it's easy to imagine the friends she has made dealing tools over the years. Some planes are obviously usable, molders made to shape some profile such as curved window mullions (see the bottom photo on p. 187). Others are tiny bench planes for working in tight places, and a few resemble salesman samples. All are craftsman-made, needed for some

Intriguing objects only an inch or two long, these miniature planes are beautifully made from beech and boxwood.

fine work where no commercial planes were available. As far as she knows, only the English maker Edward Preston made small planes, though they were larger than most of these. Looking at them I was awed by their precise workmanship and felt the lure we all feel for small, exquisite objects.

AN ADVANCED STANLEY COLLECTOR

Scotty Carter's small planes would disappear with hardly a trace into a Houston collection I visited a couple of months later. I had met this collector a few years before at a tool show when I was intrigued by the small number of extremely rare (and expensive) Stanley tools he was offering for sale—a hand beader, #4½H, and a blind nailer. In a thick southern accent, he described himself as an advanced Stanley collector, but this in no way prepared me for his

collection. What I found was a Texas-sized array of tools—planes, braces, rules and measuring instruments, levels, plumb bobs, tool parts, and related memorabilia, such as trade signs, store displays (many with original tools), and catalogs.

The collection is mostly housed on the top floor of a small office building that at one time was used for grading cotton samples from bales traded at the nearby Cotton Exchange. Half the floor is living space—a harmonious and eclectic mix of pre-Columbian figures, Thonet bentwood furniture, colorful Art Deco lamps, modern Texas paintings, religious icons, and glass cases filled with small and special tool collections. The other half of the floor includes a wood-working shop with a neat benchroom, a small machine room, and a library surrounded with old drugstore glass cases filled with more planes and tools.

It didn't take long to realize the value of this tool collection, both monetarily and for its breadth and completeness. Whole sections of shelves displayed examples of highly sought #2 bench planes, showing the subtle changes in the Stanley line and comparing them with similar tools made by Ohio, Sargent, Chaplin, and others. Some shelves held one-of-a-kind Stanley prototypes or two of the only three known examples of certain tools. The same thoroughness and rarity was represented in all parts of the collection.

This collector (who requested anonymity) grew up in Jackson, Mississippi, into a very old family, the son of a doctor and avid collector of medical paraphernalia. It was from his father that he inherited a passion for collecting, or "shopping" as he now calls it, and an awareness of tools and woodworking. He remembers being a typical boy, "drilling my father's auger into the dirt and planing the sidewalk." Gradually he started collecting good tools for his own use—planes, levels, rules, and whatever caught his eye—yet with less discipline than he wishes he had then or now.

He collected by buying from dealers, from auctions throughout the United States and England, from parking-lot swap meets and flea markets every-where, all the while refining his high-speed shopping technique. From his experience and careful study of the tools he can recognize an overlooked part of a scarce plane in a 50-cent box of rusty screwdrivers and hardware. Looking for highly sought after tools in original boxes, he has gotten his foot in the door and into the cellar shelves of more than one hardware store by asking for level bubbles. "But I had no discipline," he freely admits, and he bought quantity over condition. Often he would ask himself if he already had four, why buy

A Texas-sized collection of everything from the common to one-of-a-kind tools. Housed in glass cases are examples of #2s made by Stanley and its competitors, early and unusual block planes, rare Sargent planes, and collections of other interesting woodworking tools.

In the same Texas collection are Balinese planes, many carved in the shape of humans and mythic animals. Curiously, it's rare to find any with irons.

another. He summed up his passion by quoting his wife: "the thrill of acquisition and the boredom of possession."

Where a passion for collecting can lead was evident when we visited the cellar (or "concourse," as they elegantly call it in Texas). A huge area was stacked with row after row of boxes, all neatly labeled and mentally catalogued. Only about half were tools, the rest were the results of his wife's passion for collecting. It seems he became a bit of a legend at one of the local flea markets when he bought an entire truckload of chicken boxes, those heavy waxed boxes and lids for shipping iced chicken parts. Each box contained a dozen or more planes of every variety: Bed Rocks, Baileys, #45s and #55s, Sargents, Gages, and many,

many others. We joked about what would happen to the tool market if all of these and the rest of his collection were auctioned off all at once.

His collecting goes on, as he searches for rare tools, parts and complete planes in the original boxes, and examples of Stanley's present tool production to keep his collection current. At one time he almost bought the famous Studley tool chest now in the Smithsonian. As he talks about subtle differences between tools in his collection, it's obvious that much time goes into studying and thinking about them, how they work, and how designs evolved. Often he offers help to other tool historians doing a "type study" of specific tools, freely lending parts of his collection or catalogs from his archives. As a woodworker, he

understands and appreciates the tools from a different perspective, although he uses few of them in his real passion—turning beautiful large bowls.

Upon leaving I pressed him for advice to others getting started collecting or to those already caught up in the passion. "Collecting takes discipline and judgment," he advised, although admitting at the same time that he has less than he would like. As for investing in tools, "Stick with CDs or stocks and bonds and use your earnings to buy tools. Too many men convince their wives what a great investment they're making and guiltlessly go out and spend more money on tools." Luckily for him, his wife is just as passionate a collector as he is.

BIBLIOGRAPHY

Allen, Sam. *Plane Basics.* New York: Sterling, 1993.

Basing, Patricia. *Trades and Crafts in Medieval Manuscripts.* New York: New Amsterdam, 1990.

Bealer, Alex W. *Old Ways of Working Wood.* Barre, Mass.: Barre Publishers, 1972.

Blandford, Percy W. *The Woodworker's Bible.* New York: Crown Publishers, 1984.

The Book of Trades, or Library of the Useful Arts. Jacob Johnson Publisher, 1807. Reprinted as *Little Book of Early American Crafts and Trades,* edited by Peter Stockman. New York: Dover, 1976.

Chinn, Gary, and John Sainsbury. *The Garrett Wade Book of Woodworking Tools.* New York: Gallery Press, 1979.

The Cutting Edge: An Exhibition of Sheffield Tools. Sheffield, England: Ruskin Gallery, 1992.

Dunbar, Michael. *Restoring, Tuning, and Using Classic Woodworking Tools.* New York: Sterling, 1989.

Garvin, James L. *Instruments of Change: New Hampshire Hand Tools and Their Makers 1800–1900.* Catalog of exhibition at New Hampshire Historical Society, December 20, 1984–May 30, 1985.

Gaynor, James, and Nancy Hagedorn. *Tools: Working Wood in Eighteenth-Century America.* Williamsburg, Va.: Colonial Williamsburg Foundation, 1993.

Goodman, W. L. *British Planemakers from 1700.* 3rd. ed., enlarged and revised by Jane and Mark Rees. Mendham, N.J.: Astragal Press, 1993.

——. *The History of Woodworking Tools.* London: G. Bell and Sons, 1962.

Graham, Frank D., and Thomas J. Emery. *Audels Carpenters and Builders Guide #1.* New York: Audel, 1946.

Greber, Josef M. *The History of the Woodworking Plane.* Translated by Seth Burchard. Zurich: 1956. Reprint, Albany, N.Y.: Early American Industries Association, 1991.

Hayward, Charles. *Cabinet Making for Beginners.* New York: Drake, 1971.

——. *Tools for Woodwork.* New York: Drake, 1976.

Hazen, Edward. *Popular Technology; or, Professions and Trades.* New York: Harper and Brothers, 1846. Reprint, Albany, N.Y.: Early American Industries Association, 1981.

Henry, Bernard. *Des Métiers et des Hommes au Village.* Paris: Seuil, 1978.

Hibben, Thomas. *The Carpenter's Tool Chest.* London: George Routledge and Sons, 1933.

Hoadley, R. Bruce. *Understanding Wood.* Newtown, Conn.: Taunton Press, 1980.

Holtzapffel, Charles. *Turning and Mechanical Manipulation.* London: Holtzapffel & Co., 1875.

Jenkins, J. Geraint. *Traditional Country Craftsmen.* London: Routledge and Kegan Paul, 1978.

Joyce, Ernest. *The Encyclopedia of Furniture Making.* New York: Drake, 1978.

Kean, Herbert P., and Emil S. Pollak. *Collecting Antique Tools.* Morristown, N.J.: Astragal Press, 1990.

Kebabian, Paul B. "A Rarity: The Shoe Peg Plane." *Plane Talk* 11 (#4, 1987): 52-53.

Kebabian, Paul B., and Dudley Witney. *American Woodworking Tools.* Boston: New York Graphic Society, 1978.

Kebabian, Paul B., and William C. Lipke (eds.) *Tools and Technologies–America's Wooden Age.* Robert Hull Fleming Museum, University of Vermont, Burlington, Vt., 1979.

Kingshott, Jim. *Making and Modifying Woodworking Tools.* East Sussex, England: Guild of Master Craftsmen Publications, 1992.

Landis, Scott. *The Workbench Book.* Newtown, Conn.: Taunton Press, 1987.

——. *The Workshop Book.* Newtown, Conn.: Taunton Press, 1991.

Lee, Leonard. *The Complete Guide to Sharpening.* Newtown, Conn.: Taunton Press, 1995.

Mercer, Henry C. *Ancient Carpenters' Tools.* 5th ed. New York: Horizon Press (for the Bucks County Historical Society), 1975.

Mowat, Alexander and William. *A Treatise on Stairbuilding and Handrailing.* Barrow-in-Furness, England: 1900. Reprint, Fresno, Calif.: Linden Publishing, 1985.

Moxon, Joseph. *Mechanick Exercises: or the Doctrine of Handy-Works.* 3rd ed., London: 1703. Reprint, Albany, N.Y.: Early American Industries Association, 1975.

Newlands, James. *The Carpenter's and Jointer's Assistant.* Edinburgh and London: Blackie & Sons, 1860.

Nicholson, Peter. *New Carpenter's Guide.* Improved and enlarged edition. London: Jones, 1826.

Odate, Toshio. *Japanese Woodworking Tools: Their Tradition, Spirit, and Use.* Newtown, Conn.: Taunton Press, 1984.

Proudfoot, Christopher, and Philip Walker. *Woodworking Tools.* Oxford, England: Phaidon, Christies Ltd., 1984.

Rees, Jane and Mark. *Tools, A Guide for Collectors.* Suffolk, England: Roy Arnold, Ipswich Book Co., 1996.

Rees, Mark. "The Lid of a Cabinetmaker's Tool Chest." *Tools and Trades* 40 (Winter 1993).

Roberts, Kenneth D. *Scottish and English Metal Planes by Spiers and Norris.* Fitzwilliam, N.H.: Ken Roberts Publishing, 1991.

——. *Some 19th Century English Woodworking Tools.* Fitzwilliam, N.H.: Ken Roberts Publishing, 1980.

——. *The Stanley Rule and Level Company's Combination Planes.* Fitzwilliam, N.H.: Ken Roberts Publishing, 1975.

——. *Wooden Planes in 19th Century America Volume II.* Fitzwilliam, N.H.: Ken Roberts Publishing, 1983.

Sellens, Alvin. *Dictionary of American Hand Tools.* Augusta, Kans.: Alvin Sellens, 1990.

——. *The Stanley Plane: A History and Descriptive Inventory.* Albany, N.Y.: Early American Industries Association, 1975.

——. *Woodworking Planes: A Descriptive Register of Wooden Planes.* Augusta, Kans.: Alvin Sellens, 1978.

Sainsbury, John. *Planecraft: A Woodworker's Handbook.* New York: Sterling, 1984.

Salaman, R. A. *Dictionary of Woodworking Tools.* Newtown, Conn.: Taunton Press, 1990.

The Sargent Tool Catalog Collection. Foreword by Paul Weidenschilling. Mendham, N.J.: Astragal Press, 1993.

Seymour, John. *The Forgotten Crafts.* New York: Portland House, 1984.

Sloane, Eric. *A Museum of Early American Tools.* New York: Funk and Wagnalls, 1964.

Smith, Roger K. *Patented Transitional and Metallic Planes in America 1827–1927.* Athol, Mass.: Roger Smith, 1981.

——. *Patented Transitional and Metallic Planes in America, Volume II.* Athol, Mass.: Roger Smith, 1992.

Stanley Rule and Level Co. *How to Work with Tools and Wood.* New Britain, Conn.: Stanley Rule and Level, 1927.

Starr, Richard. *Woodworking with Kids.* Newtown, Conn.: Taunton Press, 1982.

The Tool Chest of Benjamin Seaton. Swanley, England: Tool and Trades Historical Society, 1994.

Welsh, Peter C. *Woodworking Tools 1600–1900.* United States National Museum Bulletin 241. Washington, D.C.: Smithsonian Institution, 1966.

Whelan, John M. *Making Traditional Wooden Planes.* Mendham, N.J.: Astragal Press, 1996.

——. *The Wooden Plane: Its History, Form, and Function.* Mendham, N.J.: Astragal Press, 1993.

Wildung, Frank H. *Woodworking Tools at Shelburne Museum.* Shelburne, Vt.: Shelburne Museum, 1957.

TOOL CATALOGS AND PRICE LISTS

Hammacher, Schlemmer & Co. *Tools for all Trades, and Supplies.* Catalog #355. New York, c. 1905.

Illustrated Catalogue and Invoice Price List. Greenfield, Mass.: Greenfield Tool Co., 1872. Reprint, Fitzwilliam, N.H.: Ken Roberts Publishing, 1978.

Illustrated List of Planes, Plane Irons,... Sandusky, Ohio: Sandusky Tool Co., 1877. Reprint, Fitzwilliam, N.H.: Ken Roberts Publishing, 1978.

Illustrated Supplement to the Catalog and Invoice Price List of Bench Planes, Molding Tools, &c. Middletown, Conn.: Arrow-mammett Works, 1857. Reprint, Fitzwilliam, N.H.: Ken Roberts Publishing, 1976.

Major, Robert. *Masterpiece Tools.* Suncook, N.H.: Mahogany Masterpieces, 1984.

Orr and Lockett Hardware Co. Chicago, Ill., 1898.

Stanley Rule and Level Co. Various price and pocket catalogs from 1870–1915. New Britain, Conn.

Chas. A. Strelinger. Detroit, Mich., 1895.

Tool Catalogue 1938. Alex Mathieson and Sons, Ltd., Saracen Tool Works.

A. J. Wilkinson & Co. *Wood-Workers' Catalogue.* Boston, c. 1888.

INDEX

TOOL CREDITS

Many people and museums were kind enough to lend me tools to photograph. The tools in the following photographs (and, where noted, the photographs themselves) are courtesy of:

Jonathan Binzen (p. 157; Krenov plane)

M. S. Carter (pgs. 4, 10 bottom, 11 top, 17, 35 bottom, 42, 56 bottom, 62 bottom, 146, 186, 187, 193, 198 top, 204 bottom, 245 left, 254, 256)

Jonathan Cooper (p. 214 bottom)

Michael Dunbar (pgs. 24, 34 top, 90, 173, 189, 198 bottom, 215 top left, bottom right)

Ted Ingraham (pgs. 74, 83 top, 193, 216 left, 223, 224, 255 left)

Jamestown Tool Company (p. 241, planes and photos)

Paul Kebabian (pgs. 6, 20, 33 top left, 43 top, 57, 81 bottom, 137, 168, 201 top, 222, 227, 242)

Ron Raiselis, Strawbery Banke Museum, Portsmouth, N.H. (pgs. 210, 212, 213, 214 top)

Shelburne Museum, Shelburne, Vt. (pgs. 2, 94 bottom, 123, 132 top, 134 bottom, 142, 148 top, 149, 170, 174 right, 215 top right, 216 right, 217 top, 218 top, 220 right)

Roger Smith (p. 209; illustration from *Patented Transitional and Metallic Planes in America, Vol. II*)

Windsor Precision Museum, Windsor, Vt. (p. 22)

Dean Zoerheide (pgs. 8 bottom, 9 right, 18, 19, 33 bottom right, 36, 50, 133 bottom, 136 bottom, 204 top, 208 left)

PUBLISHER: James P. Chiavelli

ACQUISITIONS EDITOR: Rick Peters

PUBLISHING COORDINATOR: Joanne Renna

EDITOR: Peter Chapman

LAYOUT ARTIST: Carol Singer

ILLUSTRATOR: Kathleen Rushton

TYPEFACE: Berling

PAPER: Warren Patina Matte, 70 lb., neutral pH

PRINTER: Quebecor Printing/Kingsport, Kingsport, Tennessee